# LINGERING INLAND

# LINGERING INLAND

## A Literary Tour of the Midwest

Edited by ANDY OLER

Foreword by José Olivarez

3 FIELDS BOOKS
An imprint of the University of Illinois Press

3 Fields Books is an imprint of the University of Illinois Press.


Manufactured in the United States of America
P 5 4 3 2 1
♾ This book is printed on acid-free paper.

Library of Congress Cataloging-in-Publication Data
Names: Oler, Andy editor | Olivarez, José writer of foreword
Title: Lingering inland: a literary tour of the Midwest / edited by Andy Oler; foreword by José Olivarez.
Description: Urbana: 3 Fields Books, 2025. | Includes bibliographical references.
Identifiers: LCCN 2025022587 (print) | LCCN 2025022588 (ebook) | ISBN 9780252088971 paperback | ISBN 9780252048418 ebook
Subjects: LCSH: American literature—Middle West—History and criticism | Place (Philosophy) in literature | Middle West—In literature | LCGFT: Essays | Creative nonfiction
Classification: LCC PS273.L56 2025 (print) | LCC PS273 (ebook) | DDC 810.9/977--dc23/eng/20250623
LC record available at https://lccn.loc.gov/2025022587
LC ebook record available at https://lccn.loc.gov/2025022588

# CONTENTS

**Foreword** *by José Olivarez* ix
**Acknowledgments** xi
**Introduction** *by Andy Oler* 1

**Mari Sandoz** Sheridan County, Nebraska *by C. J. Janovy* 9
**James Emanuel** Alliance, Nebraska *by Sean Theodore Stewart* 12
**Wright Morris** Central City, Nebraska *by Nathan Tye* 14
**Ted Kooser** Seward County, Nebraska *by Matt Miller* 16
**Malcolm X** Omaha, Nebraska *by Ashley Howard* 18

**WILLA CATHER**
Taos, New Mexico *by Tracy Sanford Tucker* 22
Bladen, Nebraska *by Christine Pivovar* 24
Omaha, Nebraska *by Conor Gearin* 26
Chicago, Illinois *by Jesse Raber* 29
Jaffrey, New Hampshire *by Catherine Seiberling Pond* 32

**Langston Hughes** Lawrence, Kansas *by John Edgar Tidwell* 34
**William Least Heat-Moon** Columbia, Missouri *by Kit Salter* 36
**Henry Bellamann** Fulton, Missouri *by Alex Dzurick* 38
**Edgar Lee Masters** Petersburg, Illinois *by Jason Stacy* 40
**Mary Hunter Austin** Carlinville, Illinois *by Karen Dillon and Naomi Crummey* 42

## ST. LOUIS

**Kathleen Finneran** St. Louis, Missouri *by Marina Henke* 46
**Naomi Shihab Nye** Ferguson, Missouri *by Taylor Fox* 49
**William Gass** St. Louis, Missouri *by Devin Thomas O'Shea* 51
**Peter H. Clark** St. Louis, Missouri *by Marc Blanc* 54
**Kate Chopin** St. Louis, Missouri *by Michaella A. Thornton* 58
**Tennessee Williams** St. Louis, Missouri *by Devin Thomas O'Shea* 61

**Gordon Parks** Fort Scott, Kansas *by Jeromiah Taylor* 64
**James Tate** Pittsburg, Kansas *by Leslie VonHolten* 66
**Meridel Le Sueur** Picher, Oklahoma *by Joe Schiller* 68
**John Joseph Mathews** Osage County, Oklahoma *by Mason Whitehorn Powell* 71
**S. E. Hinton** Tulsa, Oklahoma *by Caleb Freeman* 74
**R. A. Lafferty** Tulsa, Oklahoma *by Michael Helsem* 77
**Thomas Hart Benton** Shell Knob, Missouri *by Aaron Hadlow* 80
**Maya Angelou** Stamps, Arkansas *by Greer Veon* 83
**Elijah Lovejoy** Alton, Illinois *by Evan Allen Wood* 86
**Rachel** Prairie du Chien, Wisconsin *by Christy Clark-Pujara* 89

## MARK TWAIN

Hannibal, Missouri *by Cindy Lovell* 93
Hannibal, Missouri *by Avery Gregurich* 96
Elmira, New York *by Matt Seybold* 99
Hartford, Connecticut *by Jacques Lamarre* 102
London, England *by Susan Kumin Harris* 105
London, England *by Thomas Ruys Smith* 108

**F. Scott Fitzgerald** St. Paul, Minnesota *by Ross K. Tangedal* 111
**Heid E. Erdrich** Minneapolis, Minnesota *by Elizabeth Wilkinson* 113
**Louis L'Amour** Jamestown, North Dakota *by Sheila Liming* 115
**John Bartlow Martin** Herman, Michigan *by Ray E. Boomhower* 118
**Norbert Blei** Sister Bay, Wisconsin *by Jenna Goldsmith* 121

**Aldo Leopold** Baraboo, Wisconsin *by Marc Seals* 123
**August Derleth** Sauk City, Wisconsin *by Kassie Jo Baron* 125
**Lorine Niedecker** Blackhawk Island, Wisconsin *by Shanley Wells-Rau* 128

**CHICAGOLAND**

**Lisel Mueller** Forest Haven, Illinois *by Jenny Mueller* 132
**Sandra Cisneros** Chicago, Illinois *by Olga L. Herrera* 136
**Gwendolyn Brooks** Chicago, Illinois *by Angie Chatman* 138
**Richard Wright** Chicago, Illinois *by Joseph S. Pete* 141
**Hugo Martinez-Serros** Chicago, Illinois *by Emiliano Aguilar Jr.* 144
**José Olivarez** Calumet City, Illinois *by Ava Tomasula y Garcia* 147
**Jean Shepherd** Hammond, Indiana *by Samuel Love* 150

**Lew Wallace** Porter County, Indiana *by Matthew A. Werner* 152
**Michael Martone** LaPorte County, Indiana *by Dawn Burns* 155
**Bonnie Jo Campbell** Comstock, Michigan *by Lisa DuRose* 159
**Sojourner Truth** Battle Creek, Michigan *by Jeffrey Insko* 162
**Jim Harrison** Osceola County, Michigan *by Camden Burd* 165
**Robert Hayden** Detroit, Michigan *by Ayesha K. Hardison* 168
**Paul Vasey** Michigan—Ontario Border *by Ramya Swayamprakash* 171
**Philip Levine** Waawiiyaatanong *by Daniel A. Lockhart* 174

**TONI MORRISON**

Lorain, Ohio *by Tara L. Conley* 177
Lorain, Ohio *by Ashley Burge* 180
Cleveland, Ohio *by Monique Wingard* 183
West Point, New York *by Trivius G. Caldwell* 186
Chesapeake Bay, Maryland *by Alice Sundman* 189

**Sherwood Anderson** Elyria, Ohio *by Doug Sheldon* 192
**Kurt Vonnegut** Indianapolis, Indiana *by Laura Beadling* 195
**Booth Tarkington** Indianapolis, Indiana *by Wesley R. Bishop* 197

**Hunter S. Thompson** Louisville, Kentucky *by Charlie Cy* 200
**Sarah Morgan Bryan Piatt** North Bend, Ohio *by Sean E. Andres* 204
**John Augustus Stone** Metamora, Indiana *by Heather Chacón* 207
**Helen Hooven Santmyer** Xenia, Ohio *by Jacob A. Bruggeman* 210
**Zitkála-Šá** Richmond, Indiana *by Leah Abuan Milne* 213

**Appendix** 215
**Contributors** 218
**Photo Credits** 228

# FOREWORD

The first rapper I knew was from Chicago was Twista. My cousins in Los Angeles visited every other year, and when they did, they'd demand we play Cypress Hill, 2Pac, Snoop Dogg, Doctor Dre. Listening to rap music from Los Angeles was like listening to music from another country: the language was different. It's easy to imagine a different vocabulary coming out of Los Angeles, but it was more than that. Our landscapes were different. I had never seen a palm tree in real life. I didn't know what it felt like to drive up or down a mountain. My ocean was called Lake Michigan.

When I discovered Twista's music, I was a preteen. On "Mobster's Anthem," one of the Speedknot Mobstaz raps, "Chicago ain't a city, it's a nation." I don't know how much of the raps I really understood, but I felt that line. Chicago ain't a city, it's a nation. Look, it would be naive to pretend Twista and I had all that much in common. I was a Mexican American growing up in Calumet City, just south of Chicago, and Twista was a Black man from the West Side. In reality, we grew up in two distinct times and in two distinct but related places. Relation is important. Listening to Twista's music was the first time I understood that Chicago was a literary landscape. There was art to be made from the steel mills and the concrete and the mall and hours spent on the expressway. There was song in the suburbs. There was literature in the flash-fried foods. There was sculpture to be made from our distinctive drawl.

Reading the essays in *Lingering Inland*, I'm struck by the diversity of the Midwest. Though much of the country flattens us into a culturally barren flatlands, the Midwest is not a fixed or singular identity. For example, I was surprised and delighted to see Greer Veon's essay for Maya Angelou in Stamps, Arkansas. I hadn't considered Arkansas Midwestern, but I think that's my own bias as a northern Midwesterner.

So what does it mean to be from the Midwest? Like all identities, Midwestern is made up, and yet I can't deny that I swooned when a friend offered to take me to a cheese barn on a trip to Ohio. To be Midwestern is to love cheese. Unless you're a vegan Midwesterner. Maybe to be Midwestern is to be from a land and a people that are considered artifacts of the past.

By the time I graduated from high school, the steel mills in Chicago, Gary, and Pittsburgh had closed. Individual and small farms in Kansas were getting forced out by corporate farms and imports. We were considered expendable. Yet brilliant writers continue to emerge from the Midwest. Reports of our demise are greatly exaggerated. Because no one is looking to the Midwest for innovation, it has become an excellent place to experiment. The worst has already happened. Our former industries have collapsed or are on life support. What is there to do but dream a new way of living?

Our writers continue this tradition. They imagine a life where we are told none is sustainable. *Lingering Inland* is a testimony to the genius of the Midwest. It is a legacy I will honor by playing Twista and dreaming about Wisconsin cheese curds.

With hope,
*José Olivarez*

# ACKNOWLEDGMENTS

The making of a book is never as solitary as it sometimes feels, and that's especially true for this one. *Lingering Inland* grew out of the Literary Landscapes series at *The New Territory* magazine. Literary Landscapes began as a pandemic project, with all the acute feelings of isolation that came with the emergency closures of 2020 and the public health measures that continued for the next few years. During that anxiety-riddled period, reading and editing these essays was a lifeline. I am grateful to each of the seventy-three contributors for sharing their words and enthusiasm and to all the readers who have perused, shared, and supported the project.

Literary Landscapes could not have happened without Tina Casagrand Foss, the editor-in-chief of *The New Territory*, who found a place for it within the magazine's ecosystem and has helped it grow beyond our modest beginnings. Over the years, I've had the pleasure to work with many excellent editors and other members of the team, including Katie Young Foster, Sara Maillacheruvu, Shannon Silberman, Melanie Pierce, Jenna Dobyns, Julia Shiota, and Kevin Mahler. Grace Datil recently joined the team as an intern, and she has been instrumental to this book, performing research and communicating with contributors. The time and expertise devoted by this group of volunteers generates a beautiful, essential magazine, and they're a dream to work with.

I'm also grateful to the friends and colleagues who helped turn this idea into a book. Tina Casagrand Foss, Lisa DuRose, Katie Young Foster, Annika Mann, Steve Master, Jessica McKee, Jenny Smith, and Ross K. Tangedal all read and commented on drafts of the proposal and/or the introduction. Their feedback smoothed out rough edges and helped me speak to the multiple audiences who will one day (I hope!) select it from the shelf, take it home, and read it.

*Lingering Inland* is supported by a subsidy from the College of Arts and Sciences of Embry-Riddle Aeronautical University in Daytona Beach, Florida. A sincere thanks to Dean Peter Hoffmann and Senior Associate Dean Donna Barbie, who swim against some strong currents yet manage to make a felt difference in the working lives of faculty. As with any project, a good community makes the work easier, and while I could name any number of my department colleagues, I'll single out Steve Master, Jessica McKee, Sandy Branham, and Jen Wojton for their encouragement and support. Brie Cooper gets special mention for figuring things out and solving problems and keeping it all steady.

Thanks to Martha Bayne and the team at University of Illinois Press for helping to shape the book and guide it through the review and editing process.

My mom and aunts have been dedicated readers of Literary Landscapes; over the years, I've gotten to share their praise with a lot of contributors. So Mom, Aunt Nancy, Aunt Tracy, and Aunt Lisa, thank you, and I love you.

None of this would have been possible without Elin Grimes or my kids, Ada, Silas, and Miriam. Elin swears she did no work for this book, but that's a fiction—we made it together through a hard couple of years when this project was just beginning. I wouldn't have wanted to be locked down with anyone else, and even now that we have the choice to go out in the world, I'm usually happier to sit down to a Mario Karty with the four of you. I love you very much.

# LINGERING INLAND

# INTRODUCTION

*Andy Oler*

In 1989 or thereabouts, I posed on the side of US 40 in Greenfield, Indiana, and recited biographical facts about James Whitcomb Riley. I was standing under a sign outside Riley's childhood home, which wasn't open. Mom was filming, my grandparents' bulky camcorder perched on her shoulder. I believe it was cold. I know, at least, the wind was blowing, buffeting the mic. We did our best with the poor sound, editing that VHS into a short video for the Hagerstown Elementary media fair, which took place in the school's cafeteria, where the video played on a TV stacked up high on a rolling cart.

The video has since been lost, so I can't confirm what media fair attendees learned about Riley's life and work, but I bet it was some version of this: known as "The Hoosier Poet," James Whitcomb Riley was one of the most popular poets of the late nineteenth century. He was born in 1849 in Greenfield and lived his whole life in the Indianapolis area, until he died at home in 1916, after suffering a stroke. Riley began his career as a newspaperman and published his first book, *"The Old Swimmin'-Hole" and 'Leven More Poems*, in 1883. He was a charismatic reader, and his poem "Little Orphant Annie" originated the character that has spawned more than a century of comics, movies, and stage plays.[1] His most famous poems, including "The Raggedy Man" and "When the Frost Is on the Punkin," are written in rhyming couplets, in a dialect that Riley presented as the plain language of nineteenth-century Indiana farmers.

Riley is often read nostalgically, as dialect poetry tends to be, and I doubt as a fifth grader I would have been able to challenge that inclination.[2] I can hardly blame child me, though, because Riley is a master of the wistful, as you can see in the first few lines of "The Old Swimmin'-Hole":

> Oh! the old swimmin'-hole! whare the crick so still and deep
> Looked like a baby-river that was laying half asleep,
> And the gurgle of the worter round the drift jest below
> Sounded like the laugh of something we onc't ust to know[3]

Even as a child, I imagine I understood that the deep spot in this creek is familiar to Riley's speaker. As an adult, I notice how the movement of water downstream only slightly interrupts the scene's somnolence, but that minor disturbance doesn't shake the speaker out of the moment so much as send him into a daydream. It prompts a memory, a hazy one, of an experience at this place, or one much like it, that leads him to reflect on his mortality.

Considering my own recollection of the media fair, Riley's storytelling structure feels familiar: he begins with a scene, which recalls a sense memory, which turns into a more in-depth, personal contemplation that reveals an inherent or bittersweet complexity. The main difference, I suppose, is that Riley's poem begins with his own creation, and my writing begins with Riley's. The seventy-three essays in this book proceed similarly, with some writing and a place that matters—to both the contributor and their subject. Each chapter begins to show how the stories we tell about a place resonate personally as well as collectively. The book's title, *Lingering Inland*, signals those resonances by pointing to the land in the interior of the United States, the Midwest, a region that, like all regions, lays bare the desire for collectivity across vast landscapes.[4] The title also refers to contributors' physical lingering in these places and then their contemplation, over time, while writing and revising. I hope that readers, too, will have this experience: a lingering over both story and space that elicits a feeling of connection and prompts the reader to imagine their own literary landscapes.

## The Stories We Tell

"The Old Swimmin'-Hole" renders nineteenth-century Indiana a stage for "the merry days of youth," a place and time in which children could play, sometimes together, with minimal supervision, at an idyllic swimming hole just a short walk from their homes. The poem's speaker muses on loss but gets there through the description of the swimming hole. It's an image and a story that's easy for many (not all, but many) readers to connect to their own lives, and that way of engaging with creative and evocative writing is one of the reasons why this book centers literature. As a project, *Lingering Inland* asks these questions: How do the stories we tell about ourselves and our places influence or reflect our actual experiences? How is the literature of a place or a region relevant to the people who live there?

In answering those questions, contributors engage with a wide range of what might be considered "literary"—and a few texts challenging that definition. Many of this book's chapters think through the relationship between the contributor and the most commonly known (and assigned) types of literature, such as novels, poetry, short stories, and plays. Contributors also immerse themselves in recognizable literary nonfiction such as memoir, journalism, and travel writing. The subjects within this book, however, are not limited to what twentieth- and twenty-first-century readers might call "literary." Whatever the period, we define literature capaciously, as the writing that circulates, informs, and reflects the cultural life of our region and communities. *Lingering Inland* thus features a wide variety of texts, including those aforementioned forms alongside oratory, legal writing, and abolitionist tracts, as well as letters and other personal writing.

Combining readers' connections to different kinds of writing with a general openness to what counts as "Midwestern literature," then, helps achieve one of the main goals of this book: to present a version of the region that doesn't stop at the stereotypical.

## The Stories We Tell About Our Places

*Lingering Inland* is not simply about Midwestern literature—actual physical places are equally important. Contributors explore sites ranging from author houses to gravesites, rivers to railroads, existing structures to their remains. When I was doing my media-fair project, I stood outside the James Whitcomb Riley Boyhood Home and Museum, which is listed on the National Register of Historic Places (NRHP).[5] We didn't get to go inside because the museum was closed that day (pre-internet planning error), but from the outside it is a well-preserved, two-story white clapboard home with dark shutters and a porch stretching across the front with a balcony above. The roofline is adorned with corbels, their ornateness consistent with the balustrade and columns below. An inviting statue of Riley sitting on a bench out front was added some time later, during the state's bicentennial celebration.[6]

Mom drove me the hour to Greenfield because of this museum, a trip that serves as a lesson in the importance of historic preservation, which helps literary sites remain alive in

the popular imagination. The Riley home entered the public record in multiple ways, all related to Riley's reputation as "The Hoosier Poet." For example, this photo of Riley's home was taken in 1928 as part of the US Department of Commerce's Bureau of Public Roads project, which documented the nation's public roads and the commercial structures alongside them, including sites that would attract interest from tourists, such as the Riley birthplace. A few years later, in 1935, the City of Greenfield purchased the home from Riley's sister-in-law and has been operating the house as a museum ever since. The home was listed with the Indiana Department of Natural Resources Division of Historic Preservation in 1972, and the City of Greenfield filed for historic designation of the building with the NRHP in 1977. In the application, prepared by the president of the Riley Old Home Society, the site's area of significance is designated as "literature," one of twenty-eight possibilities listed by NRHP.[7]

Many contributors to this book visited designated or otherwise preserved historical landmarks and could therefore tell a similar story of their subject's validation in official discourse. More of them, however, write about sites that have fallen into ruin or include only traces of their literary significance. Throughout *Lingering Inland*, lost and diminished sites serve a comparative function, either between past and present or between the subject's experience (or imagination!) and the contributor's. In some essays, these differences reveal past improvements or new possibilities. For others, as with Riley's poem, they provoke a lament for the loss of a desirable past or an accumulated understanding of what the future may hold. Whether the place has been altered or preserved, these essays demonstrate how Midwestern stories are rooted in Midwestern places.

## The Stories We Tell About Ourselves

They also show how those places and stories are significant to Midwestern people. The personal aspect of this book stands alongside the literary and place-based elements and, in fact, is what sets it apart from other books about literary places. In these essays, personal reflection is the bridge between literature and place. Riley's nostalgia prompts a similar contemplative mode, as he opens the stanza above with these lines: "Oh! the old swimmin'-hole! When I last saw the place, / The scenes was all changed, like the change in my face." Thinking back on my media-fair project, from a distance of several states and thirty-plus years, it's hard not to recognize the change in my face (when I returned home for Christmas after moving away for a job, my mom said to me, "There's a lot of gray in that beard, Andy Oler"). There's an element of nostalgia in my own reflection, as there is with Riley's poem, and that feels personally significant. It might also be culturally significant, as Svetlana Boym tells us, because nostalgia offers a way to uncover the "unrealized possibilities" of modern life.[8]

Individual nostalgic reflection, for instance, can expose gaps of knowledge or understanding, revealing broader cultural bias. In the case of my media fair project, I presented a poet who told stories about people who had a lot in common with my family: white, working Hoosier farmers. Later, I found out how "the scenes was all changed." Upon reading Anna-Lisa Cox's *The Bone and Sinew of the Land*, I learned that in the first half of the nineteenth century there were thirteen African American farming settlements within about twenty miles of where I grew up.[9] As a kid, I did local history projects and then even got a degree in history, and yet this was news to me. Black history in my part of Indiana was taught by centering the Quakers for their role in the Underground Railroad—meaning, we learned that we lived in a place where Black people passed through, not where they settled. This is obviously a problematic way to impart the history of east-central Indiana. There is a more complete story to tell. (The book ends with an essay about Indigenous writer Zitkála-Šá at Earlham College in my county seat of Richmond, Indiana—another aspect of local history I never learned until recently.)

This collection doesn't presume that any one person can tell the whole story. Rather, building on scholars who emphasize the contradictory images and shifts in outlook that shape our view of the region, this book offers a multiplicity of personal perspectives.[10] Those many voices also demonstrate the distinct ways that literature circulates in our region. Midwestern literature is not relevant because any single reader, writer, or scholar says so; these stories are relevant because people encounter versions of them in their everyday lives, because they think about literature, and because it helps them understand their world or their experiences or their places in a different or more complete way. *Lingering Inland* aspires to develop a greater understanding of Midwestern life and literature through the dozens of personal experiences, perspectives, and reflections found in its chapters.

## The Stories We Tell About the Midwest

This book has its origins in the Literary Landscapes series published by *The New Territory* magazine, which bills itself as "the autobiography of the Lower Midwest." I pitched the series to Editor-in-Chief Tina Casagrand Foss in early 2020, just before the COVID pandemic began, and we decided that the series would publish in volumes of five essays to mimic the feel of a print magazine, which is *The New Territory*'s main identity. The essays would be built on each contributor's enthusiasm, or their revulsion, or their guardedness. They were conceived to be bite-size, easy to read, something a reader might peruse with their morning coffee that would spark their own reflections throughout the rest of the day. We published the first issue of Literary Landscapes in June 2020 and attracted widespread interest; in the first sixteen volumes, there has been only one repeat contributor. Much like the print magazine markets itself to people "who believe a sense of belonging in a place is possible no matter where they started," the Literary Landscapes series and this book amplify the people and stories of the Midwest.[11] Accordingly, each volume of Literary Landscapes is organized around a principle of geographical diversity, featuring locations and stories from all over the Midwest and Great Plains, often with quite some distance between them.

*Lingering Inland*, on the other hand, juxtaposes pieces of literature and contributor experiences that take place somewhat near each other. This book is arranged almost as if the reader were on a road trip (with a voyage up the Mississippi River in the middle). Taking its cue from Kristin L. Hoganson's *The Heartland: An American History*, this book offers a story of the Midwest emphasizing circulation.[12] Contrary to histories inspired by Manifest

Destiny or Frederick Jackson Turner's frontier thesis, this version of the Midwest is not based on westward expansion.[13] Instead, it accentuates proximity, moving from place to place, rambling through the region in an uneven, occasionally crisscrossing path. Sometimes the links between chapters are clear; at other times they are more tenuous. There are five clusters in the book. Two of them highlight Chicago and St. Louis, conglomerations based more on contributor interest than on a specific attempt to feature those cities (Tulsa, Indianapolis, Omaha, Detroit, and the Twin Cities have their own mini-clusters and might have developed into larger ones). The other three are focused on revered Midwestern authors Willa Cather, Mark Twain, and Toni Morrison, whom I selected as representatives of the sweep of Midwestern writing. They show the diversity of the region, its people, and its literature, as well as how long Midwesterners have been among the nation's premier authors. The essays about Cather, Twain, and Morrison also stretch the book's geography, making a case that the significance of Midwestern literature is not confined within the boundaries of the region.

This organization puts canonical and underrepresented authors in conversation with each other, and through it we travel from country to city and everywhere in between. The goal, then, is to show how literature is all around us—not just in the books we read but on our walk down main street or as we cross the railroad tracks or when we sense the river tucked behind that stand of trees. The stories we tell about our region and about ourselves are in our backyards as much as our historical sites. They are as relevant to us today as they were to Riley when he conjured his old swimming hole, where "the sunshine and shadder fell over it all."

Whether you read straight through or drop in and out, as time and circumstance allow, please enjoy.

## Notes

1. See George C. Hitt, "James Whitcomb Riley," *Indiana Magazine of History* 32, no. 3 (1936): 200–201; Barbara Olenyik Morrow, *From Ben-Hur to Sister Carrie: Remembering the Lives and Works of Five Indiana Authors* (Indianapolis: Guild Press of Indiana, 1995), 56–59; and H. J. Burrell, "From Curls to Color: A Cinematic Evolution of Little Orphan Annie," *Film Matters* 8, no. 1 (2017): 52.

2. See Nadia Nurhussein, *Rhetorics of Literacy: The Cultivation of American Dialect Poetry* (Columbus: Ohio State University Press, 2013); Angela Sorby, "Performing Class: James Whitcomb Riley's Poetry of Distinction," *Modern Language Quarterly* 60, no. 2 (1999): 197–222; and Morrow, *From Ben-Hur to Sister Carrie*.

3. James Whitcomb Riley, "The Old Swimmin'-Hole," in *"The Old Swimmin'-Hole" and 'Leven More Poems* (Indianapolis: Bobbs-Merrill, 1920), 9–12, http://purl.dlib.indiana.edu/iudl/general/VAA4391.

4. See Benedict Anderson, *Imagined Communities: Reflections on the Origin and Spread of Nationalism* (London: Verso, 1983).

5. "James Whitcomb Riley Boyhood Home and Museum," Greenfield Parks and Recreation, accessed May 14, 2024, https://parksingreenfield.com/riley-home/.

6. "Reading with Riley Bicentennial Statue Project," IN.gov, accessed May 14, 2024, https://www.in.gov/ibc/legacyprojects/3706.htm.

7. Thomas E. Q. Williams, "James Whitcomb Riley Birthplace," National Register of Historic Places Nomination Form (Washington, DC: US Department of the Interior, National Park Service, 1977), 3.

8. Svetlana Boym, *The Future of Nostalgia* (New York: Basic, 2001), xvi.

9. Anna-Lisa Cox, *The Bone and Sinew of the Land: America's Forgotten Black Pioneers and the Struggle for Equality* (New York: PublicAffairs, 2018).

10. See James R. Shortridge, *The Middle West: Its Meaning in American Culture* (Lawrence: University Press of Kansas, 1989); Jason Weems, *Barnstorming the Prairies: How Aerial Vision Shaped the Midwest* (Minneapolis: University of Minnesota Press, 2015); Janet Galligani Casey, *A New Heartland: Women, Modernity, and the Agrarian Ideal in America* (New York: Oxford University Press, 2009); Terrion L. Williamson, ed., *Black in the Middle: An Anthology of the Black Midwest* (Cleveland: Belt, 2020); Sujey Vega, *Latino Heartland: Of Borders and Belonging in the Midwest* (New York: New York University Press, 2015); Adam R. Ochonicky, *The American Midwest in Film and Literature: Nostalgia, Violence, and Regionalism* (Bloomington: Indiana University Press, 2020); and Phil Christman, *Midwest Futures* (Cleveland: Belt, 2020).

11. "About," New Territory, accessed May 14, 2024, https://newterritorymag.com/about/the-magazine/.

12. Kristin L. Hoganson, *The Heartland: An American History* (New York: Penguin, 2019).

13. Frederick Jackson Turner, *The Frontier in American History* (New York: Henry Holt, 1921).

# MARI SANDOZ

## Gravesite
## Sheridan County, Nebraska

*By C. J. Janovy*

It's not easy to get to the final resting place of Nebraska writer Mari Sandoz, whose books, I'll go ahead and argue, evoke one region of America as powerfully as William Faulkner's portray another.

Paying respects to Sandoz in the traditional way of visiting her gravesite requires a pilgrimage far from the interstate, through sandhill counties so thinly populated one can drive twenty minutes (it feels longer) without seeing another moving vehicle, on a two-lane highway dipping and rising through a forbidding grass-covered Sahara. Finally, about twenty-seven miles north of unincorporated Ellsworth, a historical marker affirms that this is Sandoz country. A faded sign across from the Deer Meadows hunting outfitters confirms she is buried three miles farther back in the hills.

Getting to this point requires first knowing who Mari Sandoz was. I never encountered her name on any syllabus despite graduating from the Lincoln Public Schools and earning two fancy English degrees (I hope syllabi have changed). I made this pilgrimage only after reconciling a childhood mystery.

## MARI SANDOZ

**Born: May 11, 1896, in Hay Springs, Nebraska**

**Died: March 10, 1966, in New York, New York**

**Forms: Novels, Biographies, Short Stories**

**Recommended Works: *Old Jules* (1935), *Capital City* (1939), *Crazy Horse* (1942), *The Strange Man of the Oglalas* (1942), *Cheyenne Autumn* (1953), *The Horsecatcher* (1957), *The Story Catcher* (1963)**

When I was a kid, Mari Sandoz's name stared back at me from the bookshelves above the fireplace at my grandparents' house in Oklahoma City. The book's yellow spine sang out like a meadowlark, while tall red letters spelled two simple words: *Old Jules*. Below that was the author's name in simple yet elegant black. The dramatic block letters told me the subject of this book was important. But what kind of name was "Jules"? It must be a man (tall red letters were for men). He was "old," like the grandfather I loved, whose fireplace was where Santa delivered gifts, but this book was on high shelves where only the adults could reach it. The writer had a strange name, too. Was "Mari" a boy or a girl? How was I supposed to pronounce it in my mind? Decades later, after my folks cleaned out my grandparents' mid-century-modern house, this book was the only thing I wanted. And I finally read it.

The Swiss immigrant Jules Sandoz was an awful human, literally filthy and abusive but also educated enough to deliver breech babies on the frontier in the 1880s. Once the United States government had murdered or moved the region's Indians, Old Jules helped colonize his part of the country through cussedness, luck, marksmanship, and the help of obedient women, one of whom wound up in the insane asylum. I don't know how often Sandoz uses the word "pounded" in this portrait of her father, but it's a lot.

Generations of readers have put up with this man for 424 pages of what is now considered Mari Sandoz's masterpiece. In this way, Sandoz's accomplishment is far greater than her father's legacy of towns and services in western Nebraska. Given the difficulties of making a life in this harsh place and time, one might wonder: Why bother? I think it was so his daughter could write such a beautiful book. "In Jules," she observed, "as in every man, there lurks something ready to destroy the finest in him as the frosts of the earth destroy her flowers."

Mari Sandoz Memorial Drive is a sand road that winds past a clanking windmill and ends in a patch of grass on a hill. Farther up is a plot surrounded by barbed wire, with a white gate. The plum-colored headstone reads simply "Mari Sandoz 1896–1966." A metal glider allows visitors to sit and contemplate the view.

Near the gate is a mailbox; inside is a spiral-bound notebook whose messages reveal it hasn't been long since someone else was here.

"She was an admirable person & wonderful writer!" wrote one visitor from Windsor, Colorado. "I heard her speak at Kearney State College in 1965, approx. 1 yr. before she died. I can still hear her exclaim, 'read my books.'"

Dan Kusek, vice president of the Mari Sandoz Heritage Society, had started a fresh notebook six weeks before my most recent visit.

“When they were bringing Mari’s casket here for burial, the hearse could climb no further,” Kusek wrote at the top of the first page. “Mari’s wish was to be buried at the TOP of the hill but they could get no further. A hawk came over us here while we were cutting grass & weeds. I have no doubt it was Mari’s spirit!!”

The only spirit I felt was the unnamed woman in *Old Jules* who tried to walk home to her one-year-old baby in a blizzard. “When the sun shone warm again over the glistening, drifted plains,” Sandoz wrote, “she was found curled up in a blanket in the slat-bottomed cart, a mile from home, frozen.”

Sitting in the sun on the metal glider, pondering the hills where Mari and Jules last lived, it was tempting to imagine her voice in the wind-stirring grasses. But even with a breeze, the place was so profoundly silent that all my own thoughts were too loud.

# JAMES EMANUEL

## Alliance Public Library
## Alliance, Nebraska

*By Sean Theodore Stewart*

Alliance, Nebraska, does not remember James Emanuel. There is no plaque, no statue. His poetry is not assigned to high school students. Despite the lofty architecture of the public library and museum, there is no display, no exhibit. Just two or three dusty books kept in the staff room of the library alongside genealogy tomes protected behind glass cases. Protected from being discovered.

I grew up craving art in a town that didn't have any. I read about other places—any other place I could—and the figures who put those places on the map. I decried the emptiness of the prairie I found myself in. I was scared the small world of my beginning had set the limits for all I could be.

Alliance had no bookstore, no venue for musical or theatrical performances to speak of, no university. In this town of eight thousand, I gravitated to the place where stories could be found. The public library was a lifeline. Everywhere else my world felt small, but when I stepped inside the library it became limitless. The old library building, built in 1912 with a Carnegie grant, boasts classical columns and resilient stone. The current library is equally grand: skylight windows fifty feet up seem to usher the world in. The place grabbed me. I got a job as a library page, and as I shelved books, a new geography imprinted itself on my mind. Even if no section of the library was especially thorough, I could see the hints of everything not present. And I wanted to learn it all.

## JAMES EMANUEL

**Born: June 15, 1921, in Alliance, Nebraska**

**Died: September 28, 2013, in Paris, France**

**Forms: Poetry, Literary Criticism**

**Recommended Works: *Black Man Abroad: The Toulouse Poems* (1970), *The Force and the Reckoning* (1984), *Whole Grain: Collected Poems, 1958–1989* (1991), *Jazz from the Haiku King* (1999)**

I'd been working there for years before I discovered James Emanuel. His faded books were kept with the archives in the staff room. When I was tasked with rearranging the archival shelves I was, as far as I could tell, the first to look at them in decades.

What I found left me breathless. James Emanuel was a poet pushing against the very bounds of what it's possible for one life to contain.

He was born in Alliance in 1921 and grew up with the same quiet streets that I did, the same railroad engines droning in the distance, the same treeless sandhills stretching to every horizon. He read his first poem at Alliance Junior High. As a teenager, he worked on a cattle ranch before leaving the area and moving East.

Emanuel attended Howard, Northwestern, and Columbia universities. He was mentored by Langston Hughes, about whom Emanuel went on to write an influential book-length analysis. Emanuel then cemented his own scholarly reputation with *Dark Symphony: Negro Literature in America*, a groundbreaking anthology of African American literature.

From the relatively pastoral beginning of early poems, Emanuel shifted the focus of his later works to racial injustice. Their topical change is matched by their uptick in rhythm. Poems like "Panther Man," his scorching condemnation of the murder of Fred Hampton, are marvels of energy and anger. Emanuel later disavowed America entirely. His son was brutalized by police and took his own life in the aftermath. James Emanuel renounced the United States and spent the rest of his life an expatriate in France, pioneering a new form he called the jazz haiku.

I have to think that Emanuel's artistic and personal evolution in a direction his country was unwilling to follow is at least partly responsible for his anonymity in Alliance. When he died in 2013, the Alliance Times Herald ran one of his early poems called "Poet as Fisherman," sidestepping his real legacy as a poet of startling rhythm, fierce critiques, and unfettered experimentation. I'm proud, now, to be from the home of the blistering jazz haiku king, James Emanuel—from the town whose streets and surrounding oceans of dry tallgrass shaped Emanuel's early world.

When I began looking for traces of him in Alliance, I learned that Emanuel said of the public library—the 1912 iteration—"the Alliance town library was in biblical terms 'my truth and my refuge.'" I wish I could tell him that it was for me, too. I wish I could tell him that his own books that I discovered there are no small part of why.

# WRIGHT MORRIS

## 304 D Street
## Central City, Nebraska

*By Nathan Tye*

For Wright Morris, home was both a physical place and an emotional ache. Born in Central City, Nebraska, in 1910, Morris made his life elsewhere but returned to the Platte Valley in his writing and photography. His childhood home remains, now a museum maintained by the Lone Tree Literary Society, and in it I find a shared weight of homecoming. Like him, I was born in the Platte Valley, built a life elsewhere, and returned. Morris's labor to excavate the homes and memories resonates as I uncover connections fallen into disrepair and begin to build a new life on the old.

Carefully restored, this single-story white frame house, built amid the Panic of 1893 by a real estate agent, carries the faded wealth of a smalltown businessman. Certainly, it must have felt like that when a widower, his son, and his housekeeper moved in two decades later. Morris's earliest memory of "lampglow and shadows on a low ceiling" is likely tied to this home. A window topped with a row of colored glass faces northeast. Bedbound with pneumonia, Morris traced the colored beams as they moved across his sheets in that room. In his first memoir, he admits that such memories left him with "the ache of a nameless longing," which he threaded through his work until he died.

## WRIGHT MORRIS

**Born: January 6, 1910, in Central City, Nebraska**

**Died: April 25, 1998, in Mill Valley, California**

**Forms: Novels, Photography, Essays, Memoir**

**Recommended Works: *The Inhabitants* (1946), *The Home Place* (1948), *The Field of Vision* (1956), *Love Among the Cannibals* (1957), *Ceremony in Lone Tree* (1960), *Plains Song* (1980)**

In *The Home Place* (1948), Clyde Muncy returns to Lone Tree, a stand-in for Central City. Nearly thirty years gone, Clyde has a new family, a new place, and memories ill fitted to Lone Tree's present. Clyde's futile attempt at placemaking is framed by images of debris and empty farmsteads, a subject Morris first explored in *The Inhabitants* (1946). In both books he captures a world worn over—abandoned homes, barren storefronts, footfall-worn carpets, frayed familial ties—and finds those spaces inhabited by absence. These homebound texts are all the sharper in our homebound epoch, for our own places are now populated with days upon days of unbroken living.

Morris relished patina, the worn, and the lived in. For him, abandonment closes distances in time. Or as the art critic and novelist John Berger found, "Home is the return to where distance did not yet count." What though, does home mean, in Central City and the elsewheres we find ourselves ordered in? Where do our ties to the past take us when the future is so uncertain? Morris returned to escape and, by documenting these visits, laid the foundation for the preservation of his home. The connection to the past "was the important thing. It had to be established," Morris wrote in *The Home Place*. "I had to be born again." Morris's texts and images commingled the present and past to forward a vision of living nostalgia.

The Lone Tree Literary Society has reversed the decay Morris documented and made his childhood home available to curious publics. And while what Morris called "the inhabitants" of these structures may now be obscured by respectful restorations, in Morris's work, their absence persists. Later in his career, Morris commented that photographs came from "the most durable of ghosts, nostalgia." In his early images of Central City, he reached back to the remnants he left in order to move forward. Nostalgia is a welcome escape given the uncertainty of our present, but as Morris's struggle with his homebound ghosts underscores, our worn-over homes are points of departure, not occupation.

At home with ourselves, we're learning to live with our inhabitants. Like Morris's photographs, COVID-19 emptied the streets, turned homes into lived-in voids, and blurred delineations between past, present, and future. Yet by documenting deterioration and distance, Morris pointed toward a restorative future. Now, in the stillness of an uncertain time, the inhabitants of Morris's home and those of our own become clearer, and the possibilities they hold emerge.

# TED KOOSER

## Gravel Roads
## Seward County, Nebraska

*By Matt Miller*

For all his stature as former US Poet Laureate, Ted Kooser remains a poet of Nebraska, and so he is a poet of gravel roads. Consider "So This Is Nebraska," his best-known poem about his home state:

> The gravel road rides with a slow gallop
> over the fields, the telephone lines
> streaming behind, its billow of dust
> full of the sparks of redwing blackbirds.
> . . .
> So this is Nebraska. A Sunday
> afternoon; July. Driving along
> with your hand out squeezing the air,
> a meadowlark waiting on every post.

I grew up in Seward County, just outside of Milford, about sixteen miles from Kooser's home in the village of Garland. Our cars never lacked a thin coat of dust that I found embarrassing any time we went "to town" in Lincoln; the city seemed so clean, with all its white concrete. Still, the gravel roads were our life in Seward County. We met our neighbors there, stopping our cars right in the middle of the lane to chat through open windows. We explored nature and culture on the roads, tossing rocks in Coon Creek or gawking at somebody's private landfill, posted "NO DUPING" (exact spelling). Sometimes the roads became our grocery store—we knew where elderberries or wild plums grew in the ditches. Once, we found a stand of edible crabapples and picked gallons of them. As we drove home, we trailed one out the back window of our Chevy Astro with a reel of dental floss, a spot of red leaping on the tan of the washboards.

## TED KOOSER

**Born: April 25, 1939, in Ames, Iowa**

**Died: —**

**Forms: Poetry, Essays, Children's Literature**

**Recommended Works: *Local Wonders: Seasons in the Bohemian Alps* (2002), *Delights and Shadows* (2004), *Flying at Night: Poems 1965–1985* (2005), *The Poetry Home Repair Manual: Practical Advice for Beginning Poets* (2005), *Kindest Regards: New and Selected Poems* (2018)**

It is from time spent on those gravel roads that Nebraskans can tell you the shape of our country, that we know where to find the old German church or the local fishing hole. It is because of gravel roads that we know, as Kooser puts it in the voice of a radiator in a broken-down Chevy, "the names of all these / tattered moths and broken grasshoppers / the rest of you've forgotten."

The gravel roads have their limitations as a public square, however. If somebody turns onto your lane, you had better stop gossiping with the neighbor and get out of the way. And Kooser, in his 2002 memoir *Local Wonders*, highlights another limitation in a rare moment of political commentary. At the start of the book's consideration of summer in Seward County, Kooser observes two contractors spraying herbicide on the roadside: "the Fourth of July parade float for this year's Poison Queen." "While these two hapless men are killing the things they're paid to be killing," Kooser laments, "they're spraying nearly everything else as well: the sunflowers, the pink wild roses, the wild grapevines, the chokecherries." The public benefit of the gravel roads extends only so far as public willingness to preserve them.

Some of that willingness has grown since Kooser wrote *Local Wonders*. Now, when I go home, milkweed and yellow signs marking organic crops are commonplace in the ditches. The spraying regimen may have loosened a bit, to judge by the milkweed. And the new prevalence of organic growers testifies to some rising ecological concern, however market driven. At least some of Kooser's neighbors in Seward County have understood how these roads and the creatures about them still contour our lives as they do the landscape.

And those contours have lasting meaning. Near the end of *Local Wonders*, Kooser recounts how the roads helped him endure cancer: "Each day when I came home, I stopped at the head of our lane and picked up a pebble from the road. I lined these up along the kitchen windowsill to count off the treatments."

Mercifully, Kooser survived, and so we might imagine that line of pebbles continuing on, day by day, joining up into a road. Beside them on the sill, a wild rose.

# MALCOLM X

## 3448 Pinkney Street
## Omaha, Nebraska

*By Ashley Howard*

My 1980s childhood included reading to my Cabbage Patch Kid in a neon bean bag and practicing my moves so that I could dance with MC Skat Kat. I was (am) a nerd. I loved school. And with the exception of the week set aside for standardized testing (shout out to Iowa Test of Basic Skills), field trips reigned as the most exciting occasions.

In Omaha, where I grew up, trips to the railroad museum and zoo were standard. Once when we visited the Mormon Pioneer Cemetery, I tripped and fell face first into a spiked wrought-iron fence. Relatively unscathed, I returned to the school cafeteria where my third-grade classmates and I shook a mason jar filled with cold cream until our little arms turned to mush.

It was a good day. We ate fresh-baked bread and homemade butter. I didn't lose an eye.

Another time our plaid-clad mob loaded onto a yellow bus bound for Hastings. At the end of the two-hour drive, we met global legend—well at least *People* magazine feature fowl and *Tonight Show* guest—Andy the Footless Goose.

These trips reinforced the mythologized stories taught to me about Nebraska history. Wide-open prairies, bustling stockyards, brave pioneers, and wholesome heartland values.

Absent were the stories of the displaced Pawnee, Ponca, Omaha, and Oto-Missouria peoples. Erased were the Black, Asian, and Latinx workers who butchered livestock and built railroads. The state's ugliest moments, those that challenged claims of Midwestern meritocracy, were swept under the rug.

Both within the popular imagination and much of the scholarly discourse, the Midwest is normalized as an exclusively white place—frozen in the past, albeit one dissociated from actual historical reality. Politicians, journalists, and everyday citizens regard the region with deep nostalgia; a "museum-piece" of a bygone era in times of great uncertainty.

## MALCOLM X

**Born: May 19, 1925, in Omaha, Nebraska**

**Died: February 21, 1965, in New York, New York**

**Forms: Autobiography, Oratory**

**Recommended Works: *The Autobiography of Malcolm X* (1965, with Alex Haley), *Malcolm X Speaks: Selected Speeches and Statements* (1965), *By Any Means Necessary: Speeches, Interviews, and a Letter* (1970), *Malcolm X: The Last Speeches* (1989)**

I was in my thirties and a professor of African American history when I finally took my own field trip to the birth site of Malcolm X, Omaha's oft-forgotten native son.

The opening pages of Malcolm X's autobiography, and arguably of his political radicalization, begin in Omaha. In the chapter "Nightmare," Malcolm shares a vivid description, recounted to him by his mother, Louise Little. One evening the Ku Klux Klan rode on their home to intimidate the family into fleeing. Heavily pregnant with her fourth child, while her husband was traveling, Mrs. Little stood her ground as the terrorists "galloped around the house, shattering every windowpane with their gun butts. Then they rode off into the night, their torches flaring, as suddenly as they had come." The Littles welcomed their son Malcolm a few months later and remained for two more years. Although Omaha is not mentioned again in the five-hundred-page book, the violence his family experienced throughout the region looms large.

In death, as he was in life, Malcolm X is a divisive figure. An admitted hustler, convicted felon, racial separatist, Muslim, and provocative orator, his brilliance resonated deeply with millions across the African diaspora. Yet the memorialization of his first home at 3448 Pinkney proceeded at a near glacial pace, due in part to his political views and widespread skepticism that one of the nation's most prominent Black leaders hailed from Nebraska. This delay is especially stark when compared to Atlanta's thirty-eight-acre Martin Luther King, Jr. National Historical Park, consisting of dozens of buildings managed by the National Parks Service.

If we consider that physical sites promote our most sacred historical myths, this really should come as no surprise. America now embraces King and the sanitized narrative of his activism as proof of this nation's redemptive, triumphalist narrative arc. Narrators distill racism as contained to the south and eradicated through the efforts of activists and federal legislation. The blocks-long King site affirms this illusion.

The Littles' Omaha experience and the ongoing struggle to create an adequate memorial of their son challenges this framework and breaks open the comfortable history of the Midwest. The Klan threatened the young family on account of Earl and Louise Little successfully organizing with the Omaha branch of the Universal Negro Improvement Association. Founded by Marcus Garvey in 1914, the pan-Africanist organization promoted Black economic independence and racial pride, representing a freedom agenda distinct from the integrationist model.

The struggle for recognition of Malcolm X's home is a continuation of this tension. The city razed the modest house on Pinkney in 1965, the year Malcom was assassinated. That building's destruction was the result of ignorance, not malice. But the wholesale demolition of homes on the surrounding blocks is indicative of the inherent racism of urban renewal.

In 1970 activist and former resident of the home Rowena Moore began the Malcolm X Memorial Foundation. While the Nebraska Historical Marker Program quickly approved the sign, another two decades passed before it was placed. On May 19, 1987, on what should have been Malcolm X's sixty-second birthday, the official state marker was dedicated. When I visited over a decade ago the marker stood, a lone sentinel in an overgrown lot, isolated from Malcolm X's activism and the vibrant community.

Today that spirit is renewed. In 2018 artist and land activist Jordan Weber constructed the 4MX greenhouse, conceived as a place to nurture seedlings and people. When standing in the greenhouse, X's historical marker is perfectly framed between the wide-open double doors. The marker's final four words read, "His teaching lives on."

What might schoolchildren learn from a visit to this site? By reinscribing Malcolm X onto the landscape, his legacy comes to the fore. Put simply, this means a radical retelling of Omaha's history. That retelling includes stories about Moore's work organizing women meatpackers as well as about Black high school students staging a walkout on May 19, 1969, demanding racially affirming educational experiences.

These histories also generate new questions: What were the work and educational experiences of Black Omahans? Why are there no local streets, government buildings, or schools bearing Malcolm's name? Why were 311 historical markers erected around the state before one honored the contributions of a Black Nebraskan?

Neighborhood divestment and stigmatization ensures that no one will happen upon Malcolm X's birthplace. One must intentionally seek it out. And like I sought out the physical marker, Omahans must also journey to seek answers to the above questions.

Through a deep engagement with Malcolm X's Omaha experience, students will locate the rich social, intellectual, cultural, and political life of the city's Black residents. In (re) visiting these sites, a more complex portrait of the construction and maintenance of Midwestern mythologies emerges. Such field trips to the past provide a roadmap to a more inclusive history and future. To supplement the white bread snack (and history) of my youth with colorful, community-grown veggies is delicious indeed.

WILLA CATHER

## WILLA CATHER

Born: December 7, 1873, near Winchester, Virginia

Died: April 24, 1947, in New York, New York

Forms: Novels, Short Stories, Essays, Poetry

Recommended Works: *O Pioneers!* (1913), *The Song of the Lark* (1915), *My Ántonia* (1918), *One of Ours* (1922), *A Lost Lady* (1923), *The Professor's House* (1925), *Death Comes for the Archbishop* (1927)

# WILLA CATHER

## The Mesa
## Taos, New Mexico

*By Tracy Sanford Tucker*

I am an American pilgrim. I've visited a hundred holy sites trying to find my way, seeking an intercession, hoping to meet my gods in the air. I've found myself at Walden Pond, naturally, and the stone wall at Robert Frost's farm, but there are many stations on this journey: the American Gothic house, Steinbeck's "Mother Road," First Avenue in Minneapolis, and a spot on the side of a Missouri highway where Ira Louvin died.

But by profession, as a writer, as an archivist, I hold one figure above them all—Willa Cather. I've traveled where she traveled, slept where she slept, and chased the horizons that populate her novels and short stories. From her birth house in Gore, Virginia, to her grave in Jaffrey, New Hampshire, and to so many places she wandered in between, I've been there, trailing after her spirit, looking for my own.

Cather wrote in a 1912 letter that, for the first time, she was glad to be away from New Mexico and Arizona; though she enjoyed the summer, she "was ready to leave when the time came. . . . The country," she continued, "is wonderful, fabulous; but after all, 'dans le desert,' as Balzac said, 'il y a tout, et il n'y a rien; Dieu sans les hommes.'" The desert is everything and nothing. God without men.

And so I am in Taos, seeing the sights, but it's the desert that calls me. For days, I let myself be led and, while I keep in mind a place to sleep, the roads just run. I think of Cather's letter quoting Balzac. I see everything and nothing.

On the mesa west of town, the road runs out, but I walk on, the scent of Chamiso pardo and rabbitbrush rising like prayers as I brush by. I breathe in their incense. Cactus spikes whisper against my pack. I have visions. I try to fathom Cather in this land. She rides through at a distance, but I can barely make her out. Between us are other figures, but they might be mirages. Smoke and sand. Wind shaking the wild oats.

A dried fruit of a tree cholla clings to the back of my coat. I don't discover it until I'm back in Nebraska, and I tuck it away in the console with other relics: sea glass from Nantucket Harbor and limestone from my family's farm and corroded buttons found buried in the dirt of an abandoned Colorado soddy.

At home I look at Cather's letter again. After she quotes Balzac, she writes, "You see, you get so lonely (I mean your soul gets lonely) in a land which has had only a geological history. Your spirit can't find anything to hang on by!" But it can, I think, and mine has hung on to that mesa, returning again and again, a lost traveler walking in circles in the only place that feels real, independent of man.

Back in Cather's Nebraska, the cholla fruit, dense and desiccated, splits its skin, and its seeds pour out, tiny miracles. Their prickles are everywhere I touch, snagging. When I think I'm rid of them, I notice tiny cholla growing in the sand at the edge of the yard. I tease them out, nurture them, but I don't think they need me. The desert is real. I'm the mirage.

# WILLA CATHER

## Pavelka Farmstead
## Bladen, Nebraska

*By Christine Pivovar*

Willa Cather's *My Ántonia* (1918) contains the first written use of the word *kolaches* in English, according to the OED. It comes in at the end of the novel, when the narrator, Jim, visits his childhood friend Ántonia at her "wide farmhouse, with a red barn and an ash grove" and meets her brood of boisterous children. The sweet, fruit-filled Czech pastries they serve him are still commonplace in bakeries throughout Nebraska today, but I'd never expected to find such a small, prosaic piece of our culture appear in one of the twentieth century's great American novels. I've made kolaches myself, using my grandma's recipe, which can't be much different from the one Ántonia's daughters used. Reading that scene, I had a powerful sense of seeing myself in a novel in a different way than I ever had before. Ántonia could have been my own great-grandmother.

Part of why I could picture that scene so vividly is because I have been to the "wide farmhouse" Cather describes. A few miles north of Cather's hometown of Red Cloud, Nebraska, it was the home of her friend Annie Pavelka, who became the inspiration for the character of Ántonia.

Situated near the geographical center of the continental US, Red Cloud is a town of brick streets, charming Victorian houses and a wide-open sky. It's the kind of town where cowboys in full gear stroll into the Subway and two of the town's three restaurants close for the weekend because of a family wedding. It was founded in 1871, and when the railroad came through in 1879 it brought settlers from all over Europe and the eastern United States. Born in Virginia, Cather moved to Nebraska with her family in 1883. She lived in and around Red Cloud until she left for college in Lincoln. Her memories of this place, in particular the hard but vibrant lives of the pioneer farmers, inspired many of her novels and stories.

Today the Pavelka Farmstead is one of the sites maintained by the Willa Cather Foundation, which provides guided tours of significant places in the author's life and work. The tour guides can tell you which of Cather's friends were the models for which characters, what living room a particular scene takes place in. Although their close reading can feel restrictive at times—the books are fiction, after all—there seems to be a kind of pragmatic Nebraskan mindset that looks for these concrete connections. Readers and tourists are used to hunting down literary settings in New York and Boston. Why shouldn't they also do so in Red Cloud?

In 2020, the Foundation restored the farmhouse: upgrading the foundation, installing electricity, and returning it to its "period of significance." As works of preservation, the farmhouse restoration and Cather's books both allow the visitor to step into a world that's passed out of firsthand memory. Taken together, the physical space can cement the fictional scenes in real experience. When I visited the Pavelka house, it was empty and gutted, but even from the building's bones, from its sloping yard surrounded by head-high rows of corn, I could picture the lives lived there. I could imagine myself as one of Ántonia's daughters, kneading the dough for kolaches.

# WILLA CATHER

## Glacier Creek Preserve
## Omaha, Nebraska

*By Conor Gearin*

"The red of the grass made all the great prairie the color of wine-stains, or of certain seaweeds when they are first washed up." One of Cather's most famous lines, from the 1918 novel *My Ántonia,* mainly refers to the color of little bluestem (*Schizachyrium scoparium*), one of the keystone grasses of the mixed-grass prairie where she grew up in Red Cloud, Nebraska. The species has a bluish color in spring but in autumn matures to a copper red that reflects the fire of a Great Plains sunset.

The first place I made this connection wasn't in farm country but instead at Glacier Creek Preserve on the outskirts of Omaha. Years of restoration transformed terraced crop fields into a glimpse at the flora of mixed-grass and tallgrass prairies accessible to city dwellers. In the Midwest, we've lost nearly all our native grasslands to agriculture, meaning that if you grew up in a city like Omaha or St. Louis—my hometown—your first look at a grassland was probably a restored site down the road like Glacier Creek. This modest-sized preserve offers a glimpse of the most threatened type of ecosystem in the world. As a biology teaching assistant, I would help lead university students at the preserve in collecting soil samples, estimating plant biomass, and identifying bird species.

When Cather was a student at the University of Nebraska Lincoln in the 1890s, Omaha was a cultural destination, and she wrote incisive theater reviews to help establish herself as a writer. Her fiction reflects this early view of the big city. Especially in *My Ántonia* and *O Pioneers!,* Omaha looms as an urban hub, reachable by train for a cosmopolitan weekend outing, the place to go for fancy fabric and renowned actors. Cather's careful depictions of small-town Nebraska take their meaning partly from the contrast she draws to these growing cities a few rail stops away.

Later in her career, Cather returned to Omaha on a brief Midwestern speaking tour. At a 1921 gathering of the Nebraska League of Women Voters in the tea room of the stately Brandeis department store in downtown Omaha, Cather advised the audience not to imitate other places. "It seems to me as I travel out through the great middle west, the people are trying to imitate New York," she said, as quoted by the *Omaha World-Herald.* "Red Cloud and Hastings are trying to be like Omaha; Omaha and Chicago are trying to be like New York. One thing I like about New York is that there we wear the kinds of hats we like, we wear the kind of clothes that please us."

The remark feels strikingly contemporary. Reading it, I think of how today's Midwestern communities often converge on a suburban sameness: small towns grasping for big box stores, larger cities sprawling out subdivisions into farm country. The result is a landscape that's hard to distinguish from hundreds of others, their quirks of ecology smoothed over and refashioned with evenly distributed brand names. But I think, too, of the distinguishing features that remain: the grasses and herbs of eastern Nebraska I saw in the field and through the microscope; the improbably steep slopes of the Loess Hills across the Missouri River; all the different kinds of live music wafting out of bars in Omaha's Benson neighborhood on a First Friday. I think of Omaha's cultural legacies—the Indigenous peoples of the Oceti Sakowin; Black families that arrived in the Great Migration; generations of immigrants from throughout Europe, Mexico, Central America, and more recently Sudan, Nigeria, and other African nations—and how those legacies often appeared in the students of my commuter campus. Foregrounding these, it's harder to write off the city as interchangeable with any other in the corn belt.

Historically, Omaha has looked to Cather's words for help in establishing a sense of place. When I lived there, my local library was the Willa Cather Branch. There's a Willa Cather elementary school and a Willa Cather playground. Despite living two hundred miles from Red Cloud, many people in Omaha (like their fellow Nebraskans) have felt better represented in her fiction than in contemporary works like *The Great Gatsby*—where the Great Plains are a grim wasteland, a place to escape.

But it would be a mistake to portray Cather as some kind of saint of Midwestern culture. Her legacy is more complex than that. She left Nebraska for New York to make her way in the literary world. She also largely erased Native Americans in her writing and essentially celebrated white settlement on Indigenous lands. Her view of Midwestern uniqueness was hitched to pioneer exploitation.

We're not beholden to that limited view. Instead, I see Cather's work as a starting point that many writers have riffed on throughout the past century. The thread of her legacy that stands out to me now is the awakening of a Midwestern ecological consciousness, distinguishing the particularity of one place from another. That awareness offers another way to envision the future of a place, one away from evenly spread amenities and toward a unique trajectory linked to local ecology and culture—a celebration of difference.

If I imagine standing at Glacier Creek Preserve now, I can look southeast toward downtown Omaha, north and west toward farmland, and south toward recently built subdivisions. Despite suburban sprawl, I wouldn't mistake the view for St. Louis or Chicago. The sources of Omaha's uniqueness haven't been completely smothered. But the threats to grassland habitats are as dire as ever. Looking around at the little bluestem, switchgrass, and side oats grama, I think about Cather's hunch that if we could articulate the special character, the thisness of a landscape, that might tell us something about how best to relate to that place. If writers and naturalists—myself included—could help more people see grasslands as vital, with inhabitants who have names and life histories, I wonder what new shape our communities might take.

# WILLA CATHER

## The Fine Arts Building
## Chicago, Illinois

*By Jesse Raber*

Chicago isn't an iconic setting for Willa Cather, the great novelist of the prairies. Yet in a sense, during Cather's time Chicago writing *was* prairie writing. When H. L. Mencken crowned Chicago "The Literary Capital of the United States" in 1920, he credited the city's literature to the "remote wheat-towns and far-flung railway junctions" of its hinterland. "The newcomers who pour in from the wheat lands," he wrote, full of "elemental curiosity" and "prairie energy," seek in the city's cultural scene "some imaginative equivalent for the stupendous activity they were bred to." Mencken's description of country talent "pour[ing] in" to the city seems to imagine Chicago writing as a river fed by the vast "Middle Empire that has Chicago for its capital."

But where Mencken, the consummate urbanite, saw brain drain, Cather saw back-and-forth circulation between country and city. Chicago drummers teach the townsfolk the latest songs in *My Ántonia*, and the South Dakota grande dame in *A Lost Lady* often entertains Chicago friends. The Chicago voice teacher Madison Bowers, in *The Song of the Lark*, trains soloists from across the Midwest and takes "long journeys to hear and instruct a chorus." The closing paragraph of *The Song of the Lark* sums up the dynamic:

> The many naked little sandbars which lie between Venice and the mainland, in the seemingly stagnant water of the lagoons, are made habitable and wholesome only because, every night, a foot and a half of tide creeps in from the sea and winds its fresh brine up through all that network of shining waterways. So, into all the little settlements of quiet people, tidings of what their boys and girls are doing in the world bring real refreshment; bring to the old, memories, and to the young, dreams.

The prairie towns aren't unsoiled streams flowing into the urban river; they are points in a "network" that regularly communicates, through Chicago, with a wider world.

Cather's Chicago itself is a symbol of hypercirculation, a "blur of smoke and wind and noise" whose disorienting flux creates eddies of creativity. "In little towns," Cather writes in *Lucy Gayheart*, "lives roll along so close to one another; loves and hates beat about, their wings almost touching." By contrast Chicago, with its uncaring crowds, allows Cather's prairie-bred artists to make themselves secret nests. Rather than exposing them to a wider swath of humanity, the city helps them find themselves and their own kind.

The most memorable of these artistic aeries is the singer Clement Sebastian's studio in the Fine Arts Building. Practicing there, Lucy Gayheart feels "it was as if they were on the lonely spur of a mountain, enveloped by mist. They saw no one . . . heard no one; the city below was blotted out." Located a few blocks south of the Art Institute on Michigan Avenue, the Fine Arts Building has cultivated artistic tenants since 1898. A ten-story structure in the Richardsonian Romanesque style of rusticated stones and stately arches, in Lucy's day it was the city's literary epicenter, and many of its greatest occupants presented themselves obscure "little" niches in the big boisterous city. There was the Little Room, an aesthetic society featuring Hamlin Garland and Harriet Monroe (among many others); Margaret Anderson's *Little Review*, which faced obscenity charges for publishing parts of *Ulysses*; and Ellen von Volkenburg and Maurice Browne's movement-launching Little Theater.

Today the Fine Arts Building still has some of that cloistral spirit. When I first went inside, during an open studio night, it was like stepping between worlds. Lush Art Deco murals cover the lobby walls, and the antique elevators have human operators. The upper floors are all dark wood trim and muted white paint, like the outside of a Tudor house. That evening, drifting between studios, each its own aesthetic universe, I bought a post-card-sized watercolor of Colorado pines, painted at the western fringe of Chicago's old railroad kingdom.

Years later I returned to visit the new Dial Bookshop, named for the old magazine and decorated with portraits of Chicago writers, including fellow Fine Arts tenant L. Frank Baum. The store was lovely, but I wondered if this veneration of the building's past meant that creativity had lapsed into nostalgia. This question bothered me as I thought about what the Fine Arts Building represents today.

One evening, as I was brainstorming this vignette, I joined a six-foot-spaced circle around a fire pit on my friends' lawn. "Does anybody happen to have any stories," I asked, "about the Fine Arts Building?" It turned out they did. I heard about a filmmaker with an office there, working for years on a documentary about feuding martial artists. Another friend recalled her amazement at wandering into a violin-maker's workshop—a *luthier's* shop, she insists—while looking for a replacement guitar string. (The luthiers were unhelpful.) A third reminisced about how the old movie theater there casually mixed art-house and mainstream films. Some of that old spirit of hidden wonders lives on, it seems. My favorite story, though, was a little older—about one friend's dad who used to take the Greyhound there to see films that didn't play in his hometown. He sometimes had to leave the movie early to catch the bus back to DeKalb, Illinois, way out in Chicago's Middle Empire.

# WILLA CATHER

## Old Burying Ground
## Jaffrey, New Hampshire

*By Catherine Seiberling Pond*

In her first known correspondence from Jaffrey, New Hampshire, Willa Cather wrote to her brother Roscoe on a postcard from the Shattuck Inn, "I am working well in this lovely country." It was 1917, and the acclaimed writer was forty-three years old, midcareer, and making revisions to her novel *My Ántonia*.

For her first few stays, Cather often wrote in a large canvas tent in the lower pasture of "High Mowing," a nearby summer home. I first heard about Cather's tent retreats and her association with the farm in the late 1970s from my best friend's mother, an English professor and owner of the property for twenty-five years. I had recently read *O Pioneers!* and *My Ántonia*, both novels inspired by the Nebraska prairie and Cather's childhood home of Red Cloud, over 1,500 miles from Jaffrey.

Over the next three decades, Cather spent part of many years at "this quiet hotel in the woods," as she described it in one letter, often with her partner, Edith Lewis. The sublime and solitary presence of Mount Monadnock loomed just to the west of the inn, and mornings of writing were followed by long walks in the afternoon. Cather's time in Jaffrey was restorative and a needed place of "happy solitude" for her writing. Here she was able to work "in comfort and quiet"—something her busy and parallel life in New York seldom allowed.

In her last known letter from the Shattuck Inn, written in 1945 to her brother Roscoe, Cather discussed her room, which was appointed in stained matchboard and simply but comfortably furnished. She compared it to her teenage bedroom, which, along with its original "rose bower" wallpaper, is still preserved today in the Willa Cather Childhood Home in Red Cloud:

> I have a funny little room in the attic here, with a sloping ceiling, like my "rose bower" in our old first house. Do you remember? I can always work best in a low room under the roof. All my best books were written in Jaffrey N. H. in a little room where I could almost touch the ceiling with my hand.

Cather once wrote of being "homesick for New England" in the autumn, a trait that I share. Having spent much of my life in the region, it's not hard to picture Jaffrey's stunning foliage, or the invigorating air and azure skies of fall in New Hampshire—and the best sleeping weather of the year. Still, not everything is the same. The original Shattuck Inn has been torn down, though the Annex remains, now refurbished into condominiums.

A few years before Cather died, she wrote to a childhood friend that she was traveling to her "old resting place in Jaffrey, New Hampshire." It would, indeed, become just that. After her death in 1947, she was buried at the Old Burying Ground behind the historic Jaffrey Meetinghouse. With availability always a question in the Colonial cemetery, her innkeeper friends, George and Eleanor Austermann, arranged for a plot near their own. No one knows exactly why Cather chose Jaffrey over Red Cloud, where she often returned to visit dear family and friends, but I believe that her own letters reveal much of that answer. In 1972 Edith Lewis was buried alongside her—while she outlived Cather by twenty-five years, they had been together for almost forty.

The gravesite in the southwest corner is framed by white pines and an old stone wall. It is a place of pilgrimage for Cather enthusiasts—and for me, whenever I can return. Since I moved to Kentucky in 2008, I have often been homesick for my grandparents' old Jaffrey farm, for the people and places of my childhood, and for the landscapes of New England. The Old Burying Ground, with its adjacent meetinghouse and classic village setting, provides sturdy mooring. Many family friends are also buried there, so visiting is now its own kind of homecoming.

The last time I stopped by Cather's grave, I was on my way to visit my mother for what would be the last time before her death. It was autumn and the leaves were glowing, the air clear and intoxicating, and Mount Monadnock a comforting fixture against the bluest sky. Later I would learn that this was also Willa Cather's favorite time to be in Jaffrey.

Other visitors leave small stones, flowers, even jewelry, and ponder the words on her granite headstone: "The truth and charity of her great spirit will live on in the work which is her enduring gift to her country and all its people." Cather's writing is deeply connected to both the people she loved and the places where she lived and wrote. For me, it will forever illuminate the wonder of our collective human experience, starting with my first reading of *My Ántonia* and continuing into the cosmos with a quotation from it inscribed near the base of her headstone: "That is happiness; to be dissolved into something complete and great." We can only speculate, but perhaps in that longer passage from the novel that Cather edited on her first visit to the Shattuck Inn thirty years earlier is the very answer for why she wanted to be buried in the place where she felt she had done her best work.

# LANGSTON HUGHES

## Woodland Park
## Lawrence, Kansas

*By John Edgar Tidwell*

In the weeks leading up to August 19, 1910, all the children in Lawrence, Kansas, were aglow with excitement and energy. To honor the birthday of editor J. Leeford Brady, the *Lawrence Daily Journal* set about hosting a Children's Day party at Woodland Park in East Lawrence. For young Langston Hughes and the other children of color, anticipation turned into anxiety and disappointment when the Daily Journal clarified the meaning of *invitees*. In response to the question about Black children attending, a front-page article confidently asserted: "The Journal knows the colored children have no desire to attend a social event of this kind and that they will not want to go. This is purely a social affair and of course everyone in town knows what that means."

How could the Black children *not* want to go?! The amusement park would have special vaudeville and picture shows, bands would entertain, a Ferris wheel and a merry-go-round would provide free rides, and such favorites as lemonade and popcorn would be available too. Without knowing it, the Black children had run up against the prohibition made legal by the US Supreme Court in *Plessy v. Ferguson* (1896). The law of the land now defined "social" to mean "forced or unwanted relations." As protection against undesired interracial interaction, the court endorsed the concept of "separate but equal." Unfortunately, as Black children in Lawrence and everywhere else learned, this legal interpretation granted society permission to practice racial separation *without* racial equality.

Hughes recreates this incident in *Not Without Laughter*. He deftly enters into the Black children's high expectations, which rise to a crescendo of excitement, only to be crushed when the admissions attendant refuses to accept the coupons that would admit them to the Ferris wheel, the shoot-the-shoots, and the merry-go-round as well as the entertainment and food. Later, he would capture this feeling of emotional confusion in his poem "Merry-Go-Round." The speaker in the poem, a little Black girl who had moved from the South to the North, sought to ride the merry-go-round at a carnival. Not knowing if she would be allowed to mount a horse at all, she attempts to find the back of the ride. She asks, "Where is the Jim Crow section / On this merry-go-round / Mister, cause I want to ride?" She then closes the poem by lamenting, "Where's the horse / For a kid that's black?"

## LANGSTON HUGHES

**Born: February 1, 1902, in Joplin, Missouri**

**Died: May 22, 1967, in New York, New York**

**Forms: Poetry, Short Stories, Novels, Memoir, Drama, Children's Literature**

**Recommended Works: *The Weary Blues* (1926), "The Negro Artist and the Racial Mountain" (1926), *Fine Clothes to the Jew* (1927), *Not Without Laughter* (1930), *The Ways of White Folks* (1934), *The Big Sea* (1940), *Montage of a Dream Deferred* (1951)**

Pernicious racism dogged young Langston Hughes throughout his formative years in Lawrence. To his credit, he never allowed bitterness and hatred to jade his vision of humankind. Instead of blaming *all* whites for preserving the racial status quo, he learned that "*most* people are generally good." This quality, no doubt, inspired the city of Lawrence to begin embracing him as one of its own shining lights.

# WILLIAM LEAST HEAT-MOON

## River-Horse Pavilion
## Columbia, Missouri

*By Kit Salter*

In March 1995 my wife Cathy and I went to wish Godspeed to Columbia, Missouri, resident William Lewis Trogdon as he was leaving for New York City to begin a 103-day nautical journey, which he would chronicle in the 1999 book, *River-Horse: A Voyage Across America*, under the pen name of William Least Heat-Moon.

Trogdon called his newly acquired boat *Nikawa*, which means "river-horse" in the Osage language. This twenty-two-foot C-Dory with twin engines was nestled in a solid towing trailer. As the author prepared to ease both his boat and his hopes into motion, Cathy presented him with an ivory amulet of a sea otter. I handed him a Timex Expedition watch that had been my trusty travel companion. On that spring day, little did we know that the C-Dory being carefully pulled into traffic would later stand in a bold wooden pavilion just outside Columbia.

Today, as you drive north on Highway 63 just coming into Columbia from the direction of Jefferson City, the red metal roof of the Boone County History and Culture Center catches your eye. Then you see an open structure next to the parking lot. This is the River-Horse Pavilion, built in 2006 to celebrate Heat-Moon's journey in *Nikawa,* the very boat we saw leave his home some years earlier.

## WILLIAM LEAST HEAT-MOON

**Born: August 27, 1939, In Kansas City, Missouri**

**Died: —**

**Forms: Travel Writing, Memoir, History**

**Recommended Works: *Blue Highways* (1982), *PrairyErth* (1991), *River-Horse* (1999), *Roads to Quoz: An American Mosey* (2008)**

Heat-Moon wrote on the final page of *River-Horse* that he had ridden *Nikawa* "5,288 watery miles from the Atlantic." At the very end of that trip, to celebrate his arrival at the Pacific, he reached for a pint of Atlantic water he had safeguarded for 103 days. He writes, "I raised the bottle high, sunlight striking through the glass, salt waves rising to it as if thirsty, and I said, 'We bring this gift from your sister sea—our voyage is done. Then I poured the stream into the Pacific and went back to the wheel of our river horse, and I turned her toward home."

Some years after completing that adventure, Heat-Moon presented his already fabled C-Dory to the Boone County Historical Society. The society was proud to have such a fine bit of Missouriana from one of the state's most productive and creative authors, but they had to ask, "How do we display it?"

The historical society wanted to make *Nikawa* available twenty-four seven yet protect it from the weather and potential pilfering. Local architect Nick Peckham (himself a marine engineer) worked with volunteers to design and build the wooden pavilion that stands adjacent to the society's main building. This open structure provides easy viewing of the boat (behind plexiglass), a map of *Nikawa*'s route from the Atlantic to the Pacific, and photographs of the craft and the author. *Nikawa*, in fact, was now home, resting and lending its stature to all of Boone County.

But the backstory of this literary landscape possesses two more elements. In 1978 Heat-Moon was teaching at Stephens College in Columbia, Missouri, when he was let go because of declining enrollments. At the same time, he and his wife decided to divorce.

Heat-Moon reacted to that pair of events by undertaking a thirteen-thousand-mile solo trip in his 1975 Ford Econoline van. That ninety-day journey (which began on Earth Day in 1978) resulted in the 1982 book, *Blue Highways: A Journey into America*, which spent forty-two weeks on the *New York Times* bestseller list and has never been out of print. In the early pages of *Blue Highways*, Heat-Moon declares, "A man who couldn't make things go right, could at least go. He could quit trying to get out of the way of life."

With *Nikawa*'s historic voyage across the continent, William Least Heat-Moon showed again that he "could at least go," and this time he took contemporary travel exploration to a new level of innovation. To complete the circle, I have my Timex back—but the amulet remains with the author.

# HENRY BELLAMANN

## Brick District Playhouse
## Fulton, Missouri

*By Alex Dzurick*

The 1940 novel *Kings Row* once so offended residents of Fulton, Missouri, that you couldn't find a copy on the shelves of the local library. You could, however, in the very same town, find a copy on my mother's bookshelf. She was a history teacher who taught classes on Missouri history, so even as a child I had heard the rumors: *Kings Row* was based on Henry Bellamann's life growing up in Fulton, and his frank portrayal of the darker side of life in my hometown did not earn him admiration by its social elites.

With all my mother's connections to the book, I'm not surprised her copy occupied such a prominent place in our home, next to heirlooms and family photographs. In middle school I asked if I could read it to complete a book challenge. She said that I could, as long as I was careful with her copy, and I remember stretching out on the living room sofa, devouring the novel over just a few days. It's a shocking story, exploring topics like euthanasia and incest, so looking back I'm surprised that I was trusted enough as a young teenager to handle the material.

Take a drive down Fulton's Court Street today, and you'll still see the Victorian-style homes that those social elites once lived in. It's easy to imagine how young Mr. Bellamann must have felt seeing those homes and knowing it was their occupants who bullied him, ostensibly for his German heritage and friendships with kids from the poorer, industrial neighborhoods. In *Kings Row*, on the other hand, Bellamann's alter ego Parris Mitchell is quite well liked by everyone. Still, he discovers the sinister side of those wealthy residents while apprenticing under the secretive Dr. Tower, who is likely based on a real local doctor.

## HENRY BELLAMANN

**Born: April 28, 1882, in Fulton, Missouri**

**Died: June 16, 1945, in New York, New York**

**Forms: Novels, Poetry**

**Recommended Works: *Kings Row* (1940), *Floods of Spring* (1942), *Victoria Grandolet* (1943), *Parris Mitchell of Kings Row* (1948, published posthumously, completed by his wife, Katherine Bellamann)**

A bit farther down Court Street, you'll find the Brick District Playhouse, which served as the town's only movie theater from 1928 to 2006. My mother worked there, part-time, for decades, and I followed in her footsteps when I turned sixteen. The small cinema had just two screens, with one built into a former balcony, and the lobby doors opened directly onto the brick streets of downtown Fulton. The brick building's marquee was changed by hand even in its last years, and it wasn't unheard of for birds and bats to swoop down from the ceiling during a film. Today, the building has been converted into a live performance venue, hosting plays, concerts, and lectures.

The theater itself is part of *Kings Row* lore, thanks to a 1942 film adaptation starring Robert Cummings as Parris Mitchell and future president Ronald Reagan as Drake, one of Parris's wealthy friends. The movie did little to appease Fulton's residents, exposing their town's secrets to an even wider audience. Tensions had eased by the later part of the century, however, and several cast members came to Fulton in June 1988 to celebrate their source material (Reagan did not attend, as he was busy politicking). My mom had the opportunity to meet them at the theater. Her copy of *Kings Row* has a red autograph inside the front cover—"To Beautiful Lola. Love, Bob Cummings."

Later, I had the chance to watch the film, which brought characters like Parris, Drake, and Dr. Tower to life in new ways for me. The novel's darkest themes were removed to satisfy film codes, but it remained a tale of small-town hypocrisy. And the film's visuals are eerily reminiscent of the older parts of Fulton, as evidenced by the historic photos and sketches that hung in our home. Despite the passage of some fifty years between the film's release and my own youth, it became apparent to me how easily Fulton's residents would have seen themselves in Bellamann's work.

I used to live just outside of Philadelphia, where Bellamann was a dean at a prestigious music school before writing *Kings Row*. These days, I live in St. Louis, much closer to my and Bellamann's shared hometown. When I return to Fulton, and I pass those grand old Court Street homes just a few blocks north of the movie theater, I can't help but look at them through Bellamann's eyes, seeing the town in its honesty, with all its grandeur and all its faults.

# EDGAR LEE MASTERS

## Ann Rutledge's Grave
## Petersburg, Illinois

*By Jason Stacy*

As a boy I found it unsettling that Edgar Lee Masters anthologized the dead in an Illinois cemetery that never existed. *Spoon River Anthology*'s ghosts haunted the same rich Illinois soil I walked on, stared out at fields like the ones that rolled by the window of my school bus, and spoke in accents that echoed mine, but these people were nowhere to be found. Doubly spectral, they were the dead neighbors that never were. Reading a frayed copy of Masters's book brought home by my mother, an English teacher, I felt as if I were peering into a legendary Illinois that dissipated the closer I got to it.

But now that I'm older, I am at peace with the legends. The trick is not to get too close.

Masters himself is buried in a very real place: Oakland Cemetery in Petersburg, Illinois, just about at the center of the state, a short drive from Springfield and down the road from New Salem, the pioneer community where Abraham Lincoln lived for a time. Petersburg is in the Illinois part of Illinois.

Masters rests only a few feet from a legend he helped make: Ann Rutledge, thought to be the one love of Abraham Lincoln's life. About twenty yards away, down one of the main paths of the cemetery, a low iron fence surrounds a solid block of granite on which is engraved a poem by Masters:

> Out of me unworthy and unknown
> The vibrations of deathless music;
> "With malice toward none, with charity
> for all."
> Out of me the forgiveness of millions
> toward millions,
> And the beneficent face of a nation
> Shining with justice and truth.
> I am Ann Rutledge who sleep beneath
> these weeds,
> Beloved in life of Abraham Lincoln,
> Wedded to him, not through union,
> But through separation.
> Bloom forever, O Republic,
> From the dust of my bosom!

## EDGAR LEE MASTERS

**Born: August 23, 1868, in Garnett, Kansas**

**Died: March 5, 1950, in Melrose Park, Pennsylvania**

**Forms: Poetry, Novels, Biography, Drama**

**Recommended Works: *Spoon River Anthology* (1915), *Domesday Book* (1920), *Mitch Miller* (1920), *The New Spoon River* (1924)**

Rutledge died of typhoid fever in 1835 and was originally buried in the Old Concord graveyard about five miles from Petersburg. After Lincoln's death, his former law partner William Herndon claimed in his biography of the president that Rutledge was the one true love of Lincoln's life. Her death at twenty-two threw the future president into an emotional crisis and, according to Herndon, Lincoln never loved any woman as much again. As the living Lincoln faded from popular memory after the Civil War, Rutledge's ghost began to haunt the legends of the fallen president. These legends turned central Illinois into a destination for secular pilgrims, and she became the key to understanding Lincoln's combination of melancholy and stoic fortitude.

To capitalize on the legend, local undertaker and furniture dealer Samuel Montgomery exhumed Rutledge in 1890 from the Old Concord graveyard and reburied what was left of her—two bones, a little hair, some bits of cloth—in Oakland Cemetery, where he was part owner. In *Lincoln Legends*, Edward Steers writes that Montgomery hoped this location would prove convenient for visitors and fortuitous for the town. Twenty-five years later, in 1915, Rutledge was reburied again, this time symbolically, when Edgar Lee Masters planted her in Spoon River's fictional cemetery. In 1921, at the height of Masters's popularity, her epitaph from *Spoon River Anthology* was engraved on a new monument in Oakland Cemetery. These days, tourists commune with the legend of Rutledge that William Herndon perpetuated, by the grave that Samuel Montgomery filled with a few remains, under a fictional epitaph written by Edgar Lee Masters.

Outside of town, in the Old Concord graveyard, a small headstone marks Ann's first resting place. It appeals to visitors' desire for authenticity by telling them that this lonely spot in an out-of-the-way field is, in fact, "where Lincoln wept." But when I drive through Petersburg, I visit Ann at Oakland Cemetery. The legend is better there.

# MARY HUNTER AUSTIN

## Blackburn College
## Carlinville, Illinois

*By Karen Dillon and Naomi Crummey*

As professors in the English department at Blackburn College, we have always been aware of the legacy of the college's most famed writer, Mary Hunter Austin, who was born in Carlinville and graduated from Blackburn in 1888. Immediately after graduation she pioneered west with her family, and in the landscapes of California and the Southwest, she became celebrated for her understanding of nature and unconventional feminism. In Austin's canonical work of American nature writing from 1903, *The Land of Little Rain*, she recounts the story of a Paiute woman, Seyavi, who survived a massacre by hiding in caves with her young son. After describing the landscape in which Seyavi struggles to survive, Austin remarks, "That was the time Seyavi learned the sufficiency of mother wit, and how much more easily one can do without a man than might at first be supposed." As Seyavi earned the respect of her people by raising her son without a husband, Austin, too, cast off convention to follow her own path. Though Blackburn played only a small and short-lived role in her life, we feel a kinship with Austin and the intellectual and artistic foundation the college laid for her.

## MARY HUNTER AUSTIN

**Born: September 9, 1868, in Carlinville, Illinois**

**Died: August 13, 1934, in Santa Fe, New Mexico**

**Forms: Nonfiction, Novels, Poetry, Drama, Autobiography**

**Recommended Works: *The Land of Little Rain* (1903), *The Basket Woman* (1904), *The Flock* (1906), *Lost Borders* (1909), *The Arrow Maker* (1911)**

Blackburn does not appeal to everyone. It is a tiny, student-managed work college in a small Midwestern town abutted on two sides by farmland; there is plenty of hard work but little glamour. Blackburn can sometimes feel isolating, but as a small, student-centered school, it also, in Austin's own words from her 1932 autobiography *Earth Horizon*, provides space for professors and students alike "to walk about in it, making fruitful contacts with [each other], as couldn't have [been] done in the larger universities." Austin briefly left Blackburn for a nearby teaching college but despised the "rasping insistence on a regime that violated all the natural motions of her own mind." Austin's fiction also emphasizes the desire for natural motions over convention. In the short story "The Walking Woman," the titular character "had walked off all sense of society-made values, and, knowing the best when the best came to her, was able to take it. . . . It was the naked thing the Walking Woman grasped, not dressed and tricked out, for instance, by prejudices in favor of certain occupations."

Austin returned to Blackburn precisely because it welcomes and nurtures the individual mind; it gave her freedom and space to learn as she was inclined, leaving her, as she wrote in *Earth Horizon*, "so far as her professional proclivities go, without so much as a thumbprint of predilection; and that I count entirely to the good. I am quite sure she could never have escaped from one of the larger, better regimented institutions with so free an intelligence and so unhampered a use of herself." The campus newspaper *The Blackburnian*, for which Austin was a writer and editor, may provide evidence of the intellectual freedom Austin was known for at Blackburn. In the March 1887 edition of the "Peculiar Characteristics" section, a nineteenth-century version of a shoutout column to students' and professors' unique talents, quirks, and physical characteristics, Mary Hunter is recognized simply for her "ideas."

As we pass the bust of Austin that presides over the halls of the science building, we continue to draw inspiration from her free-spirited feminism and artistry. In the college archives, there is a copy of the February 1888 edition of the *Blackburnian*, which notes, "Miss Mary Hunter has not been attending her classes for the past week. Too busy writing, we suppose." We like to picture Austin, confident and even a bit arrogant (she switched her studies from English to science because for the former she believed she needed only herself and books, but the latter she felt required a proper teacher), walking through the green spaces of campus, writing and imagining alternative ways of inhabiting the world. Like the seemingly arid spaces Austin's best-known works so meticulously open for readers, the Blackburn campus offers a path for those who seek a space in which to walk about unhampered and forge meaningful connections.

# ST. LOUIS

# KATHLEEN FINNERAN

## North County
## St. Louis, Missouri

*By Marina Henke*

In the middle of winter a red cardinal lands on a birdbath. It sits, jumps onto a kitchen windowsill, and flies away. A suburban backyard just north of St. Louis, Missouri. Such is the opening scene, and the near-constant backdrop, of Kathleen Finneran's piercing family memoir *The Tender Land* (2000).

In a book that traverses the faith and formation of a family of six and ultimately centers around the death of her youngest brother, Sean, Finneran takes us through the winding suburban streets and cracked brick houses of her North County suburb. Occasionally we depart the space: to her late brother's bike rides along the Alton River Road and to her days in claustrophobic Catholic schools and under the dull fluorescents of strip-mall stores. But the place that she most frequently returns to is exactly where the book begins: her family home's backyard.

It's the spot of her mother's seasonal sunbathing. It's where Finneran witnesses her youngest siblings' summer campouts, where she, in a paralleled childhood decades before, lay clouded by night with her eldest sister.

## KATHLEEN FINNERAN

**Born: December 3, 1957, in St. Louis, Missouri**

**Died: —**

**Forms: Memoir, Essays**

**Recommended Works: *The Tender Land: A Family Love Story* (2000), "Lying in the Land of Memoir: Straddling the Line Between Fact and Fiction" (2002), "Crock Pots: A Confession" (2004)**

In the years following her teenage brother's death, it is where she stumbles to. Anything to break the undulations of grief. "I went out in the backyard," Finneran writes, "and stood in the snow, everything so white around me—the house, the ground, the trees, the fence." In easier times, the snowy landscape is a simple escape. Finneran describes looking out the window at her youngest siblings: "I watched the two of them falling backwards, flapping their arms and legs, standing up to admire their creation and falling down again."

I should say, I've never been to this yard. The closest I may come is unknowingly passing it by on my frequent loops through the city. But rarely has writing on a page so convinced me of its familiarity.

Because the suburban backyards of St. Louis are ones I know well. I grew up just a few miles south of Finneran: wedged between Delmar and Olive Boulevard, a stone's throw from city lines. I am writing this now in one of the layovers of one's late twenties, overlooking my own childhood backyard of similar proportions. Big-leafed catalpas rim its grassy edges. An electrical wire that's always hung too low sways in a humid breeze. There's the rotting stump, home to a revolving family of possums. And cracking concrete from an attempted basketball court installed decades ago, bordered on its farthest edge by a fence drowning in green honeysuckle.

These backyards, both of them, are muted spaces. To the untrained eye, stumble on these spots on a gray and wickedly humid summer day, and there is little awe to be found. And yet there is awe, everywhere, and *The Tender Land* is determined to reveal it. Finneran writes and invites readers to look at such spaces through something akin to a kaleidoscope: one that splinters, refracts images of itself across its mirror, and ultimately catapults the earthen plots of our homes into masterpieces.

In most common depictions, the suburban backyard does not frequently escape categorizations of banality. This is a space where, supposedly, lives are languished, where the complexity of culture is sacrificed for one's green-grassed homestead. Finneran, though, puts to words what I—and I suspect many who grew up in these spaces—can viscerally feel. In family joy, in family turmoil, in family tragedy, these are the places, for better or for worse, so many have to turn to. All it takes is a look through Finneran's kaleidoscope to lay plain what we've always known.

Sure enough, her backyard feels changed after this kaleidoscope treatment. It's a place of beauty—of caterpillars caught in jars, of refuge found beneath basement steps. A place to hold oneself when that beauty is so ruthlessly disrupted, in which a red cardinal landing on a birdbath can provide a reprieve, or at least a fixation, in times of senseless grief.

As its opening pages began, the memoir closes in the same space, with a description of Finneran's late brother gathering rainwater during a summer storm. "Through the basement windows I could see you in the backyard with your buckets, collecting rainwater for your fish." It's a scene that holds the impossible layering of sorrow and joy. "That was happiness. That *is* happiness, Sean, everything dissolved into its simplest, purest form that day; for me, something complete and great."

Finneran puts words to a fact that I suspect many of us know is true—these backyard spaces hold the memories of a life lived through raging grief and easy joy. They are simultaneously the refuge and the battleground.

Just now I watched two squirrels chase each other in endless circles around our oak tree, their claws scratching loudly across the bark. The catalpa leaves above envelop the tinny sound. Soon it's quiet again.

# NAOMI SHIHAB NYE

## Central Elementary School
## Ferguson, Missouri

*By Taylor Fox*

There's a haunted feeling that comes with walking around an empty schoolyard. Barren playgrounds and darkened windows convey emptiness, dejection. It's unnatural for playgrounds to go quiet. Yet outside the historic Central Elementary School in Ferguson, Missouri, that eerie feeling is missing, replaced by a comforting glow provided by the towering trees, climbing vines, and community garden of fragrant herbs.

"Did you know there was a time Ferguson was all a farm?"

Central alumna Naomi Shihab Nye's poetry is filled with imagery that conjures up the aura of her former school. She specifically reflects on the Ferguson of her youth in a poem honoring Jamyla Bolden, a nine-year-old Black girl killed in her Ferguson home in 2015 when a man shot into her house, targeting someone he believed stole from him.

The poem illustrates the commonalities between the author and Jamyla, who attended Koch Elementary School, just over three miles east of Central. In the poem, Nye wishes she could pass her own lived years on to the girl who was taken too soon.

Drive down Florissant Road today, and it is hard to imagine it as farmland. The asphalt street is lined with barbecue restaurants and dozens of murals honoring the Black Lives

Matter movement. Outside the Ferguson Police Department stands a row of signs and artwork remembering those killed by police violence in the United States.

## NAOMI SHIHAB NYE

**Born: March 12, 1952, in St. Louis, Missouri**

**Died: —**

**Forms: Poetry, Essays, Short Stories, Young Adult**

**Recommended Works: *Different Ways to Pray* (1980), *Words Under the Worlds: Selected Poems* (1995), *Fuel* (1998), *19 Varieties of Gazelle: Poems of the Middle East* (2002), *You and Yours* (2005)**

Leaving Florissant Road and all its restaurants, you immediately enter the quiet, calm neighborhood surrounding Central Elementary. Nye has described the area as a "leafy green historic suburb" and fondly remembers her old brick school. Built in 1880, the school flaunts a plaque acknowledging its listing on the National Register of Historic Places. The original bell tower—visible from both the playground and the community garden—still crowns the old building.

Considering Nye drafted her first poem when she was six years old, it's easy to imagine the young artist gazing out the school's wrought iron windows onto the large garden below and piecing together her earliest works.

Nye attended Central from kindergarten until sixth grade, and in 1966 her family moved to Palestine, her father's country of origin. She has often spoken on her experiences as a Palestinian American going to a then all-white school and, in a 2014 essay, wrote, "In Ferguson, an invisible line separated white and black communities. In Jerusalem, a no-man's land separated people, designated by barbed wire."

Nye's poetry often reflects the parallels between her two childhood homes. Her first published collection, *Different Ways to Pray*, is entirely on the topic of cultural similarities and differences, using her own Palestinian American identity as a model.

As a first-generation Cuban American with an ethnically Jewish heritage, my own parallels to Nye are too striking to ignore. I can imagine the feeling of otherness she must have endured in Ferguson, accepted in neither the white nor Black communities. After moving to Palestine, where she may have felt even more of an outsider, she began to study culture and identity, perhaps to find her own sense of belonging. I too have felt the drive to study my heritage in order to feel *enough*, to feel like I deserve to claim my roots.

Despite our commonalities, it is also not lost on me that, while I cannot trace my ancestry back to Israel, we are from opposite sides of that barbed wire fence, belonging to two cultures with more in common than they are willing to admit. We are from two cultures that historically villainize the other without the effort of understanding and respect.

We share this severing too with Ferguson itself, represented by the seeming innocence of the empty Central Elementary School across town from the home where Jamyla was killed and next to a street so often shown as a scene of violence against Black people—violence portrayed to make a point, without respect for the motivation behind the movement or any attempt to amend the systemic issues that have led to this point.

# WILLIAM GASS

## Parkview
## St. Louis, Missouri

*By Devin Thomas O'Shea*

The epigraph of *The Tunnel* reads, "The descent to hell is the same from every place," but William Gass chose to set his magnum opus in a leafy suburb of St. Louis, Missouri, called Parkview.

Parkview is one of the first white-flight subdivisions ever constructed. It was a planned neighborhood, a prototype that would use winding lanes and a single outlet to discourage "traffic." In the basement of one of these darling mansions, based on William Gass's real house, Gass imagined a history professor at an upscale *cough* Wash. U. *cough* Midwestern university. Professor Koehler sits to write the introduction to his career-defining work, *Guilt and Innocence in Hitler's Germany*. But he faces a block and pens *The Tunnel* instead—a messy, dark, lyrical portrayal of Koehler himself.

Instead of the neat, well-researched book dissecting the Nazis, Koehler describes the fascism in his own heart. In his basement, digging down in the soil of his soul, he also literally tunnels in the dirt floor of his Parkview cellar.

## WILLIAM GASS

**Born: July 30, 1924, in Fargo, North Dakota**

**Died: December 6, 2017, in St. Louis, Missouri**

**Forms: Novels, Short Stories, Nonfiction**

**Recommended Works: *Omensetter's Luck* (1966), *In the Heart of the Heart of the Country* (1968), *Willie Master's Lonesome Wife* (1968), *The Tunnel* (1995), *Middle C* (2013)**

According to Gass, "The reader is to feel, as he or she doubtless will, as if they are crawling through an unpleasant and narrow darkness." We learn Koehler threw a brick on Kristallnacht. He kills his wife's cat when it gets in the way of his digging. He runs out of space for all his soil, but luckily the history professor's wife, Martha, is an antique-shop owner. Their second floor is lined with Martha's restored bureaus, and though Koehler fears Martha's gaze—and wants to hide the tunnel (and *The Tunnel*) from her—he loads soil from his basement dig into her furniture, where she'll surely find it one day. At the end, Martha finds Koehler's filth and confronts him in the basement. She tips a drawer onto his manuscript, and the dirt goes everywhere: in his lap and all over his pages. Martha orders him to clean her cabinets, and Koehler wonders if she understood his pun about soiling her drawers.

Gass and Koehler both lived in secluded Parkview, a neighborhood built on the philosophy that rich people shouldn't have to share the sidewalks with poor people. In the 1900s downtown St. Louis was busy and dirty. The rich built Parkview far away, just across the city limit, literally on the edge of the county. *The Tunnel*—written and set in the center of this planned community—is a deeply moral book about filth hiding below the surface of respectability. Like Gass, Koehler is an esteemed American intellectual with a wife, a house, and tenure. His research aims to find what was so unusually nasty about the villains of history, but long before he starts digging in the St. Louis mud, Koehler concludes that the Germans were just like you and me. Fascism is not aberrant. It has always been down in our subconscious basement; it lives in everyday hatreds.

Parkview's wealth has been resilient in the face of St. Louis's century-long economic decline, but just down the street, the city's racial segregation has made poverty in the Black community worse every day. The so-called Delmar Divide represents one of the largest economic cliffs in the country. On the south side, White professors raise families in leafy, historic neighborhoods with old-timey gas lamps. Just up the street from Koehler's basement, the redlining starts. Black suburbs like Mill Creek were destroyed to ghettoize Black St. Louisans in the Pruitt-Igoe housing projects. The city defunded Pruitt-Igoe soon after it was completed in 1956 and then condemned and demolished it in the 1970s. Now, even the North County homes are falling down or being deconstructed because the bricks are worth more than the walls. Beauty is everywhere in North St. Louis—but people go hungry, police violence runs rampant, schools are pipelines to the prisons, and poverty abounds. And you don't have to dig to find it.

# PETER H. CLARK

## 1909 Annie Malone Dr.
## St. Louis, Missouri

*By Marc Blanc*

Peter H. Clark lived in St. Louis when it felt like its brightest days were still ahead. Relocating from Cincinnati to the north St. Louis neighborhood called The Ville, in 1888, the teacher and political orator found a river town on the brink of becoming a national metropolis. Starting in the 1880s, St. Louis would add one hundred thousand residents to its population every ten years for the next half-century, arguably reaching the peak of its cultural power in 1904 when it hosted both the World's Fair and the Olympics. Part of this growth was driven by Black migrants from the unreconstructed South, many of whom began to settle in The Ville shortly before Clark's arrival.

Clark's neighborhood was also home to St. Louis's significant German and Irish populations, and the social mixing between the European emigres and Black migrants was often tense; by the 1920s most whites had left The Ville. However, some residents labored to build relationships across the color line. Clark, a Black socialist who had been collaborating with

German radicals in Cincinnati since the days of abolitionism, was well prepared for the task.

## PETER H. CLARK

**Born: March 29, 1829, in Cincinnati, Ohio**

**Died: June 21, 1925, in St. Louis, Missouri**

**Forms: Political Writing, Oratory, History**

**Recommended Works: *Herald of Freedom* (1855), *The Black Brigade of Cincinnati: Being a Report of Its Labors and a Muster-Roll of Its Members* (1864), "Socialism: The Remedy for the Evils of Society" (1877)**

Known just as much for his work on behalf of racial equality as he was for his activism in the German-dominated socialist movement, Clark was in the rare position of having the ear of both Black and white Midwesterners. He used his platform to mend ethnic divisions sewn by racial capitalism, reminding workers that the boss was not their friend even if they shared the same skin tone. "Go into the South and see the capitalists banded together over the poor whites," he implored an overflow crowd at Cincinnati's Robinson Opera House in March 1877. Invited to the opera house to give a stump speech for the Workingmen's Party ticket ahead of local midterm elections, Clark seized the opportunity to address what he saw as intersecting national crises: monopoly capitalism in the North and the re-entrenchment of a racist caste system in the South.

In the same speech, Clark showed how the postbellum marriage of Southern plantation power to Northern financial capital weighed particularly heavily on Black sharecroppers, who in 1877 were more vulnerable to virtual re-enslavement than at any point since the Civil War. For Clark, the same wealthy landowners and financiers who lorded over poor whites "carefully calculate[d] how much, and no more, it will require to feed and clothe the black laborer to keep him alive from one year to another. That much they will give him for his hard labor, on which the aristocracy live, and not a cent more . . . . Not a foot of land will they sell to the oppressed race who are trying to crowd out the degradation into which capital has plunged them."

Clark's orations reveal a man who was aware that people experience economic exploitation and political domination differently depending on their race and region. At the same time, his speeches attempt to make these different experiences of oppression legible across the diverse groups that he addressed. We know that Clark was thinking about Cincinnati's and St. Louis's sizable communities of German revolutionaries in his March 1877 speech because he pointed out that "capital," the same force that German socialists knew to be dominating industrial laborers in the north, was also weighing heavily on Black farmers in the South.

Clark thereby legitimized Black agricultural labor in the context of the early Marxist movement, which too often considered the factory and its generally white proletariat as the sole sources of revolution. Similarly, his description of Southern planters as an "aristocracy" appealed to the Midwest's Irish immigrants, starved and subjugated by the English monarchy. Despite the Workingmen's Party having only a handful of Black members, Clark never separated antiracism from anticapitalism. With varying degrees of subtlety, all the speeches that he delivered on behalf of the party encouraged Europeans and white Americans to understand and ally with his race in the struggle for freedom.

Clark exhibited a striking hope that his efforts to build an interracial coalition of political radicals would pay off sooner rather than later. On July 21, 1877, when the United States was in the throes of a national railway labor strike, Clark delivered his most famous oration, "Socialism: The Remedy for the Evils of Society." He predicted, "Twenty years from today there will not be a railroad belonging to a private corporation; all will be owned by the government and worked in the interests of the people."

This, of course, did not happen. The railroad monopolies coordinated with the federal government to violently crush the strikes, and today a handful of behemoth corporations continue to dominate the country's major freightways. Knowing that Clark believed the US would nationalize its railroads by 1900, it is difficult to stomach our twenty-first-century economy's acceleration of privatization and deindustrialization.

Today, as I drive north from my inner ring suburb to The Ville, I survey a city that has been hollowed out. Clark's house, like many structures from St. Louis's boom years, has crumbled and disintegrated. However, traces of it remain. The foundations of a brick facade guard the edge of what was once Clark's property, with two concrete steps ascending into a now clover-covered lot. If his house resembled the few that still flank the empty lot, then it would have been a modest shotgun-style abode, perhaps with a small front porch for Clark and his wife, Frances, to talk and watch their neighbors stroll by on languid summer evenings. The home kept Clark within walking distance of the school where he taught, the stately Charles Sumner High, which looks as magnificent today as it did during Clark's tenure.

Shortly after Clark's death in 1925, his neighborhood began to prosper. In the mid-twentieth century, The Ville was a crucible of Black wealth and talent. For such a small square of urban land, the number of famous figures whom the neighborhood raised is astounding. Josephine Baker (b. 1906), Chuck Berry (b. 1926), and Rep. Maxine Waters (b. 1938) are just the beginning of a roster stacked with cultural, political, and athletic luminaries; I could pull three different names as recognizable as these from the neighborhood's historical census. Partially in recognition of The Ville's sterling legacy, Clark's street, Goode Avenue, was renamed, in 1986, after Annie Turnbo Malone, a twentieth-century entrepreneur and philanthropist who was one of the first Black women millionaires in American history. With names as prominent as these, it's not surprising that Clark does not often turn up in lists of The Ville's famous residents.

However, with national trends of economic precarity amplified in Black Midwestern neighborhoods like The Ville, the words of America's first Black socialist may once again command people's attention. To read Clark in present-day St. Louis is to experience temporal vertigo. Although the speeches that he delivered a century and a half ago anticipate an egalitarian future, his critiques of inequality remain as applicable to the 2020s as they were to the Gilded Age. But what if the 1877 labor strikes had resulted in a victory for the workers? Would Clark's speeches from that fiery July have been recorded in history books? Would Clark's house have remained standing, preserved to honor its visionary resident?

That is not the present we're living in—Clark's political and oratorical contributions belong to the American people's dissident counterhistory, not the dominant, institutionalized historical narrative. This is not necessarily a reason to despair. The inequality and unrest of Clark's time did not prevent him from believing that he would live to see peace and universal prosperity prevail in every region of the United States. In his nearly one hundred years of life, Clark witnessed slavery and its abolition, Reconstruction and its betrayal, racist massacres and cross-racial labor solidarity. Through it all he maintained faith in the possibility for a social order that was not simply better than what presently existed but even ideal. What reasons for political hope might I glimpse in a sleepy postindustrial city or an empty lot? It will take some searching, but I am confident that signs of the cooperative spirit and human perseverance that led Clark to believe in a better world are still visible in St. Louis, like the brick foundations of a house waiting to be rebuilt.

# KATE CHOPIN

## 4232 McPherson Avenue
## St. Louis, Missouri

*By Michaella A. Thornton*

The Central West End neighborhood where Kate Chopin spent her final year boasts some of the loveliest homes in St. Louis, Missouri. Dormers and cornices and stained glass, lush gardens bedecked in hydrangeas and peonies, birdsong and wrought-iron fences.

The house at 4232 McPherson Avenue isn't far from the domed, devout beauty of the Cathedral Basilica or the local coffee roaster who prides himself on not using computers to roast the beans.

## KATE CHOPIN

**Born: February 8, 1850, in St. Louis, Missouri**

**Died: August 22, 1904, in St. Louis, Missouri**

**Forms: Short Stories, Novels**

**Recommended Works: *At Fault* (1890), "Désirée's Baby" (1892), *Bayou Folk* (1894), "The Story of an Hour" (1894), *A Night in Acadie* (1897), *The Awakening* (1899)**

I haunt Kate Chopin's last earthly home on the weekends I don't have my child. Sitting on the stoop, death all around me, I want to know how to continue writing through a pandemic. Here's what I would love to ask Chopin as I sit on the front steps of this historic home: How did you do it?

How did you write two novels and numerous short stories and poems *and* support six children as a single, widowed mother? How did you remember your worth as a writer and human being when polite society shunned you after *The Awakening* was published in 1899?

Before your death at age fifty-four, you suffered many fools. How did you put up with T. S. Eliot's bore of a mother for two years in the Wednesday Club? You were right to roast the hell out of "club women" in your writing.

We didn't deserve you, Kate.

But I've loved you since I taught "The Story of an Hour" to my community college students. Intuitively, readers understand the feeling of being trapped, the lure of freedom. We recognize "the joy that kills," which is why I'm taking notes at this underwhelming two-story brick house.

Did you need smelling salts or brandy, as your friend Lewis B. Ely joked you might, when the local newspaper printed a bad review of *The Awakening*? How about when Willa Cather wondered out loud in a Pittsburgh newspaper how you could waste "so exquisite and sensitive . . . a style on so trite and sordid a theme"?

I mean, *How dare she? Trite?*

You studied Guy de Maupassant. You revolutionized flash fiction. Plot twists? Hello, "The Storm" and "Désirée's Baby." Realistic fiction? You debunked the saccharine stench of motherhood as martyrdom, and you wrote women's sexuality as ripe, rich, and complicated as any man's.

Only after your death would the literary world realize your brilliance. What a fucking shame, and also so typical. Even now, there's no plaque marking this house.

Did the critics make you doubt what you had to say? That kills me. Some say you wrote less because of the criticism. *The Awakening* was out of print two years after your death. It took more than sixty years for scholars and readers to rediscover your prose.

Many days, for me at least, it feels impossible to write in the margins of one's life, especially as a single mother. To care for my child, myself, and my home, let alone my art, is hard. There are Zoom meetings and work in ten-minute bursts and snacks and walks and groceries to buy and a face mask to secure to my three-year-old daughter's nose and mouth.

And I am one of the lucky ones.

But also like Edna Pontellier, many days I'm drowning.

I cannot imagine doing what you did, Kate. You began a writing career at age forty. You navigated the straightjacket of women's social conventions at the turn of the nineteenth and twentieth centuries. You were the first to write unflinchingly about sexuality, divorce, and a woman's desire to govern herself. As literary scholar Per Seyersted wrote in your biography in 1969: "She was the first woman writer in her country to accept passion as a legitimate subject for serious, outspoken fiction."

As a former farmgirl who once dreamed of secret gardens and women who refused to remain silent, I sit on these cracked, crooked steps and breathe. If homes hold onto a small piece of their former inhabitants, I feel respite here. I can finally catch my breath.

# TENNESSEE WILLIAMS

## 4633 Westminster Place
## St. Louis, Missouri

*By Devin Thomas O'Shea*

Tennessee Williams called St. Louis "cold, smug, complacent, intolerant, stupid and provincial" in a 1947 interview with the *St. Louis Post-Dispatch*, playing the heel to his childhood home as he was on his way to becoming one of the most influential and celebrated American playwrights of the twentieth century.

Williams's relationship to the Midwest is the antithesis of *The New Territory*'s ethos, "Here is Good." For Tom, as he was known as a young man, here was very bad. But the repression St. Louis represented was a creative pressure cooker, according to Henry Schvey in *Blue Song: St. Louis in the Life and Work of Tennessee Williams*. Wild birds would become a ubiquitous symbol throughout Williams's work: "I feel uncomfortable in the house with Dad when I know he thinks I'm a hopeless loafer," Tom journaled. "Soon as I gather my forces (and I shall!) I must make a definite break . . . . I have pinned pictures of wild birds on my lavatory screen—significant—I'm anxious to escape—But where & how?— . . . What a terrible trap to be caught in!"

## TENNESSEE WILLIAMS

**Born: March 26, 1911, in Columbus, Mississippi**

**Died: February 25, 1983, in New York, New York**

**Forms: Drama, Short Stories, Novels, Poetry, Memoir**

**Recommended Works: *The Glass Menagerie* (1944), *A Streetcar Named Desire* (1947), *Cat on a Hot Tin Roof* (1955), *Suddenly, Last Summer* (1958), *The Night of the Iguana* (1961)**

Williams nicknamed his river-city home "Saint Pollution," and indeed the city had a few characteristics of a sulfuric runoff swamp. In the 1920s St. Louis was the fourth largest city in America, following New York, Chicago, and Philadelphia, and it was one of the most polluted urban spaces on the planet, culminating in "the day the sun didn't shine" in November 1939.

On Black Tuesday, as it came to be known, a weather pattern trapped coal emissions close to the ground, blanketing the entire city in a thick smog that smelled of ash. The streetlamps were lit all day, and in his poem "Demon Smoke," written in 1925, Williams captured the noisy, smelly, industrialized hellscape:

> crash and clap of Olive Street
> Where nature and man's work compete
> For mastery in the dingy sky;
> Where clouds of smoke
> And jets of steam
> Defy pure air and sunlight's gleam.

Saint Pollution was no place for wild birds, though as Schvey points out, Tom's true antagonist lay "not in the physical city, but within his own family." His father, Cornelius C. Williams, was either absent, drunk, abusive or some combination of all three. Tom's mother, Edwina Williams, was a repressed socialite never contented with her station in St. Louis society. Tom's older sister, Rose, was schizophrenic—diagnosed with "dementia praecox" and confined to a mental institution in Farmington, Missouri. "She is like a person half-asleep now," Tom wrote of his sister. "Quiet, gentle and thank God—not in any way revolting like so many of the others."

All three members of the Williams family were inspiration for various characters throughout Williams' writing career. "So much of this writer's work was forged in a crucible of anger and self-conscious rebellion against both family and home," Schvey writes.

The smokestacks poisoning downtown with demonic coal ash caused all kinds of people to flee west, touching off St. Louis's westward suburbia as early as the 1880s. The rich built mansion neighborhoods in the clean air, in neighborhoods at the periphery of the city, like the Central West End where the Williams family lived for a time and which is now the site of the Tennessee Williams Festival.

In 2021, confronted with COVID-19 restrictions, the festival staged a production of *The Glass Menagerie* outside of Williams's childhood home on Westminster Avenue. The production made use of the fire escapes that Williams once walked on, which inspired scenes in the play, as part of the outdoor theater set.

When the Williams family moved out of Westminster Place to their residence on South Taylor, Tom noted a corresponding decline in social standing. He explains, "It was a radical step down in the social scale, a thing we'd never had to consider in Mississippi; and all our former friends dropped us completely—St. Louis being a place where location of residence was of prime importance." A sensitive, shy Tom Williams seemed to adopt many of his mother's opinions of the city. "Social status in St. Louis depended on how much money you possessed," Edwina Williams complained in her memoir *Remember Me to Tom.* His mother's inveterate disdain for the city was based largely on her failure to find a social position equivalent to what she possessed as the rector's beautiful daughter in her previous homes, Columbus and Clarksdale.

Meanwhile, Tom's father, Cornelius, was often drunk and fighting with Edwina—complaining loudly about his wife's disdain for sexual intercourse, warring over the bottle hidden behind the bathtub. Williams describes a Cornelius-like figure in his short story, "Hot Milk at Three in the Morning," noting that his father often entered the house with "the intention of tearing it down from the inside."

With this kind of family life, surely a bookish young man could find sanctuary in school, right? As the historian David Loth points out, St. Louis was a booming metropolis known for the "best city school system in the Midwest, and by several years of national ratings, it was considered one of the best school systems in America." In University City High, Tom learned Latin and received a classical education in art, reading, and writing, but he was teased for his Southern accent and "effeminate" manner.

College was not much better. Williams was so ashamed of failing to graduate from Washington University that he omitted mention of his enrollment from his memoir. "I was a very slight youth," Williams describes himself. A young man beginning to come into his queer sexuality, he writes, "Somewhere deep in my nerves there was imprisoned a young girl, a sort of blushing school maiden."

"Williams was addicted to escaping St. Louis from first to last," Schvey writes in *Blue Song*. "It was the great triumph of his life that, unlike his sister, he did manage to literally leave it behind." After a lifetime of flight, it seems ironic that Williams would be returned to Missouri and buried in Calvary Cemetery alongside his family, but as Schvey notes, "Williams remained tethered to the city for the rest of his life. . . . It was his tragedy that for all his desperate attempts, Tom Williams never really left home. The imagination and willpower that allowed him to devote his life to writing also kept forcing him to return home again in his imagination."

The restrictive turmoil of the city is a symbolic throughline in Williams's work—a wound he returned to over and over.

The Tennessee Williams Festival now carries on his legacy in the Central West End, projecting the author's words from the cast iron balconies of his former home. A sculpture of the writer decorates the corner of McPherson and Euclid Avenue, across the street from the historic Left Bank Books, capturing a moment in bronze of Williams emphasizing something profound with a cigarette. But St. Louis still owes a debt to Tom Williams—an obligation to prevent yesterday's traumas and protect the city's LGBTQ+ community, its wild birds, and its artists.

# GORDON PARKS

## Marmaton River
## Fort Scott, Kansas

*By Jeromiah Taylor*

The grass is fuchsia, the sky bluntly cold, and the horizon swathed in haze. It is late November on the Osage Plains. In southeast Kansas the distinction between grassland and woodland, or plain and hill, is blurred by the mile. Technically speaking, it is a tree savanna. As for creeks and rivers, we've got a few. On my little stretch of highway between Wichita and Fort Scott I encountered the Osage, Cedar Hollow, Bachelor, and Owl creeks. There were also the Little Walnut River, the Fall River, and the Neosho River. And then, roping through the 155-acre Gunn Park in Fort Scott, the river I'd come to see: the Marmaton.

It took some time to find the river on foot. Like most Kansas rivers right now, the Marmaton is low. In fact, one offshoot was completely dry, allowing me to walk the cracked bottom of the gulch. While I stood in the Marmaton's dusty vein, the ground as I knew it rested ten feet above my head, with only the ombre sediment at eye level. In my silent memories, the idle river moves slowly, its wooded sentinels bending in the sharp gust.

At eleven years of age, the photographer, director, composer, and writer Gordon Parks was thrown into this river by some white boys under the impression that he couldn't swim.

These events and his circuitous path to fame and fortune are documented in his 2005 memoir *A Hungry Heart*, a Kansas Notable Book. The river itself is part of a driving tour commemorating the filming locations of the 1969 film *The Learning Tree*, Park's landmark film debut, which he wrote, directed, and scored. The film is based on his autobiographical novel of the same name.

## GORDON PARKS

**Born: November 30, 1912, in Fort Scott, Kansas**

**Died: March 7, 2006, in New York, New York**

**Forms: Photography, Film, Music, Poetry, Novels, Memoir**

**Recommended Works: *The Learning Tree* (1963), *A Choice of Weapons* (1966), *A Poet and His Camera* (1968), *Voices in the Mirror* (1990), *A Hungry Heart* (2005)**

In *A Hungry Heart*, Parks describes Fort Scott as "touched by all the hands of nature," and also as "the mecca of bigotry." A place he refuses to flatten: "bathed in lovely twilights," yet where "bigotry spewed its venom," and where he "ate hatred, a lot of it," as well as "cabbage, cornbread, [and] strawberries." It was in Fort Scott that Park's parents and siblings "sowed love's harvest," which he learned to share with those "who asked for no more than also to be loved."

And it is in Fort Scott that he is buried. After traipsing in the rain through Evergreen Cemetery on 215th Street, the sun-bleached lot markers having been no help, I found Parks's grave, which bears his poem "Homecoming." Parks reflects on Fort Scott therein, while also venturing, with a heap of triumphalism, that "hatred is suddenly remaining quiet, / keeping its mouth shut!" The unhappy irony of reading that rain-splattered inscription in 2022 will not soon leave my memory.

In 1950, amid the Jim Crow–era turmoil culminating in the 1954 decision of *Brown vs. Board of Education*, Parks shot an unpublished photo-story for *LIFE* magazine called "Back to Fort Scott." The Gordon Parks Foundation later published the story in a book. Isabel Wilkerson, in her introduction, describes Fort Scott as "neither North nor South, neither East nor West, right smack in the middle of the mainland, at the intersection of what it meant to be American on the eve of The Depression and as-yet-unseen social upheaval."

As for Parks, Wilkerson deems him the "documentarian of a watershed century." That sentence caught me in its undertow, as figurative watersheds are a recent fascination of mine. Maybe because I live surrounded by literal ones. Wichita sits on the mouth of the Little Arkansas River watershed and Fort Scott is in the Little Osage River watershed. The Marmoton flows into the Little Osage which flows into the Osage which flows into the Missouri which flows into the Mississippi which empties into the Gulf of Mexico. "Right smack in the middle" starts to feel relative when discussing rivers.

Watersheds, idiomatically speaking, are dividing or turning points. Parks's writing is filled with recollections of watersheds. For example, as he lay dying, Park's older brother Leroy, told a ten-year-old Parks who'd been caught fighting, "Your brain is more powerful than your fists, try using it. You're to remember that—ok?" One year later, after being thrown in the Marmaton and left to drown, Parks stayed below the surface, swimming to the opposite bank so that his white attackers wouldn't see him escape. A brain more powerful than fists indeed.

# JAMES TATE

## Cow Creek Crossing
## Pittsburg, Kansas

*By Leslie VonHolten*

Each James Tate poem presents itself like a welcoming trailhead—happy, sunshiny even. It is not until you are deep in the woods of it all before you sense the lurking weirdness. For example, in "The Government Lake" a trip to the toy store ends with a discomfiting acceptance of violence. Or the reader of "Awkward Silence," on her porch, is annoyed by helicopters mating overhead. Or how about those late-in-life lovers, mugged by musicians in "The Hostile Philharmonic Orchestra"?

If you think these are strange setups, how about this: Tate, a surrealist, absurdist Midwestern poet, won the Pulitzer Prize (1992) and the National Book Award (1994) for his odd dreamscapes. What a world.

Tate lived many places that rightfully claim him, but it was as a student in Pittsburg, Kansas, where he learned that he was a poet. This landscape of disturbed prairie, coyote howls, and broad days opened the deep attention he needed to see the absurd in everyday life.

I'm all for the magic carpet ride Tate gives us, but it is "Manna," from his first collection, that grounds me. A little sentimental, yes, but its alignment of solitude and connection under the night sky hits me square in the sternum. It is my all-time favorite poem set in Kansas.

> it was two
> o'clock in the morning in
> Pittsburg, Kansas, I finally
> coming home from the loveliest
> drunk of them all, a train chugged,
> goddamn, struggled across a
> prairie intersection.

## JAMES TATE

**Born: December 8, 1943, in Kansas City, Missouri**

**Died: July 8, 2015, in Amherst, Massachusetts**

**Forms: Poetry, Short Stories, Essays**

**Recommended Works: *The Lost Pilot* (1967), *Selected Poems* (1991), *Worshipful Company of Fletchers* (1994), *The Route as Briefed* (1999), *The Ghost Soldiers* (2008)**

Train tracks in Pittsburg have changed since Tate wrote those lines in 1967. Many spurs have been pulled out or paved over, and the depot is now an event center. But you can still find slow, flat, and open crossings on the quieter edges of town. Tate's miraculous provision of the poem likely happened as he walked home along West Hudson Street. Poets and other bohemians were known to drink on the trestle bridge spanning nearby Cow Creek, the setting of another poem in the collection.

Rural Kansas is rarely seen as a gateway to surrealist thought, but look closer and consider. Pittsburg is surrounded by the land scars of mining, small pits and hills that undulate throughout the county. In the early twentieth century, immigrants from all over the world came to southeast Kansas to work in the "gopher hole," strip, and shaft mines. Many were from Eastern Europe, and the area became known as the Little Balkans. It's a heritage that echoes still: until the pandemic, you could polka dance at Barto's Idle Hour in neighboring Frontenac on Saturday nights. Artist-painted fiberglass replicas of coal buckets honor the town's mining past.

This is also a land of gorillas. They are everywhere. This Pittsburg State University mascot is the proud town identifier—even the trash bins in front of each house are the school's colors, gold and red, and cement silverbacks decorate yards in every neighborhood.

The historical juxtaposition exposes the absurdity: Pitt State students selected the gorilla in 1925, while just three years earlier the town made international news when six thousand women and children marched for three days to protest poor labor conditions in the mines. The Kansas National Guard was deployed to establish order; a *New York Times* reporter dubbed the women the "Amazon Army." They were lauded as heroes in the mine camps.

It's a surreal mix, these legacies of college rah-rah comingling with a socialist labor movement. "I sure miss that country; I am really beginning to feel or see the roots I have there," Tate wrote to his instructor Eugene DeGrusen in 1966. "It takes time and distance I guess to see that kind of thing, but I see it now and I'm proud of it. Not that I write bucolic verse or even use much naturalistic imagery, but I am primitive in a contemporary way, if such a phrase can be allowed."

*but I am primitive in a contemporary way,* fiberglass coal buckets, Saturday night polka music, and gorillas on the prairie. Seeing a place better after you have left. Hello absurdist poet—we know you well.

# MERIDEL LE SUEUR

## Miner's Shack
## Picher, Oklahoma

*By Joe Schiller*

The shacks huddled haphazard and crosswise, scattered between the chat piles. Leaky roofs, knotholes, and loose-swinging doors let the dust in on any decent breeze. In Picher, Oklahoma, nobody built for permanence. They leased their plots from the biggest mining companies or from the Bureau of Indian Affairs on behalf of the Quapaw people (who were then mostly excluded from mine work). They moved on short notice as the "diggin's" expanded, evicted by progress. In 1948 Meridel Le Sueur traveled to the Tri-State Mining District at its productive end. Where useful ore made up only 2 percent of the dirt, they were pulling mountains of rock to the surface to parse out any profit.

The extra stuff was called "chat." The shack she stayed in during her visit, like most in Picher, had come to town in pieces on family migrations from area farms and older district camps.

## MERIDEL LE SUEUR

**Born: February 22, 1900, in Murray, Iowa**

**Died: November 14, 1996, in Hudson, Wisconsin**

**Forms: Novels, Short Stories, Journalism, Creative Nonfiction, Children's Literature, Poetry, History**

**Recommended Works: *The Girl* (1930s/1978), *Salute to Spring* (1940), *North Star Country* (1945), *Ripening: Selected Work, 1927–1980* (1982), *Sparrow Hawk* (1987)**

Le Sueur is identified mostly with the Upper Midwest, but this landscape of the Lower Midwest epitomizes her life's work: proletarian literature and reportage about industrial capitalism's paired assaults on women and land. Her mother's home on Minneapolis's tony Lowry Hill, where Le Sueur taught writing after World War II, will not do as a landscape for Le Sueur. The "wasteland of ruined earth and human refuse" she encountered in extreme northeast Oklahoma will.

"It's the chat, overn everything," explained Le Sueur's interview subject, the titular "Eroded Woman" of this trip's product, an article for the left-wing *Masses and Mainstream*. The woman wiped a chair for the writer. "Her eyes seemed dusted" with chat, wrote Le Sueur, "their blueness dimmed and yet wide open and upon me." The Eroded Woman was the wife and mother of mine workers, and she nursed her husband through the district's environmental scourge, silicosis. "You drown in your own blood, you do," lamented their son.

The Eroded Woman and her family were partisans of the International Union of Mine, Mill and Smelter Workers, which was affiliated with the Congress of Industrial Organizations (CIO). That made them outcasts in a district of proud, American-born laborers who had violently excluded Black Americans, immigrants, and labor organizers from their camps, certain that they were future bosses themselves and didn't need a radical union. Just Le Sueur's kind of person, the Eroded Woman repaired the son's wounds from "the Klan, the bosses, pickhandlers," who beat every man with a union button during mid-1930s labor strife. "I'm mighty proud of him not to lick the boots of the company," she declared. She and her men resisted their town's xenophobia. They exemplified the ideal of what the historian Julia Mickenberg has called Le Sueur's "alternative Americanism."

The shack is most certainly gone. Nothing in Picher met a dignified end when the mines closed across the 1950s and '60s, except proud citizens, who willed theirs, usually by moving away. Even the landmark Connell Hotel was razed, its rubble filling an abandoned mine shaft in 1972.

In the 1980s a new generation of feminists rediscovered Le Sueur. More recently have come the regionalists. Late in life she said she was "a passionate, partisan Midwest lover," but that didn't tell it all. More accurately, she loved the Midwest at its margins, and no place was more marginal than the Tri-State mines in the late 1940s.

"Eroded Woman" and its landscape embodied what Le Sueur's editor Elaine Hedges called her "central formulation of female experience." It focused on one woman haunted by the deaths of children and "the plunge into the darkness of the underground, the woman (or the earth) as wounded, invaded, and raped." "Eroded Woman" was suffused with agrarian longing for what was lost on the land when capitalists extracted progress from beneath it. Amid shifting political winds in the late 1940s, perhaps Le Sueur felt her McCarthy-era persecution coming. She closed:

> All over mid-America now lamplight reveals the old earth, reveals the story of water, and the sound of water in the darkness repeats the myth and legends of old struggles. The fields lie there, the plow handles wet, standing useless in the mud, the countless seeds, the little houses, the big houses, the vast spider network of us all in the womb of history, looking fearful, not knowing at this moment the strength, doubting the strength, often fearful of giant menace, fearful of peculiar strains and wild boar power and small eyes of the fox.
>
> The lower continent underlying all, speaks below us, the gulf, the black old land.

Meridel Le Sueur's life and work remind us of the hopeful and radical potential of regionalism and place—that tradition and history, rather than being reactionary, can gird people for progressive struggle. Picher, down from ten thousand people to about two thousand, unincorporated in 2009 after a contentious buyout process and the coup de grâce of a tornado that killed seven people and destroyed more than one hundred homes. The Quapaws remain, remediating mine waste with the Environmental Protection Agency.

The chat piles, once the symbol of a proud community's work, stand now like monuments to folly, leaching their payload of heavy metals into Tar Creek and rendering a large area uninhabitable. Without the shacks and the people who built them, the piles memorialize only the bankruptcy of past racial and ethnic exclusion. The "white man's camp" of the early twentieth century proved to be no bulwark against economic and environmental collapse. As Meridel Le Sueur could surely have told us, it's a good lesson for our time of climate crisis, economic precarity, hardening borders, and rising xenophobia.

# JOHN JOSEPH MATHEWS

## Tallgrass Prairie Preserve
## Osage County, Oklahoma

*By Mason Whitehorn Powell*

"Three ridges roughly boat-shaped push their prows south into the sea of prairie." The opening lines of *Talking to the Moon* by Osage author John Joseph Mathews describe the land where he would build a sandstone cabin, in 1932, to live out the remainder of his life. Published in 1945 *Talking to the Moon* is an intimate reflection on the landscape, wildlife, occasional tribal affairs, and seasonal changes that he experienced across this decade.

Mathews named his one-room cabin The Blackjacks, moored by those eponymous native oak trees and harbored by a sea of prairie. The cabin was abandoned after his death in 1979, and his grave remains on the property, which is now surrounded by a fence to keep roaming buffalo off the grounds. The Blackjacks and the land surrounding it were purchased from Mathews's descendants by The Nature Conservancy (TNC) in 2014 and, during summer 2020 I toured the cabin digitally, in a virtual event hosted by TNC and the Tallgrass Prairie Preserve.

I may have never seen The Blackjacks with my own eyes, but I know the world Mathews describes because I was cut from the same cloth. After serving as a pilot during World War I, studying at the University of Oklahoma, obtaining a degree in Natural Sciences from Oxford, and roaming around Europe, Mathews grew travel weary and was drawn back to the lands he knew intimately and loved. He returned home to allotted land on the tallgrass prairie north of Pawhuska, Oklahoma, his birth town.

## JOHN JOSEPH MATHEWS

**Born: January 27, 1894, in Pawhuska, Osage Nation, Indian Territory**

**Died: June 28, 1979, in Pawhuska, Oklahoma**

**Forms: Novels, Memoir, Short Stories, History, Biography**

**Recommended Works: *Wah'Kon-Tah: The Osage and the White Man's Road* (1929), *Sundown* (1934), *Talking to the Moon* (1945), *The Osages: Children of the Middle Waters* (1961)**

His words are familiar to me, as an Osage with the same blood quantum as Mathews, raised in Osage County, pulled between tribal traditions and the white influence on my own life. I also studied in Europe; I met my wife there and lived in Italy for a time before returning to Hominy, Oklahoma, where we lived in a native sandstone building even older than Mathews's cabin.

Mathews writes, "My coming back was dramatic in a way; a weight on the sensitive scales of nature, which I knew would eventually be adjusted if I live as I had planned to live; to become a part of the balance." Structured by and depicting the four seasons, *Talking to the Moon* is subdivided according to the traditional Osage calendar: moon phases. Everything is structured as so—one only has to look. I write this as the Yellow-Flower Moon fades into Deer-Hiding Moon. Heat enters through my window, and I notice that the yellow flowers growing in my yard have closed up. Behind my grandfather's house, a doe and fawn are beginning to stir on cooler evenings, but the bucks have already vanished as hunters ready themselves.

Under this same moon, Mathews writes of driving to Hominy to meet with the old Osage men Claremore, Abbot, and Pitts to have their portraits painted by an artist with the Public Works of Art Project. These portraits are still on display in the Osage Tribal Museum in Pawhuska, which Mathews established in 1938. From 1934 to 1942 he sat on the tribal council on that same hill rising above downtown Pawhuska, where my mother also served for two terms as an Osage congresswoman.

My grandfather never met Mathews but tells me about my family's encounter with him:

> About half those books were given to him by your [great-great-] aunt Magella. When he'd run out of things that weren't in a book somewhere he could study, or come out of the Catholic Diocese or wherever, then he'd have Magella tell him what had really happened. Where they came from. What families you were talking about.

He summed up the conversation: "My dad told my aunt, 'Don't you be giving him any more information.'"

Mathews and my blind aunt Magella Whitehorn were speaking after the "old ways" were laid to rest during her father's generation. Mathews and Magella were both born in 1894 in Osage Indian Territory, twenty-two years after our final relocation. She was a full-blood and among the last of those born onto the ground and raised with a bundle, observing the ancient Osage religion.

In the posthumously published autobiography *Twenty Thousand Mornings*, Mathews writes of his childhood bedroom, from which he "could look down into the valley." From this vantage point, he could hear Magella's father and other elders rise before dawn to greet the sun with prayers, which sounds he recounts as "the scar" of "a precocious memory." Mathews writes, "The prayer-chant that disturbed my little boy's soul to the depths was Neolithic man talking to god."

In her youth Magella was sent to boarding school and pressured to relinquish her traditional Osage identity and status grounded in our ceremonial rites. She did so because her elders said to, and it must have felt like entering an oblivion. Even though Mathews spent a career wrestling with his precocious memory of Osage mysteries—a lifelong attempt to capture and confront the past with words—there remained a painful tension between those who had to leave the old ways behind and those raised to inherit the new world. For Magella, this was a tragic episode. And her brother, Sam Whitehorn, my great-grandfather, told her not to speak with Mathews because he viewed her knowledge of the past as family business.

The land speaks in indescribable ways, and our history is mysterious in its abandonment as we are adopted into a new world. It is evident in his writings that Mathews experienced a different Osage County than I know, but my generation still faces many of the same concerns, will pass down similar traditions, and can still fully experience that immutable landscape. A cabin is just a building. That was never the point—rather that it is centered, grounded, embraced by land that knows and accepts us, that is our inheritance despite ongoing changes. Lost traditions survive both in Mathews's books and in family stories such as my own. Mathews knew that Osage history must be preserved, just as land must be conserved, because the two are inseparable.

The more I learn from the rolling hills around me, the more I know about myself. Any time I drive north from Hominy toward Pawhuska, crossing a sea of prairie and islands of blackjacks, I feel at home and overwhelmed by acceptance. I haven't needed to visit his cabin to know these things—only to truly see nature here and to listen. When the world allows and when in-person tours resume, I hope to step inside Mathews's cabin. Until then, I have the Osage landscape and my connection to Mathews in our shared culture and his books: "With word symbols as my poor tools, to sweat at the feet of a beauty, an order, a perfection, a mystery far above my comprehension."

# S. E. HINTON

## Crutchfield
## Tulsa, Oklahoma

*By Caleb Freeman*

One day in the winter of 1981, when the film adaptation of S. E. Hinton's 1967 novel *The Outsiders* was still in preproduction, Hinton and Francis Ford Coppola, the film's director, rode double on a bicycle down North Tulsa's side streets. More than sixty pounds of film equipment sat in their handlebar basket, and so they had to stop periodically to keep from falling onto the pavement. Their route took them into one of the city's oldest mixed-use neighborhoods. They rode past houses in various states of disrepair, many of them built shortly after the city was incorporated in 1898, as well as industrial sites and manufacturing plants, some empty and derelict, abandoned in the years of suburban sprawl.

Their destination was a house that Coppola had stumbled on, a dilapidated Craftsman bungalow located at 731 North St. Louis Avenue in the Crutchfield neighborhood. With its rusted chain-link fence and overgrown lawn, it was a promising candidate for the Curtis house, where Derry, Sodapop, and Ponyboy, the orphaned protagonists of *The Outsiders*, would live. Hinton agreed, and when production began the next year, that house was at the heart of it.

Hinton's novel of warring teenage gangs, written fifteen years earlier when she was a student at Will Rogers High School, has a complicated relationship with Tulsa. Hinton is from Tulsa, and by all accounts set the story here, too, but chose not to include any real names or landmarks in order to, as she told the local newspaper, "protect the guilty." When she wrote *The Outsiders,* Hinton was bearing witness to teenage alienation and violent socioeconomic segregation, and these weren't Tulsa problems; they were everywhere.

## S. E. HINTON

**Born: July 22, 1948, in Tulsa, Oklahoma**

**Died: —**

**Forms: Novels, Young Adult, Children's Literature**

**Recommended Works: *The Outsiders* (1967), *That Was Then, This Is Now* (1971), *Rumble Fish* (1975), *Tex* (1979)**

The film took a different approach, fully embedding itself in Tulsa. In March 1982 Zoetrope Studios moved into Crutchfield, setting up their production team in the former Lowell Elementary School building, which had been closed four years prior. In a type of method acting, the young cast members haunted the city as greasers, stealing from local drug stores, staying out all night, and sometimes sleeping in the Curtis house, which didn't have any heat. Local markers—the Oklahoma Steel Castings Company, the Admiral Twin Drive-In, the art deco architecture of Will Rogers High School and Boston Avenue Methodist Church—appear in the film. Hinton and Coppola even revised the story so that the Greasers would live on the north side instead of the east, a more accurate geographic representation of Tulsa's class and racial divide. When the filming was done, Coppola threw a party in Crutchfield Park, complete with carnival rides, an abundance of food and beer, and an ice sculpture. He received a key to the city from the mayor and an appreciation plaque from the Crutchfield Neighborhood Association.

Then he left. The film came out in 1983, and members of the Oklahoma Film Industry Task Force, which had lobbied hard for Coppola to film in Tulsa, relished their success. Much of the young cast went on to become celebrities. Crutchfield, on the other hand, faded into memory.

The neighborhood is still here, though, just north of the historic "Frisco" Railway, which once brought hopeful settlers and cutthroat opportunists to Tulsa, back when the area was still known as Indian Territory. Now you drive through Crutchfield and see the husks of uninhabited buildings. The neighborhood kindergarten was shut down in 1986. The Oklahoma Steel Castings Company closed a year later, leaving behind a polluted ten-acre lot. The oil bust of the 1980s drove out many of the neighborhood's remaining manufacturers, and many residents who could afford to leave did. By 2007 approximately one-third of the houses in the neighborhood were abandoned. Rates of violent crime rose to become the highest in Tulsa.

The neighborhood association, led by longtime residents—truck drivers, store owners, church leaders—advocated tirelessly for Crutchfield. They organized neighborhood cleanups, met with city officials, and developed a revitalization plan that called in part for better infrastructure and more public facilities, including a new school. Although the City of Tulsa approved the plan in 2004, little has changed. In 2006 Tulsa Public Schools spent $3.3 million converting the old Lowell Elementary building, the former production site for *The Outsiders*, into a four-and-a-half-acre "state-of-the-art" ropes course. Although it was touted as a boon to the community, the course was fenced off and inaccessible to the neighborhood's residents. The course was later closed in 2017 due to budget cuts, and the site once again sits abandoned.

Today Crutchfield is still without a school or a grocery store. Its predominately Hispanic population experiences some of the worst health outcomes and rates of poverty in the city. Although the neighborhood is one of Tulsa's oldest, the city has never treated it with the same significance as its other historic neighborhoods.

As my girlfriend and I drive through Crutchfield in the winter of 2021, I wonder about the decision to bring *The Outsiders* film to Tulsa. When the novel was released, local media was quick to absolve the city. The *Tulsa World* suggested that, although the setting was Tulsa, "it could be any city." After watching the film, though, I wonder if Hinton might say otherwise.

*The Outsiders* is a story about boundary lines, divisions that we create and perpetuate. It's a fitting story for Tulsa, a city whose inclination toward boosterism—as the self-proclaimed "Magic City" and "Oil Capital of the World"—frequently has sanitized and distorted its history, almost always at the expense of its marginalized communities.

Crutchfield sits just north of the line that divided Cherokee Nation and Muscogee (Creek) Nation land, one of the lines established by the Indian Removal Act of 1830. The neighborhood was named after Vinita Crutchfield, who was allotted the land after the General Allotment Act. She appears on the Dawes Roll as a nine-year-old Cherokee girl living with her mother. Growing up, Crutchfield would have lived on the dividing line much like the characters in Hinton's novel.

One mile to the east of Crutchfield is Tulsa's Greenwood district, which was once forty square blocks of Black-owned land known as "Black Wall Street." Born of entrepreneurship, Greenwood was a precarious haven for Black Oklahomans during a time when the state adopted strict Jim Crow laws. Local newspapermen disparaged Greenwood as "Little Africa," and the growth of the KKK in Tulsa posed an increasing threat. In May 1921 a white mob invaded, razed, and in the end, partially annexed Greenwood, killing its residents in a state-sanctioned slaughter. For decades, the Tulsa Race Massacre, as it would come to be known, remained a secret, a part of Tulsa's history hidden from people like me who never learned about it in school. From Crutchfield, just beyond the borderlines of Lansing Ave. and the Midland Valley railway tracks, you would have been able to see the smoke of Greenwood's burning buildings.

When we arrive at the Curtis home, which was purchased in 2016 and converted into a small museum dedicated to *The Outsiders*, I think about the people of Crutchfield. Surrounding the home are boarded-up houses flying tattered American flags. Stray dogs roam the area. Less than a block away from the house is an auto shop, the same type of place where Ponyboy might have worked. We stay for a little while, driving around the neighborhood. When we leave, I think about the tyranny of boundaries and the exorbitant privilege of being able to cross them.

# R. A. LAFFERTY

## 1724 S. Trenton Ave.
## Tulsa, Oklahoma

*By Michael Helsem*

> Everything, including dreams, is meteorological.
> —R. A. Lafferty, "Narrow Valley"

A couple of years ago my wife and I were visiting my young niece and her husband in Tulsa, Oklahoma, where they had moved—a place I had never been. At first all I could think of was that immense, windswept plain, many times traversed by me, with speeding wheels, with wings, never stopping, the very incarnation of a blur. Then it dawned on me that the science fiction author R. A. Lafferty, whom I had idolized in the '70s, had spent almost his entire life in Tulsa. In the same house.

I had no luck finding any of his books in a bookstore there to show my niece, but at one point we were out on a walk, and I had summoned up from the internet a not-quite-exact location of the house he had lived in. According to Natasha Ball on "Lafferty Lost and Found," the house is "a shaded brick bungalow where Trenton comes to a T." We went looking and found what seemed to be it, the corner house at 1724 South Trenton Avenue. I didn't have a camera along, but it was satisfying to have seen it, anyway. It was a quiet, slightly gentrified neighborhood of older houses near a small lake, with good-sized trees on every block, which reminded me of the place in Oak Cliff I myself had grown up in—a good place to be a kid running wild on bicycles, where it seemed nothing bad could ever happen.

## R. A. LAFFERTY

**Born: November 7, 1914, in Neola, Iowa**

**Died: March 18, 2002, in Broken Arrow, Oklahoma**

**Forms: Novels, Short Stories, History**

**Recommended Works: *Past Master* (1968), *Fourth Mansions* (1969), *Nine Hundred Grandmothers* (1970), *The Devil Is Dead* (1971), *Okla Hannali* (1972)**

> Their brains differed from ours, their concepts must have been different, and therefore they lived in a different world.
> —*The Devil is Dead*

*Who*, you may ask, *is R. A. Lafferty?* He has fallen into obscurity but seems to be making a little bit of a comeback these days, praised by the likes of Neil Gaiman. To know him better, first run out and grab a copy of *Nine Hundred Grandmothers*. That's a good start. Lafferty is best known for his inimitable short stories, which are only incidentally concerned with the tropes and themes of regular science fiction, and told in a jocular but slightly jarring voice that is a little like a tall tale and a little like a homegrown surrealist who has some really important things to say that he absolutely will not divulge, except in hints and sideways jokes. If you read enough of him, you start to dimly discern the vast, convoluted architecture of Lafferty's universe—not an easy task, since so many of his books are out of print and not a few of them were published by small presses that never printed a large run in the first place.

To my understanding, there is a highly esoteric Thomist-Catholic aspect to his work. He apparently also believes we inhabit a multiverse in which time and space are sometimes illusory and sometimes not; survivors from the distant past (such as Neanderthals) or visitors from the future are not unheard of—and they're not often used for the science-fiction story; they're just *there*. Lafferty often makes reference to obviously bogus works, yet he's also curiously erudite in real ones. There's a wild Zen side, too, but you never can be quite sure when he's being serious and when he's pulling your leg.

> I was always for the underdog, and, doggy, you're way way under.
> —*Fourth Mansions*

It's been said that aspects of the surrounding town are always seeping into his works, and not only the more ostensibly realist ones. But by and large Tulsa is not present in any immediately named way—any more than the environs of the great mystical poets—unless you count the almost complete absence of that most twentieth-century experience: riding in a car (Lafferty didn't drive). But two things I know. One is that Lafferty always identified with the underdog, the misfit, the underclass, and the socially disfavored; he has some striking stories and one historical novel (possibly his masterpiece, *Okla Hannali*) about Native Americans, whom he invariably credits with greater perception of reality.

In his many worlds, there is a pervasive, bone-deep precarity: the irruption of personal and/or apocalyptic violence is never out of the question, at any moment. I have to think the terrible 1921 Tulsa Race Massacre, which happened about three miles from his house (although he was only seven at the time) must have been something he couldn't *not* have known about and reflected on.

> We are living in the narrow interval between the lightning and the thunder.
> —*Arrive at Easterwine*

And then there are the tornados—ninety-eight since 1950, according to the National Weather Service. Idyllic the place might be, but hardly peaceful. On the mild, sunny afternoon when I visited, we drove past two blocks of torn-up buildings that hadn't yet been rebuilt, havoc from the last big one. It looked like a bomb had gone off, levelling everything; the car fell silent. You see such scenes in newsreel footage, latterly of Ukraine maybe: never in these United States, not like this. All the other cars kept right on rolling, on to their intended destinations, untroubled and, I daresay, sound asleep. They raise their families, go to their neighborhood churches, my niece and her new husband among them. This is where they choose to live.

> "We could always make another world," said Welkin reasonably.
> "Certainly, but this one is our testing."
> —"Sky"

# THOMAS HART BENTON

## Mark Twain National Forest
## Shell Knob, Missouri

*By Aaron Hadlow*

There is a burled oak tree that stands on the knuckle of a ridge finger behind my parent's house in Shell Knob, Missouri. Despite its disfigurement, the oak is otherwise straight and tall. Given the oak's stature, the other trees around it have little choice but to stretch for sunlight and grow tall and straight too. When I was a child, I recall, that oak's bloom of leaves in the spring reached what I perceived from the Mark Twain National Forest floor to be a heaven, even if just a lower one. The oak is a way-marker tree, and many times growing up I was relieved to pass by it, knowing that the comfort of home was not far. I fear now I would become lost if I tried to find that oak, even though those woods are quite familiar. One may become lost even among the familiar.

## THOMAS HART BENTON

**Born: April 15, 1889, in Neosho, Missouri**

**Died: January 19, 1975, in Kansas City, Missouri**

**Forms: Murals, Book Illustration, Autobiography**

**Recommended Works: *America Today* (1930–31), *Indiana Murals* (1933), *A Social History of Missouri* (1936), *An Artist in America* (1951)**

Thomas Hart Benton, one of Missouri's most storied artists, knew this sense of estrangement all too well. I became acquainted with Benton's work when I was in elementary school. On a road trip from southwest Missouri to Columbia to watch the state high school basketball championships, my father stopped at the capitol building in Jefferson City. My brother and I raced through the wide polished corridors of the capitol, the stone echoing footsteps and our voices. Our father led us to the Missouri House of Representatives Lounge. Once inside the room, Benton's many-paneled mural, *The Social History of the State of Missouri* (1936), stilled our feet and voices.

As an adult I can now see the mural is characterized by Benton's depiction of laboring bodies. They are often sinewy, in fluid motion, bent under a gravity of some unidentified downward pressure that suggests the yoke of their exploiters. Their bodies rarely find repose, except for a cabal of politicians who sit smoking Roi-Tans and drinking, presumably, bathtub gin. Those bodies yield to the same gravity throughout the work but find a comfortable recumbent ease. The stylistic truth of Benton's mural is only part of its genius.

But the dissonance is striking between the way Benton writes about his own life and the way he depicts the subjects in many of his paintings. This dissonance is best exemplified by an anecdote from his autobiography, *An Artist in America* (1937), recounting a hike in the woods after he planted the plank of his father's remains in a respectable cemetery in Neosho, the site of his childhood home.

Long absented from Missouri, Benton had returned to Neosho in 1924 to sit next to his father's deathbed. Benton's father was a former US congressman, and as he neared death his "cronies" also neared to tell stories. In those long hours of vigil, Benton listened, and his father's friends became his friends. Benton was "moved by a great desire to know more about the America" he'd glimpsed in Neosho. He declared that "for the hangovers of idealistic social theory, Missouri is a grand pickup," going so far as to laud the "individual will" deeply grooved in the "American character."

Not long after, the artist set out on a walk in the "White River country along the Arkansas-Missouri line," in an effort to discover the America he'd been missing. Benton stumbled through the hollows and hills of this area, growing increasingly weary of snakes and cursing the "distrusting" locals, who he blamed for giving him bad directions. He referred to a ferryman who initially denied him passage as a "goddamn son-of-a-bitch" because the ferryman feared Benton was the culprit of a bank robbery the night before. He eventually appraised the locals as "marauding and shiftless hill people" whose "depredations," "wild quarrels," and "wild fornications" fill the records of the county courts. Eventually he arrived at his destination in Forsyth. His evaluation of the denizens of the Ozarks was adduced from a hike he estimated to be about fifty miles. I imagine he passed by that burled oak behind my parents' house near Shell Knob without realizing how close to home he actually was.

In 1935 Benton was commissioned to paint *The Social History of the State of Missouri* by the Missouri legislature. The windfall that came with the commission must have made it easier for Benton to return to Kansas City to live, though he summered in Martha's Vineyard every year until he died in 1975.

Since his death, Benton's relevance has waxed and waned, leading the editor of my copy of *An Artist in America* to derogate Benton an "artistic nationalist," an "irretrievably out-of-date Jeffersonian," with "nineteenth century" artistic vision. As an irretrievably out-of-date Jeffersonian myself, this all sounds a bit harsh. Of course Benton is problematic for reasons that are self-evident upon reading his autobiography. A privileged heterosexual white man born below the Mason-Dixon Line shortly after the twilight of reconstruction, Benton had ethical blind spots that can be easily surmised.

Benton is also regularly criticized for what is thought to be his "provincial" subject matter, verging on caricature. Despite his upbringing in Missouri, Benton's connection to the America that he is most associated with was attenuated by the path he chose. He fled the Ozarks as soon as he could and only returned for the sort of selective excursions that permitted him to extract experience to fuel his creative work—like a gouty gourmand deigning to visit an ungentrified urban area only for a tasty treat. By the time of his trek through the woods, he'd become all but a stranger to the country.

Instead, perhaps the most salient and lasting truth of Benton's work is the politics of his curved lines. Benton's strong yet disfigured bodies—bodies that bend down and rise up—defy any theory praising the solitary individual will. It is a truth of form and structure, if not subject. It is the truth of every stand of woods.

# MAYA ANGELOU

## Angelou Memorial
## Stamps, Arkansas

*By Greer Veon*

Despite living in southwest Arkansas most of my life, my first visit to Stamps was with my parents in August 2018. We made the trip on a Sunday afternoon before my flight back north the following morning, my parents joking that Stamps was the kind of place that kept to itself. I sat in the backseat picturing the red clay that Maya Angelou once walked across and imagined feeling the breeze she once breathed.

In September 2017 a local newspaper reported that a memorial sign dedicated to Angelou disappeared from the grounds of Lake June days after Stamps elected Brenda Davis, their first Black mayor. "It makes you wonder," Mayor Davis told reporters. "But I wouldn't speculate." All the same, the mayor's suspicions resonated, coming as they did in the Southern town that served as the backdrop for *I Know Why the Caged Bird Sings*, Angelou's painful

1969 memoir about coming of age during the Jim Crow era. Over time I searched for updates, but the suspects' names were never printed, and the story went cold.

In a way, Angelou's memoir prefigures Mayor Davis's wariness:

> What sets one Southern town apart from another, or from a Northern town or hamlet, or city high rise? The answer must be in the experiences shared between the unknowing majority (it) and the knowing minority (you). All of childhood's unanswered questions must finally be passed back to the town and answered there. Heroes and bogey men, values and dislikes, are first encountered and labeled in that early environment.

## MAYA ANGELOU

**Born: April 4, 1928, in St. Louis, Missouri**

**Died: May 28, 2014, in Winston-Salem, North Carolina**

**Forms: Autobiography, Poetry, Essays, Drama, Children's Literature**

**Recommended Works: *I Know Why the Caged Bird Sings* (1969), *Just Give Me a Cool Drink of Water 'Fore I Diiie* (1971), *Gather Together in My Name* (1974), *And Still I Rise* (1978), *The Heart of a Woman* (1981)**

In the early twentieth century, Stamps served as a flag stop for the railroads that stretched across Arkansas, Texas, and Louisiana. I grew up forty-five minutes away on the state line between the twin cities of Texarkana, one of the bigger stops on that same line, the Cotton Belt Route. Many of my childhood memories are set in the backseat of our family car as we took weekend drives on local roads through one-stoplight towns filled with forgotten gas stations and churches. Most of the newer highways bypassed Stamps. So did most people. When my ninth-grade English class read Angelou's memoir, our teacher spoke less about how close we lived to the town and more about parents' letters asking that my classmates be excused from the reading.

I didn't revisit that memory until shortly after I moved away and read a piece on the Celebrate Maya Project, which was holding a 2018 celebration for the author's ninetieth birthday. Angelou's admirers gathered in Stamps to honor her and witness her childhood landscape. Still, I couldn't shake the missing sign. I wondered what remained, and I longed to visit Stamps the next time I returned home.

On the way to Stamps that afternoon, we stopped at Burge's, a retro dairy barn in nearby Lewisville, where we ordered from the front window. Minutes after stuffing ourselves with brisket and chocolate pies, we entered Stamps's historic downtown, marked by a post office and outdoor storefronts. Paint cans and a ladder leaned against a half-completed mural. As we crossed over the train tracks, I looked for Annie Henderson's merchandise store, the center of Angelou's life in *I Know Why the Caged Bird Sings*, but it's gone.

We found Lake June on the edge of town, the water drained enough to expose its bottom brush. Despite reports that the state would replace the missing sign, there, almost a year after it was stolen, stood a wooden skeleton of the memorial. There's something sobering to see that as the same place where a young Angelou spent her alone time. Even Maya Angelou, a voice of her generation, still faces these attempts at erasure, even in the town that played such a vital role in her legacy. Angelou's memoir addresses a childhood filled with love and pain that stayed with her no matter where she moved. What "heroes and bogeymen" have other children first encountered here and in other towns alike? Who decides what parts of our homes will be forgotten? Will they make space or blot out the experiences, the identities of their neighbors? I inhaled the damp air and left without answers.

# ELIJAH LOVEJOY

## Lovejoy State Memorial
## Alton, Illinois

*By Evan Allen Wood*

Elijah Parish Lovejoy was shot by members of a mob and succumbed to his wounds on the evening of November 7, 1837, in Alton, Illinois. Decades later the community erected a 110-foot-tall monument honoring him. The monument has a central granite column with a cast-bronze winged statue of victory on top. Looking at the monument from the eponymous Monument Avenue it appears neatly framed by the stone retaining wall and staircase leading into the cemetery. Beside it are two smaller columns with a curved whispering wall wrapping around behind.

## ELIJAH LOVEJOY

**Born: November 9, 1802, in Albion, Maine**

**Died: November 7, 1837, in Alton, Illinois**

**Forms: Journalism**

**Recommended Works: *St. Louis Observer* (1833–35), *Alton Observer* (1837)**

Lovejoy had been publishing *The Alton Observer*, an antislavery newspaper, for the better part of three years, and on the day he died a mob formed—not for the first time—intent on destroying the Presbyterian minister's press. Lovejoy's editorials were written in a straightforward voice, and he often invoked his Christian faith. In a characteristic example from September 8, 1837, he wrote: "It is the duty of us all to unite our hearty and zealous efforts to effect the speedy and entire emancipation of that portion of our fellowmen in bondage." Although his friends rallied to his side, an exchange of gunfire left the thirty-four-year-old editor dead. Nobody was prosecuted in the weeks that followed, and Lovejoy's body had to be buried in a secret location lest the citizens who'd participated in his killing decide to press their harassment beyond the grave.

It's hard to look past the irony of a community tacitly allowing a mob to kill one of its citizens and then several decades later erecting a grand monument heralding the same man as a defender of the free press and superior moral convictions. The cynical view might hold that the monument constitutes an attempt for the river town to paper over the reality of its past. But allowing Lovejoy to rest in an anonymous grave is an even less preferable course. It would not be unreasonable to ask how a community could best practice restorative justice for a killing that was, by that time, sixty years gone.

Abolitionist organizing wasn't a safe proposition anywhere in the United States in the 1830s. Mobs tarred and feathered or otherwise chased away abolitionist speakers, editors, and groups from Nashville to New York. It's fair to posit that the consequences tended to be more dire in states like Missouri where slavery was legal, but abolition, which entailed immediate emancipation of all people kept as slaves (as opposed to gradualism which called for a slower end to the practice), was still a fringe view among antislavery advocates in the US at this point.

Elijah Lovejoy knew he was risking his life by continuing to publish his paper, originally called *The St. Louis Observer*. He moved upriver from St. Louis to Alton to avoid mob justice on the western banks of the Mississippi, where his paper's offices had been raided and his press destroyed. Alton, despite being in a free state, was not a safe haven for Lovejoy. His press was again destroyed and tossed into the river after it had been shipped to its new home, and mobs would harass Lovejoy and his *Observer* multiple times before his death.

Each new instance of peril seemed only to strengthen Lovejoy's resolve. He spoke out on his own behalf at community meetings and walked the streets, damn the consequences. That his life was in danger was something he often acknowledged in editorials and addresses, but he was unwilling to abandon his cause. In his final recorded remarks, apparently from a public meeting of Alton citizens, he remarked, "If I die, I have determined to make my grave in Alton." Lovejoy's determination in the face of mortal danger was commendable; perhaps the monument is a fitting tribute.

But one can't help but think of the thousands of lynching victims across the nation who gave no act of provocation at all, let alone any involvement in publishing inflammatory editorials. As the National Lynching Memorial has demonstrated, these victims of racial violence are worthy of monuments as grand as can be built.

Monuments can't undo the pain caused by the deaths they commemorate any more than they can pardon the communities complicit in them. But a society with a clear sense of its own history is one that properly remembers its heroes and villains. A tour of public statues and monuments across the US at present reveals that our ideas about our past are sometimes misguided if not outright delusional. During the time it was erected, Lovejoy's monument would have stood in contrast to the statues of Confederate generals going up around the country as part of the burgeoning Lost Cause movement. Correcting the historical record in statues could be looked on as a comparatively low-cost act of civic maintenance as opposed to an activist victory, but it should be done all the same.

Lovejoy's death accomplished more for the abolitionist movement than he could have dreamed of doing with his paper. The incident made headlines across the country and generated increased sympathy for the abolitionist cause. In an 1857 letter Abraham Lincoln described Lovejoy's death as "the most important single event that ever happened in the new world." The moral implications of that statement go beyond the scope of this essay, but it is true that his sacrifice advanced the cause of abolition. The monument at Alton tells us he gave everything he could for a cause that was urgent and just. Let's hope it stands another hundred years.

# RACHEL

## Fort Crawford
## Prairie du Chien, Wisconsin

*By Christy Clark-Pujara*

On November 4, 1834, a twenty-year-old "mulatto" woman named Rachel filed a freedom suit in St. Louis, Missouri. She claimed that a military officer named Thomas Stockton held her in slavery at Fort Snelling for two years and then moved her to Fort Crawford in Prairie du Chien, Wisconsin. According to Rachel's suit, "Stockton . . . took your petitioner to . . . Prairie du Chien for about two years, holding your petitioner as a slave . . . causing her to work for & serve him & family at that place during that time as a slave at which place her child James Henry was born." Rachel argued that her residence and her son's birth in the free territories made them free people. Slavery was prohibited by federal law in the Northwest Territories. But despite the ban on slaveholding, Black Americans were held in bondage; in fact, federal military officers were given an allowance to cover the cost of hiring a servant or keeping a slave.

Rachel had been extremely vulnerable at Fort Crawford. She lived in a space dominated by armed white men, and she was regarded as property. Moreover, because Fort Crawford was under construction, Rachel was burdened with serving Thomas's family, which included two infants (born in 1831 and 1832), in extremely crude conditions. Life on the

Midwestern frontier became even more taxing when Rachel became pregnant and gave birth to a boy named James Henry, whose father is not revealed in the historical record. Rachel was not protected by status or race or law or family. She had no legal or social recourse against the sexual advances of the multitude of men who had access to her, especially Thomas. And in 1834, just months after she gave birth, Thomas took them to St. Louis and sold them to Joseph Klunk, who sold them to William Walker—a local slave trader.

## RACHEL

**Born: ca. 1814, location unknown**

**Died: Unknown**

**Forms: Legal Writing**

**Recommended Works: Petition for freedom (1834), *Rachel v. William Walker* (1836)**

Somehow, Rachel and James Henry escaped and made their way to the courthouse. Rachel petitioned for legal representation: "Your petitioner prays that your petitioner and said child may be allowed to sue as a poor person in St. Louis Circuit Court for freedom & that the said Walker may be restrained from carrying her or said child out of the Jurisdiction of the St. Louis Circuit Court till the termination of said suit." Her petition was granted, but Rachel lost the case. The circuit court ruled that slavery was not prohibited in the Northwest Territories when enslaved people were put to work serving military officers. Rachel appealed, and in June of 1836 the Missouri Supreme Court overturned the lower court's decision. They asserted that Thomas had violated the ban on slaveholding in the Northwest Territories when he purchased Rachel from the slaveholding state of Missouri after he was stationed at Fort Snelling. Rachel's courage and audacity are palpable, seen especially in her use of a legal system created to disempower her.

I first visited Fort Crawford two years after I accepted a faculty position as a historian in the Department of African American Studies at the University of Wisconsin-Madison. I knew enslaved people were held at forts throughout the Midwest, but I did not associate Midwestern frontier forts with the larger institution of race-based slavery in the United States. Mainly, I understood these frontier forts as part of American westward expansion and empire building that violently and viciously displaced Indigenous peoples. The area around Prairie du Chien, where the Mississippi River meets the Wisconsin River, has been home to Indigenous peoples for over twelve thousand years, most recently the Meskwaki, Sauk, Ho-Chunk, and Dakota peoples who had been repeatedly forced off their ancestral lands. Prairie du Chien, the oldest European settlement on the Upper Mississippi River, had been a center of French fur trading since the 1680s. Both the French and British claimed territory in the region. Fort Crawford, founded in 1816, would come to represent American hegemony in the region. Built from local oak timber, it formed a square of 340 feet on each side. In 1826 the fort was severely damaged by a flood. In 1829 construction began on a new elevated fort made of limestone, which was completed in 1834.

Rachel was brought to this contested space. She was enslaved in the hinterlands of the American empire, and she bore witness to the daily realities of the displacement and violence of "Manifest Destiny." She literally witnessed the physical building of the American empire in the "West," and she was forced to contribute to that process in service of Thomas, his wife, and his children. At least seventeen African Americans were held in race-based bondage in and around Fort Crawford between 1820 and 1845. Slaveholding at Fort Crawford, like forts throughout the Midwestern frontier, was a part of the expansion of race-based slavery in America. And slaveholding officers served to undermine the ban on slaveholding and permit its practice in the region. Race-based slaveholding was so embedded in white American culture that its practice persisted even when it was explicitly and legally banned. As a lifelong Black Midwesterner whose maternal family settled in Nebraska before it was a state and as a historian of American slavery, I was astounded about how little I knew or had even considered knowing about race-based slavery in the Midwest.

Midwestern frontier forts like Fort Crawford are places that illuminate and expand understandings of American slavery and Black people's tenacious pursuits of freedom. People like Rachel are part of a larger history of slaveholding in the United States. Stories like hers transform how we experienced these places. For me, these forts have become archives, places to contemplate Black history and experience. And while I am frustrated that stories of people like Rachel have only recently—and often marginally—been included in the historic presentation at these sites, I am inspired when I imagine that maybe I have walked where Rachel walked, maybe touched a wall she watched being built. My current book project, *Black on the Midwestern Frontier: Contested Bondage and Black Freedom in Wisconsin, 1725–1868,* seeks to tell the stories of people like Rachel and expand how we understand American slavery, the social-cultural formation of the Midwest, and Black people's pursuits of freedom and liberty.

Note: Rachel's petition and other documents related to *Rachel v. William Walker* (1834) can be found on the Digital Gateway of the Washington University in St. Louis.

MARK TWAIN

## MARK TWAIN

Born: November 30, 1835, in Florida, Missouri

Died: April 21, 1910, in Redding, Connecticut

Forms: Novels, Short Stories, Travel Writing, Journalism, Essays, Oratory, Drama, Poetry

Recommended Works: "The Celebrated Jumping Frog of Calaveras County" (1865), *The Innocents Abroad* (1869), *Roughing It* (1872), *The Gilded Age* (1873), *The Adventures of Tom Sawyer* (1876), *The Prince and the Pauper* (1881), *Life on the Mississippi* (1883), *Adventures of Huckleberry Finn* (1884), *A Connecticut Yankee in King Arthur's Court* (1889), *Following the Equator/More Tramps Abroad* (1897), *Extract from Captain Stormfield's Visit To Heaven* (1909), *The Mysterious Stranger* (1897–1908/1916), *Letters from the Earth* (1904–9/1962), *Weapons of Satire* (1900–1908/1992), *The Diaries of Adam and Eve* (1893–1906/1996), *Autobiography of Mark Twain: The Complete and Authoritative Edition*, vols. 1–3 (1906–10/2010–15)

# MARK TWAIN

## Mark Twain Boyhood Home & Museum
## Hannibal, Missouri

*By Cindy Lovell*

The best time to visit Hannibal, Missouri, is right after you've read *The Adventures of Tom Sawyer* (1876), especially if you chase it with the sequel, *Adventures of Huckleberry Finn* (1884). The other best time to visit is when you haven't read these books in many years. You see, Hannibal stands ready to awaken memories, stir dormant imaginations, and welcome you to its literary folds. The question is, are *you* ready?

I first read *Tom Sawyer* in the fourth grade. I would spend the next thirty years trying to get to Hannibal as I reread *Tom Sawyer* and learned more about its author, Samuel Clemens, pen name Mark Twain.

Although critics claim *Huck Finn* as the better book, *Tom Sawyer* provides the gateway where Clemens initially resurrects the people and haunts of his youth. No other town has served the purpose of literature as well as Hannibal. No other author fictionalized his own childhood in such a way as to constantly be inviting all who read the book to come home, come home to Hannibal . . . or "St. Petersburg." The line between fact and fiction is lovingly blurred.

My first pilgrimage was in the summer of 1996. Exiting Highway 61 past a handful of motels and diners, I steered downhill until the Mississippi River sprawled before me, a river of rafts and perils and adventures. I ditched the car and climbed across the levee to feel the power of place. Jackson's Island loomed large. The Mississippi River may border or pass through ten states, but Mark Twain staked Hannibal's claim on it when he wrote *Tom* and *Huck*.

Two kinds of tourists visit Hannibal: those who have read the books and yearn to feel the connection and those who enjoy nitpicking impossible points and whining about commercialism. Yes, that's Sam's face on the Pepsi machines. To those lacking imagination, I say: lighten up.

At the corner of Hill and Main, Sam's two-story boyhood home surveys the town, his bedroom windows facing the river and Cardiff Hill, scenes that presented irresistible temptation. Missing is the one-story ell on which Sam (and Tom) landed when climbing out the window. Imagination supplies the invisible summer kitchen where the boys landed. Across the street stands Laura Hawkins's girlhood home. Laura was the model for Becky Thatcher. Other period buildings complete the scene, such as Sam's father's Justice of the Peace Office and Grant's Drug Store, where the family lived during harder times.

If you squint, power lines and cars disappear, revealing imaginary barefoot boys scampering toward adventure, eluding an unseen Aunt Polly.

Poke your head inside the replica of Tom Blankenship's home, making sure to duck if you're on the tall side. Blankenship was Huck's real-life counterpart, and his house is catty-corner to the Clemens home, providing excellent proximity when the boys meowed to each other as a signal at night. Museum benefactors built this tiny abode on the site of the original home that housed the vast Blankenship clan. The house was rebuilt using period lumber and conjures enough cramped authenticity to remind modern visitors why Huck preferred sleeping in hogshead barrels. They were roomier.

A few blocks north, a memorial lighthouse, absent during Sam's childhood, invites visitors to climb 244 steps up Cardiff Hill. The vistas of the river are worth it. Take out your copy of *Tom Sawyer* and reread the passages describing this "Delectable Land, dreamy, reposeful, and inviting." Sam got it just right.

As twilight descends, meander farther away from the river toward the Old Baptist Cemetery, where Tom and Huck found "round-topped, worm-eaten boards staggered over the graves, leaning for support and finding none." In summer, one million lightning bugs await to enchant the devoted reader. You are forgiven if you yield to temptation and go barefoot in the grass.

In the distance a train slouches through town, each whistle unique, composed by the engineer. On Lover's Leap, out-of-towners listen expectantly.

Two miles south, the Mark Twain Cave reaffirms Clemens's meticulous memory. In *Huckleberry Finn*, he provided these directions:

> We went to a clump of bushes, and Tom made everybody swear to keep the secret, and then showed them a hole in the hill, right in the thickest part of the bushes. Then we lit the candles, and crawled in on our hands and knees.

> We went about two hundred yards, and then the cave opened up. Tom poked about amongst the passages, and pretty soon ducked under a wall where you wouldn't a noticed that there was a hole. We went along a narrow place and got into a kind of room, all damp and sweaty and cold, and there we stopped.

I have followed those directions to that room. It is uncanny that young Sam knew that cave so well as to remember these directions decades later when he wrote *Huckleberry Finn*. The oldest cave signature is in this room, dated 1819. Young Clemens himself autographed a cave wall as did his friends. I imagine Sam pulling the pencil out from behind his ear, or maybe his pocket. The cave is sacred ground. Utterly sacred.

Hannibal itself is holy to all who fall under the spell of Sam Clemens's pen. When Jorge Luis Borges, the blind Argentine writer, visited, his only wish was to touch the Mississippi River in Sam's hometown. He wept.

I have witnessed schoolteachers, students, and others respond similarly. Between my first visit in 1996 and moving there in 2007, I lost count of the dozens of people I brought to explore Sam's boyhood home. They marveled at the cracks in the plank floors where Tom poured the dreaded Pain-killer. They peered at Becky Thatcher's house from the parlor window and asked if Laura Hawkins stayed in Hannibal or moved away as Sam did. (She stayed.) They lingered in the kitchen imagining Sandy, a young enslaved boy whose services were rented by the Clemenses, sleeping on a rug.

Their questions attempted to discern fact from fiction. All were worthy visitors. They brought no snipe, no snark, no snide remarks dismissing the commercialization of Hannibal's most famous resident. They brought respect, curiosity, and imagination. And Hannibal rewards such folks.

# MARK TWAIN

## Mark Twain Cave
## Hannibal, Missouri

*By Avery Gregurich*

> It was said that one might wander days and nights together through its intricate tangle of rifts and chasms, and never find the end of the cave; and that he might go down, and down, and still down, into the Earth, and it was just the same labyrinth underneath labyrinth, and no end to any of them. No man 'knew' the cave. That was an impossible thing.
> —Mark Twain, *The Adventures of Tom Sawyer*

Dear Mark,

I haven't written in a while. By now it's August in Missouri, and I'm driving on the Avenue of the Saints, destination: Hannibal. I'm told this highway runs from St. Paul to, eventually, St. Louis. You had to take the river between, but I'm able to take this avenue through the land of the park and ride. It's midmorning, and the first leg of the commutes are already done, measured in time out from the country roads into the cities, which hold the jobs, and back again into the country, which hold a lot of anger, as they always have. Also, melons. The painted cardboard signs turned toward the highway announce that melon season is here. They're all thump ripe, I'm sure of it. At least that much is the same from both of our formative years spent here along the Mississippi.

Here are my credentials: I'm from Pike County, just south of here on the Illinois side of the river. Like you, I too had the sandbagging summers and the mayfly hatchings and the infinite boredom watching the river pass, knowing it was going somewhere and I wasn't. In the introduction to *Huck Finn*, you warned that you had written the text employing a number of dialects, including "the ordinary 'Pike County' dialect, and four modified varieties of the last." I suppose that I have used this dialect by default, confounding the rich suburban kids at college when my vowels all came out the same. I never could feign their language; so I sat real still, mostly with my mouth shut.

At the gas station, we fill up behind a hearse flanked by barefaced men in suits that have become well worn by this point in the pandemic. Back on the highway we are passed by a car careful to merge, as its back window is covered with conspiracy-theory paraphernalia. (There's too much to tell, Mark. I'm sorry. Suffice to say people are now as they always have been: vain and afraid to apologize.) Just outside the highway hunting camp with tall fences penning in the game, a truck hauling a grain auger had an elk head propped up in its truck bed. It was just the head, and a blue tarp covered its face, but the antlers couldn't be corralled. Past all this—the speed-trap towns and firework stands and corn mazes and the round bales wrapped in red-white-and-blue plastic along the edges of the fields—we finally make it, announced by your face on the welcome sign. Hannibal: America's Hometown™.

By now, all the remaining river towns look like one another. That is, if there's any money left in them. If there is, then the train depots downtown are always turned into history museums, the former factories get big murals painted on their brick that make the locals cry foul, and the habitable real estate still left down by the water can be had at worrisome prices. In the time since I grew up, Hannibal opened up a brewery with your name on it, and they turned the Wonder Hostess Discount Bakery Outlet into a vape shop. That pretty much brings us up to speed.

At the entrance to the Mark Twain Cave Complex, which holds both "America's oldest and newest show caves," I spotted our teenage tour guide sitting behind the ticket counter, brushing up on her presentation with a copy of *Tom Sawyer* that was for sale right there in the gift shop. (You won't be surprised to learn that only the heartland hits have really survived. No copies of *The Mysterious Stranger* or *The Private Life of Adam and Eve* are available for purchase. I'm still not sure Hannibal is ready for either of them.) I was tempted to buy a bobblehead barely intimating your likeness. You could sit on the dashboard of my car, passing judgement on all passing things. I settled instead for a souvenir dime my father couldn't believe cost fifty cents to smash.

My parents have joined Sara and me here at the cave. Due to ongoing circumstances, we had to skip last year's Christmas and Thanksgiving, which our pre-tour conversation reflects. After a short video introduction, we are ushered into the mouth of the cave. The air in there is cool and surely the same as when you wandered through as a kid, only today it is mixed intermittently with my father's picnic belches emanating from immediately over my shoulder. I recognize it even through the mask I wear, one of only two seen on the entire tour, the other covering my love's face. We are clearly the real tourists here. I have to forgive my mother, who says she just forgot her mask in the car.

As you are aware, the cave is unique in its almost complete lack of speleothems, those stalagmites and stalactites that make caves desirable these days. Instead, hundreds of thousands of signatures cover the limestone walls around us, lots written in black paint or candle ash or berry juice, as our tour guide tells us. The signatures all around us confirm that for as long as we've been stumbling into caves, we've wanted to leave some kind of mark. Someone from St. Louis even drew a caricature of you about a century ago, a white outline cut into a patch of black paint.

Would you believe that they finally found your signature on the bicentennial of the "discovery" of the cave? They had it authenticated and everything, put up a wooden box with a screen on it to protect it from smudges. My father points to it, his indication that I should take a picture. Photographing in the cave is futile, but still I try to capture whatever he points at. I don't think he's ever read one of your sentences.

While we follow the path you made Tom and Becky traverse, we learn about the cave's various lives as a onetime hideout for Jesse James, as a secret storeroom for Confederate weapons, and as a mausoleum for a doctor's deceased teenage daughter. None of this is particularly surprising: most of what has been "discovered" over the last few centuries here in the river basin is grisly—bones left by things once chased or killed or both. No matter how we've tried to dress them up, we still played a role in the burial, if only by coming here now to attend the funeral.

At one point, our tour guide leads us in an exercise in which she turns out the accessory lights and we experience total darkness, something she says with teenage gravity is "really rare." "So dark that you can't see the hand in front of your nose," tempting us to try. The punchline comes when she flips the lights, and we all stand there waving at one another. (Of course, we stop immediately when the lights come back on). The tour continues, more signatures are found, formations pointed out, and a prop treasure chest is revealed at the bottom of a crevice, but I keep thinking about that moment of total darkness.

Not only was there the absence of light, but it was finally quiet for a moment, even the kids in the group awed by something outside of the algorithm's reach. We shared there, for a moment, the realization of how much of our lives are consumed in light. This shared, quiet darkness felt elemental and deeply human, full of something communal, maybe grief or fear. It might have been more commonplace in your time, but as our tour guide said, it's rare these days.

I truly think the price of admission was for that one brief moment of total obscurity. I regret to admit that I really wanted to take that time to add my name to the thousands covering the cave walls. I wish I knew why. Instead, we walked out into August, said our goodbyes and drove back home beneath clouds of black gnats that seemed to follow the highway.

Let's do it again next summer. I'll bring a permanent marker. You bring a light.

# MARK TWAIN

## East Hill
## Elmira, New York

*By Matt Seybold*

Now it's just a small, oddly shaped clearing in a dense wood. At the top of the large pile of limestones we generously call a "staircase," a space opens up in the trees. It feels like a good place for a pagan ritual. And every four years, on the final night of the International Conference on the State of Mark Twain Studies, that's kind of what happens. A gaggle of scholars, creative writers, actors, filmmakers, and other Twainiacs gather in the moonlit clearing to smoke the cheapest possible cigars, their inexpensiveness a point of pride, as it had been for Sam Clemens himself. Winners of Pulitzers, National Book Awards, Emmys, Oscars, Tonys, and every imaginable academic fellowship scrape dry flakes of tobacco off their tongues and pretend to know the words to "Oft in the Stilly Night."

Mark Twain drafted the majority of the works for which he is now remembered in this very space. From 1874 to 1953, an octagonal study designed to resemble a steamboat pilothouse stood here at the top of the hill. After too many midcentury literary tourists made pilgrimage, traipsing across the property where Twain's in-laws still resided, the study was relocated to the campus of Elmira College, where his wife, Olivia Langdon Clemens, was an alumna and his niece, Ida Langdon, was a professor. Elmira College would eventually become custodian of Quarry Farm as well, and the home of the Center for Mark Twain Studies, where I work.

While I once cringed at the solemnity with which my fellow scholars sung "Will The Circle Be Unbroken?" after four days of academic panels and roundtables, I'll admit in the intervening years I have occasionally secluded myself in that clearing for a few idle minutes of, I don't know, reverence.

When Twain was here, most every summer from 1869 to 1890, and periodically thereafter, there were no woods. The study was, as he put it, "perched in complete isolation on the top of an elevation that commands leagues of valley and city and retreating ranges of distant blue hills." One can still approximate this view from the veranda of the main house at Quarry Farm, a hundred yards southeast and downhill from where the study stood. On a clear day, the blue hills are visible well across the Pennsylvania border, seven miles south.

It was this view, across the Chemung River Valley, this panorama of church steeples, lumber barges, railways bridges, and smokestacks, of commercial development buttressed by wilderness on all sides, which inspired Twain's imaginative return to antebellum Missouri. First the early chapters of *The Adventures of Tom Sawyer* (1876) and then the greater parts of *Life on the Mississippi* (1883) and *Adventures of Huckleberry Finn* (1885) were drafted here, along with dozens of other novels, memoirs, plays, essays, stories, speeches, and at least one pornographic farce solely for private circulation. Twain estimated that he wrote ten chapters in the study at Quarry Farm for every one that he wrote elsewhere.

Visitors joke, often enough for it to become something of a cliché among our staff, that Twain's productivity must have been fueled by boredom. His other regular haunts during the Gilded Age—Hartford, New York City, London, Vienna, Berlin—are so cosmopolitan and Elmira so provincial by comparison. It must have been easy for him to avoid distraction up there on East Hill. I have myself sometimes described him as looking down on Elmira like the Grinch over Whoville. But there is no evidence that Sam Clemens disdained or eluded the social scene of Elmira. To the contrary, some of his most cherished friendships were developed here, with Thomas K. Beecher, Charley Langdon, John T. Lewis, and John B. Stanchfield. And he did not vegetate at Quarry Farm, waiting for them to come to him, either.

One of Twain's most healthful habits was taking his near-daily constitutionals. He was a "pedestrianist," as he put it. Often accompanied by friends, often chain-smoking, he would walk shocking distances over tough terrain. During the seasons he spent here, downtown Elmira was connected to Quarry Farm only by what one visiting reporter described as "a winding road, which is steep, very steep, and at times is really a dangerous driveway." Twain was well aware of the danger, having witnessed the occasion in 1877 when a runaway carriage containing his sister-in-law and niece nearly careened into a deep ravine, saved only by the heroic efforts of Lewis.

The "dangerous driveway" no longer exists. It has been replaced by a pair of paved two-lane surface roads, still very steep, and treacherous when icy. This commute should be considered as essential to Twain's writing process as the porch where he read each day's work aloud to the assembled family and maybe even as the study itself.

Throughout his forties and fifties, Twain tripped his way down (and back up again) to visit the barber shop of Henry Washington, the self-emancipated man whose mother is the narrator of Twain's "A True Story, Repeated Word For Word As I Heard It"; to play pool with Beecher in the makeshift billiard parlor the radical theologian had created in the southwest corner of the Park Church; to gossip with other men of his guild at the newspaper offices of the *Elmira Advertiser, Gazette,* and *Telegram*; and to wet his whistle at Klapproth's Tavern.

Far from being a recluse during the three or four months he spent in Elmira every year, Twain was someone you were likely to bump into during a summer stroll, a fixture of the downtown scene. When Twain died, legions of well-wishers gathered in New York City for a public viewing of the celebrity who Robertus Love, in his obituary, deemed "the most famous man on earth." But Twain's eulogy, written by the first woman ordained in this state, Beecher's protégé Annis Ford Eastman, was read at the Park Church in Elmira, and he was laid to rest at Woodlawn Cemetery, next to his wife, son, and the two daughters who preceded him.

Frank Gannett, the newspaper magnate who was then the publisher of the *Elmira Star-Gazette,* noted in his obituary that, though Twain's celebrity and works belonged to the whole world, his "personal attributes, idiosyncrasies and peculiarities of disposition, temperament and moral attitude" felt like they were peculiar to Elmira. Nearly every Elmiran could recount secondhand stories, if not personal memories, of the famous author's local exploits and could testify to his "labors in the path of universal education," his "insistence on an exchange of absolutely honest and honorable relations in every business and social enterprise," and his "domestic life full of examples of faithfulness and devotion."

That steep, winding, hazardous road between Quarry Farm and downtown Elmira connected the pastoral idyll—which was undoubtedly good for Twain's productivity—to a diverse cast of quirky characters and social dynamics, which were also, I contend, generative for his art. Part of what I have elsewhere called the "Quarry Farm Style" is its dialectic of romance and realism. The novels written under these conditions move from King Arthur's Court to scathing critiques of feudal and industrial society, from vivid naturalist descriptions of the Mississippi River to violent scenes of crisis and collapse along the banks, from prevailing American myths to reportage that debunks them, from the lifestyles of deluded princes to those of grasping paupers (equally deluded).

By the time he first came to Elmira, thirty-three-year-old Mark Twain well knew what it was like to climb. How hard. How irrational. How unlikely. And I expect every time he contemplated those two miles back up East Hill, he was reminded again. The bootstrappers, the strivers, the grinders, the scrapers, the self-titled entrepreneurs: all the lunks in the streets blindly hustling some mirage of success in a society structured to ensure their defeat; aren't they ridiculous?

Well, so am I.

# MARK TWAIN

## Mark Twain House & Museum
## Hartford, Connecticut

*By Jacques Lamarre*

In 2008, with no ceremony, I was handed a simple brass key to Mark Twain's Hartford home. Having just been hired as the director of Marketing and Special Programs, I was given a few rules: do not touch anything, do not sit on the furniture, and for God's sake, don't enter the house after the alarm has been set. The key went onto my keychain alongside those for my house, my Jeep Liberty, and my shed, and I began my efforts to lure visitors into the Clemens family's house and its adjacent museum.

Up until that time, I only had been to the Twain House on an otherwise unmemorable date. I don't know who chose the house tour for a date activity, but it likely had to do with my being a resident of the West End of Hartford and, at the time, without a car. I cannot remember my date's name, but the house made an immediate impression. That was the Clemenses' intention.

One can track the trajectory of Twain's life, work, and gathering sophistication by visiting his homes. I have visited Samuel Clemens's childhood home in Hannibal, Missouri, as well as his birthplace, a humble two-room shack in Florida, Missouri. Both homes lay bare his Lower Midwest roots and illustrate the elements that would feature heavily in several of his most popular works. He left Missouri a Clemens and found his pen name of Mark Twain when he went out West.

His time in the rough-and-tumble Wild West atmosphere of Nevada would find him living in a variety of frontier structures. In California his accommodations ranged from mining camps to boarding houses. *Alta California*, a San Francisco newspaper, engaged his services as a traveling correspondent to cover the first transatlantic pleasure cruise to Europe and the Holy Land. This trip on the steamship the *Quaker City* would not only expose him to a rich world of antiquities and awe-inspiring sights—all chronicled with a wry cynicism in his first major work, *The Innocents Abroad* (1869)—it would also introduce him to his future brother-in-law Charley Langdon.

Twain experienced love at first sight after seeing an ivory miniature picture of Charley's sister Olivia "Livy" Langdon. After meeting in New York City in 1869, an ardent courtship ensued, much of it conducted in the Langdon family home in Elmira, New York. The Langdons' wealth and social prominence, along with Twain's burgeoning success as an author and lecturer, allowed him to graduate into a new circle of society and a heightened level of ambition. After their marriage, Livy and Sam moved into a gorgeous, fully furnished home on a highly desirable street in Buffalo—a gift from Sam's father-in-law. Their time in Buffalo was brief, only one year. Twain set his sights on a move to Hartford. It wasn't his first visit to a city that would loom large in his life.

In 1868 Twain visited Hartford—at the time, the wealthiest city per capita in the United States—to meet with the publisher of the forthcoming *The Innocents Abroad*. Always one to economize efforts, Twain used the visit to file one of his ongoing travelogues to the *Alta California*. "Of all the beautiful towns it has been my fortune to see this is the chief. . . . Everywhere the eye turns it is blessed with a vision of refreshing green. You do not know what beauty is if you have not been here."

Sam, Livy, and their first child Langdon moved to Hartford in 1871 to be close to the American Publishing Company. They rented a home in Hartford's West End, then known as Nook Farm. Named after a bend in the Hog River, Nook Farm was and would be home to many of Hartford's cultural and political elite, including author Harriet Beecher Stowe, suffragist Isabella Beecher Hooker, journalist Charles Dudley Warner, actor and playwright William Gillette, Senator Joseph Hawley, and eventually, Katharine Hepburn.

It was during this time that four significant events occurred. The first, the tragic death of their young son in 1872, a devastating blow for the family. This was followed by the joyful births of their daughters Susy, in 1872, and Clara, in 1874. The fourth, Sam and Livy purchased a plot of land on Farmington Avenue to begin construction of the first home that they could properly call their own.

Positioned overlooking the Park River (the new and much nicer name for the Hog River), the property sat on the edge of Hartford adjacent to Harriet Beecher Stowe's final home. Sam and Livy engaged architect Edward Tuckerman Potter to design a house that would be both a family home and a jaw-dropping showstopper that reflected the Clemenses' growing social importance. The construction of the massive Victorian Gothic home, with its ornate brick and woodwork, would cause tongues to wag around the conservative town. *The Hartford Times* wrote, "The novelty displayed in the architecture of the building, the oddity of its internal arrangement and the fame of its owner will all conspire to make it a house of note for a long time to come." They weren't wrong.

The seventeen years that the Clemenses lived in their beloved home were to be their happiest and were Sam's most prolific and productive. Ironically, it was during this time that he wrote three of the works that would lean most heavily on his Midwest roots: *The Adventures of Tom Sawyer* (1876), *Life on the Mississippi* (1883), and *Adventures of Huckleberry Finn* (1884).

Of his Hartford home Twain wrote in 1897, "To us our house was not unsentient matter—it had a heart & a soul & eyes to see us with, & approvals & solicitudes & deep sympathies; it was of us, & we were in its confidence, & lived in its grace & in the peace of its benediction. We never came home from an absence that its face did not light up & speak out its eloquent welcome—& we could not enter it unmoved."

Over my years at the Twain House, that simple brass key would grow in weight and import in my pocket. Every day when I left, I would swing by the bust of Twain in the lobby and say (quietly, so no one would question my sanity), "I hope I did right by you today." In 2016 I left the Mark Twain House for another job. I still live in the Hartford area and can visit, but I feel acutely the loss of that key and my access to the bewilderingly beautiful and eccentric home that I, too, could not enter unmoved.

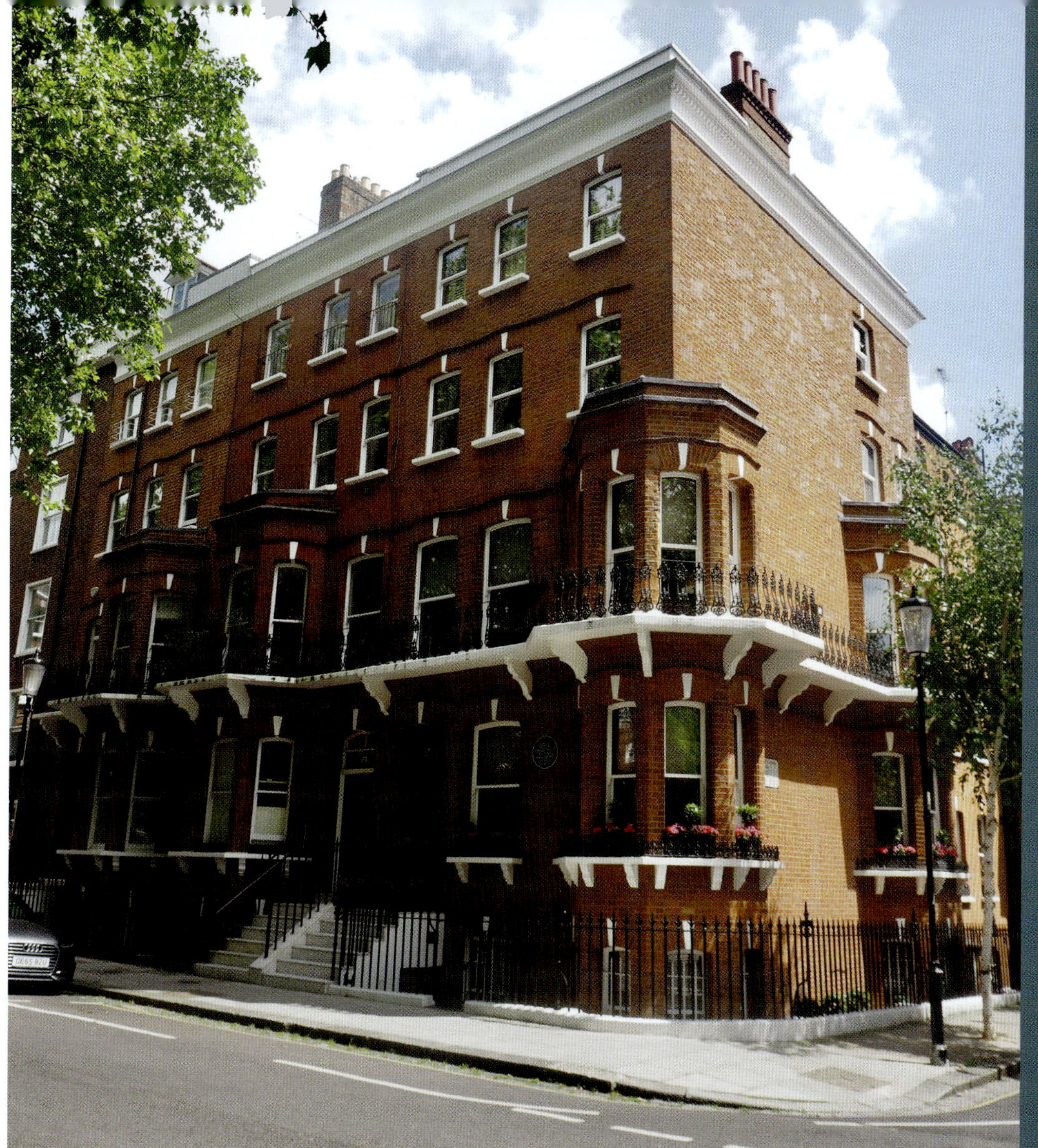

# MARK TWAIN

## 23 Tedworth Square
## London, England

*By Susan Kumin Harris*

When Mark Twain reached England at the end of his 1895–96 lecture tour around the British Empire, he first sojourned in Guildford, twenty-five miles southwest of London, where he began work on what would become *Following the Equator* (British title, *More Tramps Abroad*), his record of that trip. However, shortly after he and his travel companions—his wife, Olivia (aka Livy), and their middle daughter, Clara—moved in, his eldest daughter, Susy, died in the family home in Hartford, Connecticut, and according to Twain legend, the family fell into a period of deep mourning from which Olivia, at least, never fully recovered. In October, after their youngest, Jean, joined them, they moved to 23 Tedworth Square, London, a five-story townhouse where they would dwell for the next nine months. There, the story goes, the family lived in almost complete seclusion: Olivia grieving, the two girls faithfully attending her, and Twain alternately railing against God and knuckling down to writing. As he bitterly told his old friend Joseph Twichell, "I am working, but it is for the sake of the work—the 'surcease of sorrow' that is found there. I work all the days, and trouble vanishes away when I use that magic."

Tedworth Square is in Chelsea, a leafy section of London. In Twain's day it was a modest neighborhood; today it shows all the signs of upscale gentrification, with apartment sales starting at over £1 million. I made London my final stop when I followed Twain's route around the world in 2013–14. Like Twain, I was relieved to have my journey finished. Although I had visited Australasia, India, and South Africa in separate trips, interspersed with teaching and other domestic duties, the collective undertaking had proven far more exhausting than I had anticipated—in part because I was always conscious of being an outsider, especially in cities where the sight of a lone woman triggered outspoken commentary from male spectators. In contrast, London seemed welcoming and strangely safe. It was, I realized, a transitional space for me: familiar—I had visited often and lived there one summer—though still distant from domestic stress; a place to tie up loose research ends at the British Library, stroll through parks, and collect myself before I hit home and the myriad responsibilities awaiting me.

I suspect Twain and Livy felt the same way, despite—or perhaps because of—their bereavement. At least the family had been spared the shock of hearing about Susy's death while surrounded by strangers and unknown tongues, and London was old stomping grounds for them too. Chelsea also afforded some distractions, even for a grief-stricken writer living in (relative) seclusion. Tedworth Square enters obliquely into *Following the Equator*, in the India portion of the book. There Twain compares the flawless beauty of black and brown skins to "the white ones which are streaming past this London window now." Not only are his neighbors' skin colors "fish-belly," "sallow," and "mustard yellow"; one passerby sports a "boiled-cauliflower nose in a flabby face veined with purple crinklings." Not a generous assessment but an early marker of the angry misanthropy that Twain developed in the wake of Susy's death, I suspect.

Today's London complexions are generally better—for all our urban pollutants, at least we don't struggle with coal dust—but my journal reminds me that while I was sitting across from 23 Tedworth, a man stumbled by who did look like the people Twain described. Disheveled and unshaven, he was drinking beer at 11:00 a.m. and smelled like a horse. Even upscale Chelsea isn't entirely shut off from London's outcasts.

Nor was the Clemens family entirely shut off from London's social life. The story that the mourning family isolated themselves is, like many Twain stories, largely a myth, probably originating in Twain's attempts to fend off interviewers by claiming sequestration. In fact, all four had contacts with the world beyond the house. Although Livy rarely went out, she did see close friends at home, and Barbara Snedecor's edition of Livy's letters shows that she quickly resumed responsibility for family correspondence, including paying bills and (because Twain had shifted ownership of his copyrights to her prior to declaring bankruptcy) dealing with Twain's contract negotiations. Clara and Jean certainly supported their mother, but not 24/7; David Frears's *Mark Twain, Day by Day* notes that they acquired bicycles and learned to ride them in the Square, and Clara's memoir *My Father, Mark Twain* recounts long Sunday walks around the city with her father. With friends, both girls also attended concerts and theater performances.

Twain, always gregarious, visited friends, including Poultney Bigelow, John Hay, Bram Stoker, and Rudyard Kipling, and he willingly attended the theater as well as other social and public events, including a Zangwill reading, at least one meeting of the Savage Club, a Parliamentary session, and the Queen's Jubilee. Letters also show him keenly following the McKinley–Bryan presidential race in the US. Moreover, though resisting most demands for lectures and interviews, he allowed his friend Adele Chapin to persuade him to "tell stories" to patients at the London Hospital, an event that delighted the patients and forced Twain out of his self-absorption.

We associate sprawling cities with loneliness and alienation. But their small neighborhoods and parks can also provide shelter, quiet places to harbor while learning how to shift from one stage of life to another. London proved transitional for the Clemens family, furnishing them the physical and social spaces they needed to navigate their lives without Susy. For them, as for me, the city served as interstitial space, between the upheavals of travel and the resumption of familiar routines. They could mourn together inside the five-story house, but they could also venture beyond it: a bike ride around the square, tea with a friend, an afternoon concert, dinner at a social club. Day by day, month by month, 23 Tedworth Square harbored Livy, Clara, Jean, and Samuel Clemens while they worked through their initial shock and relearned the social skills they would need for the remainder of their lives.

# MARK TWAIN

## Dollis Hill House
## London, England

*By Thomas Ruys Smith*

It's the first real day of spring and I'm in Dollis Hill—an unremarkable suburb of North London that sits just inside the North Circular, the multilane road system that encircles the center of the capital and is synonymous with traffic congestion and an entrenched atmosphere of urban decay. Still, in Gladstone Park the sun is out and so are the local residents: in the ruins of what was once Dollis Hill House, a children's birthday party is winding down just as a group of women begin an impromptu karaoke session; our miniature schnauzer, Winifred, is making the acquaintance of a fluffy, white Pomeranian apparently named Snowflake. This might seem an unlikely location for a ghost hunt, but that's why we're here.

This is just the kind of place, however, to start seeking the restless spirit of Mark Twain, at least according to the man himself. Interviewed in 1907 as he embarked on what he knew would be his final trip across the Atlantic, Twain was clear that he intended to spend his afterlife in the modern Babylon that had often served him as a second home: "I may never go to London again until I come back to this sphere after I am dead," he told a reporter, "and then I would like to live in London."

As an academic based in the UK, I've spent much of my career exploring Mark Twain's relationship with the Mississippi River, tracing the way that the river wound its way through his life and work. In surprising ways, that muddy water often washed up at my own front door across the Atlantic: British writers had a surprising influence on the creation of the Mississippi as a powerful global emblem of America. Now, though, I'm reversing that transatlantic equation. It seemed time to pursue the traces of Mark Twain in my own backyard—in London, the city in which he spent roughly three crucial years on numerous trips, from his inaugural visit in 1872 to his final victory lap in 1907. A number of Twain's London residences still exist, most famously the Langham Hotel, which hosted his early visits, and the house he rented at 23 Tedworth Square, in affluent Chelsea, which bears a blue plaque erected by English Heritage to announce to passersby that Mark Twain, American writer, had once lived there in 1896–97.

For me, though, there is something especially evocative about Dollis Hill House, occupied by Twain with his wife, Olivia, and daughter Jean in the summer of 1900. Compared to the glamour of his first trips to London as a literary lion ensconced in the Langham, or to the awful gloom of his secluded residence in Tedworth Square after the death of his daughter Susy, there is an appealing softness to Twain's time in Dollis Hill: after years of personal turmoil, including bankruptcy, the months he spent in the house were a relatively sunny sojourn. By 1900 his fortunes had been largely restored, enough for his family to return to America after a period of financial exile in Europe, and Dollis Hill House was a final hiatus before the end of this odyssey.

Twain's description of this time exudes a warmth and peace that was rare in his later years: "Dollis Hill House comes nearer to being a paradise than any other home I have ever occupied. . . . It is within a biscuit-toss of solid London; yet it stands solitary on its airy hill, in the centre of six acres of lawn, and garden, and shrubbery, and heavy-foliaged ancient trees." His only complaint was the lack of a telephone. Today, of course, London has swallowed up Dollis Hill, and what had been "country, pure and simple" to Twain is now surrounded by urban sprawl. Even on a warm spring day, "paradise" seems a stretch. However, as Twain himself noted, the land around the house had just been "bought for a park, to be for all time a memorial to Mr. Gladstone"—a frequent visitor to the house during his time as Prime Minister—which meant that, to some extent, the landscape that

Twain loved really would "remain as it is." Unlike hotels or his other residences that still function as private homes, this Twain-imprinted place remains immediately and freely accessible to all.

There's also something about Dollis Hill House's ruin that adds a poignancy, and a piquancy, to its association with Twain. A series of fires in the late 1990s left it a derelict shell. Though money was earmarked for its restoration, it became a casualty of austerity when former Prime Minister Boris Johnson canceled the funding during his time as London mayor. A final fire in 2011 precipitated its demolition. Now it remains an absent presence in Gladstone Park: a short course of bricks marks out the building's floorplan, and a fragment of one wall remains. People make their own use of this liminal space—like today's birthday party.

An absent presence is also how I've come to think about Mark Twain as I search for him in London. Today, I can't swear that the parkgoers in Dollis Hill are thinking much about its famous former resident, but across the closing decades of the nineteenth century, London was infatuated with the writer who seemed to embody their dreams, and sometimes nightmares, about America. In 1907 local newspaper the *Hendon and Finchley Times* proudly claimed him "our friend Mark Twain, who is associated with this district owing to his residence at Dollis Hill House." Another paper judged that Twain's connection to Gladstone Park would "add a certain . . . literary flavour in the public mind to its natural attractions." These are vivid and hyperlocal examples of what Twain's sometime associate Ralph Ashcroft declared in 1907: the English—and Londoners in particular—were "part-owners with the American nation of Mark Twain."

In turn, Twain himself was infatuated with an urban space that was like no other on the face of the planet. "Everything in this monster city interests me," Twain announced during his first time in London. And it always did. I would argue that outside of America, there is no other location that meant as much to him or that had as much influence on his sense of self. Just as this ruined corner of London will always be a little paradise for Twain's ghost, so London should always be a part of our understanding of this iconically American writer. And for me there is something particularly significant about having this enigmatic shell on my doorstep, a short drive away from my own home along the gray river of the North Circular. Tracing the outlines of the rooms of Dollis Hill House as my daughters eat an ice cream purchased from the old stable block and modern life buzzes throughout this liminal shell, I can conjure up Twain as a near-neighbor, a fellow suburbanite, a Londoner, available for afternoon calls. In Gladstone Park, the sun is shining, and Mark Twain is lounging in a deck chair beneath the trees, forever.

# F. SCOTT FITZGERALD

## 599 Summit Avenue
## St. Paul, Minnesota

*By Ross K. Tangedal*

In fall 2016 my wife, CJ, was six months pregnant, and we decided to visit the Minnesota State Fair at the insistence of my cousin Michael, a Minneapolis resident and state-fair aficionado. After meandering through the massive beehive exhibit, CJ and I peeled away

## F. SCOTT FITZGERALD

**Born: September 24, 1896, in St. Paul, Minnesota**

**Died: December 21, 1940, in Hollywood, California**

**Forms: Novels, Short Stories, Essays**

**Recommended Works: *This Side of Paradise* (1920), *The Beautiful and Damned* (1922), *The Great Gatsby* (1925), *Tender Is the Night* (1934), *The Short Stories of F. Scott Fitzgerald* (1998)**

to take a quick walking tour of old St. Paul. I was excited to explore Summit Avenue, which is known for its Victorian row houses, including the birthplace of F. Scott Fitzgerald, whose work I'd been studying for the preceding five years.

The house at 599 Summit Avenue is not all that different from those around it, fitting into the line of its Victorian neighbors: two stories, with an arched entryway, a rounded bay window, and a stately turret topping the unit. One expects to be wowed when witnessing the domicile of genius, but this unimpressive house did little for my enthusiasm. We could not go inside, nor were there any definable features of the home to suggest anything but mundanity. The plaque out front says nothing about the home either, other than "F. Scott Fitzgerald House." On Summit Avenue in the early twentieth century, people dreamed of their money aging. But now, more in line with Fitzgerald's fears than his parents' dreams, this home is a broken-down shell of Romanesque revival and mediocrity.

Rarely has there been a more complicated "favorite son" than Scott. He spent his childhood in Buffalo, Hackensack, and St. Paul, wanting so much to be more than he was, more than his disappointing father had become, more than a Midwestern nobody with glittering things in his heart. After completing his military service he drank himself into such depression that, in 1919, he moved home to the last place he wanted to be, St. Paul; and lived in the house he least wanted to live in, 599 Summit Avenue; with the people he least wanted to live with, his parents. If he got his first book published, Zelda Sayre, a judge's daughter, the rich girl that poor boys like him never marry, would marry him.

I know now why I felt that way about 599 Summit Avenue during fall 2016: we don't appreciate transitions, not like we do beginnings or endings. The F. Scott Fitzgerald House in St. Paul is a transition cloaked in a beginning, a place he never cared to live in, and a place to which he never returned once he published *This Side of Paradise*. There was more for him, he thought, than a row house rented with his mother's money and populated by his father's letdowns. He was always moving away from St. Paul and the Midwest, even when he wrote about them. Fitzgerald's Midwest was behind him. His future was glittering things and people. Like his character Dexter Green in the short story "Winter Dreams," Fitzgerald was all potential.

As for CJ and I, our trip to St. Paul that summer was a beginning, too, with a pregnancy and a new job leading toward our unknowable future. Like Fitzgerald, I had a hard time appreciating the transition. Then my daughter Adeline Rose arrived just five months later, glittering with the newness of life.

# HEID E. ERDRICH

## All My Relations Art Gallery
## Minneapolis, Minnesota

*By Elizabeth Wilkinson*

All My Relations Art Gallery is on Franklin Avenue, 1.1 miles from my house, in the Ventura Village neighborhood of Minneapolis. This section of Franklin Avenue is called the American Indian Cultural Corridor. The corridor starts just as you cross over Cedar Avenue, is interrupted by Hiawatha Avenue, and extends west toward an endpoint near Maria's Café on 11th Avenue. The art gallery shares space with the Pow Wow Grounds Coffee Shop. During the summer months their joint parking lot becomes the Four Sisters Farmers Market, selling produce from Indigenous farm cooperatives. Much of what happens on the corridor is under the umbrella of the Native American Community Development Institute. Heid Erdrich, National Book Award recipient and poet from the Turtle Mountain Band of Ojibwe, is one of their board members.

Erdrich's work weaves through the Twin Cities and the cities weave through her. When I first came to Minneapolis and St. Paul, a non-Native moving from North Carolina into Anishinaabe and Dakota territory, Heid Erdrich and her poetry welcomed me in. Only a few weeks into my life in the cities, in the fall of 2008, a colleague took me to hear Heid read poems from her collection *National Monuments*, which would come out in November.

Now I weave that book of poems over and over again into the classes I teach and smile at the sharp wit:

> Guidelines for the treatment of sacred
> objects
> that appear or disappear at will
> or that appear larger in rear view
> mirrors,
> include calling in spiritual leaders such
> as librarians,
> wellness circuit speakers and financial
> aide officers.

## HEID E. ERDRICH

**Born: November 26, 1963, in Breckenridge, Minnesota**

**Died: —**

**Forms: Poetry, Essays, Cookbook**

**Recommended Works: *National Monuments* (2008), *Cell Traffic: New and Selected Poems* (2012), *Original Local: Indigenous Food, Stories, and Recipes from the Upper Midwest* (2013), *Curator of Ephemera at the New Museum for Archaic Media* (2017), *Little Big Bully* (2020)**

The Powwow Grounds is in the same building as All My Relations, and you have to go through the coffee shop to get to the art. Well, to get to the gallery. There is always some community art hanging on the coffee shop walls and some community artists hanging around drinking coffee. At Pow Wow Grounds, you can tuck into a warm corner with a cup of tea and a wild rice blueberry muffin baked by Bob Rice, the owner. Worldclass Indigenous artists show at All My Relations. Heid Erdrich has been connected with the gallery for over a decade. It makes sense; her work—poetry and prose—is often intertwined with performance and with visual art.

On her homepage, Erdrich includes links to her video poems. "Pre-Occupied" takes viewers from the comic cosmos into the churning Mississippi River, turned brown and frothy at the point of the St. Anthony Falls Lock and Dam in central Minneapolis, just a scant two miles north of All My Relations. "River, river, river," she says, "I never, never, never . . ." Her poem spills out over city scenes and archival photos and clips from a 1950s animated Superman comic, while the Crash Test Dummies' "Superman's Song" plays.

She wrote and recorded "Od'e Miikan / Heart Line" for an award-winning art project; her voice autotuned with wolf sounds and then with moose sounds echoed into the Minneapolis night sky while giant animated wolf and moose art installation sculptures, made from chicken wire and scrap plastics, howled and pawed the ground.

A few years ago, Erdrich taught ekphrastic poetry—poems that describe art, and its impact on the viewer, in vivid detail—to a small group of Indigenous women at All My Relations. Those writers traveled the gallery, pulling imaginative language meaning out of the artistic visual-meaning pieces all around. Heid sat, as she often describes herself, bear-like, watching and listening with a fierce-gentle-art-love. Inside the warm yellow walls in Minneapolis, a name that combines *mni*, the Dakota word for water, with *polis*, the Greek word for city, she connected words and images and women across space and time in the heart of the American Indian Cultural Corridor.

# LOUIS L'AMOUR

## World's Largest Buffalo
## Jamestown, North Dakota

*By Sheila Liming*

The most famous writer to ever come out of North Dakota never wrote anything that takes place there. Louis L'Amour often talked about revisiting his home state, which he left at the age of fifteen. But he didn't succeed in doing that until he was well into his seventies, when his induction into the state's hall of fame lured him back at last.

Jamestown, North Dakota, is a curious place, and one that delights in making much of its status as L'Amour's hometown, despite his reluctance about ever seeing it again. Its skyline, so to speak, is dominated by a buffalo—the world's largest buffalo, to be exact. The twenty-six-foot-tall figure, which was commissioned in the 1950s as a ploy to ensnare motorists on I-94, presides over hills that rise so gently, they barely merit use of the word *hills*. Further off the highway, and just visible through the buffalo's anatomically incorrect undercarriage, is the town itself (pop. 15,750). Its squat, brick buildings are intermixed with houses built in the American four-square, or "cornbelt cube," style, their hipped roofs designed to keep off the snow. Some of the brick buildings would have been there before L'Amour was, but the cornbelt cubes likely date from right around the time of his birth in 1902.

## LOUIS L'AMOUR

**Born: March 22, 1908, in Jamestown, North Dakota**

**Died: June 10, 1988, in Los Angeles, California**

**Forms: Novels, Short Stories, Nonfiction, Poetry**

**Recommended Works: *Hondo* (1953), *Shalako* (1962), *The Sackett Series* (1960–69), *The Quick and the Dead* (1973), *The Lonesome Gods* (1983)**

North Dakota is where the West meets the Midwest. The state is huge and thus big enough to contain the multitudes indicated by both geographical designations. L'Amour, though, was drawn to only one of them in particular—the rugged West of his fantasies, not the Midwest of his experiences. Jamestown sits about an hour west of Fargo, on the eastern side of the state, and so has more in common, topographically speaking, with its neighbor Minnesota than with the scorched and mountainous Western landscape that plays such an important role in his fiction. In drawing inspiration for his books and stories, L'Amour set his gaze westward, summoning visions of bloody battles that took place against a backdrop of desert buttes and mesas, land that he termed "Indian country." He was, as historical photos indicate, compulsively clad in a cowboy hat and oversized silver belt buckle, even after he moved to Los Angeles and settled into a career in Hollywood.

I first visited L'Amour's hometown in 2014, though not exactly by choice. Rather, I was traveling the state as part of a bus tour for new University of North Dakota faculty. The bus dropped us off at the buffalo; we were given bottles of sarsaparilla and a few hours to poke around the attached tourist facility known as Frontier Village.

Much like Louis L'Amour once did, Frontier Village combines Western identity with Midwestern geography. You can ride a horse-drawn stagecoach there; you can gaze upon a disturbing collection of hollow-eyed stares in its doll museum; and you can wander among buildings that have been plucked from their original prairie environs and deposited there for the sake of posterity. Among them is Louis L'Amour's so-called "Writer's Shack," though he never wrote or published anything while living in North Dakota. It's a one-room, wooden house—Structure? Cabin? Nay, *shack* is the only word that works here—containing paperback copies of all of his "117 published novels." (The real number is, apparently, eighty-six, though after his death, L'Amour's son Beau continued to write and publish books under his father's name, extending his oeuvre considerably). They're arranged in a plexiglass display case on the far wall alongside a few of his typewriters and a placard offering a dubiously fact-checked version of his biography.

I had heard of L'Amour before I visited his Frontier Village "Writer's Shack," of course; my grandparents' spare bedroom, located in the basement of their ranch-style home in Snohomish, Washington, was lined with his books. But I can't say that I was much of a fan or that visiting his Writer's Shack in Jamestown succeeded in turning me into one. There is an intriguing bleakness to be found at the site of this makeshift memorial to him in Jamestown, though. Much like the rest of its Frontier Village surroundings, the Writer's

Shack strives to commemorate an authentic vision of Western history via a familiar if rather problematic species of Midwestern fantasy. The Midwest, after all, is not the West; if you take I-94 out of Fargo, away from Minnesota and toward the Montana border, you'll see what I mean. The flat, level plains of the corn belt give way to arid grasslands that are only good for grazing, just as the trucker caps of beet truck drivers on the eastern side of the state give way to Stetsons on the western side.

L'Amour's career, it could be argued, was a direct product of the confrontation between the romanticized West he barely knew and the Midwestern prairies he knew all too well. In the same way that the world's largest buffalo was born as a means of coaxing tourists out of their cars, so might his literary legacy be seen as an attempt to coax the "West" out of the "Midwest" and thus renovate the conditions of culture and geography that he was born into.

# JOHN BARTLOW MARTIN

## Smith Lake Camp
## Herman, Michigan

*By Ray E. Boomhower*

Writing about the Upper Peninsula (UP) of Michigan in his classic regional history, *Call It North Country* (1944), John Bartlow Martin described the expanse as "a wild and comparative Scandinavian tract—20,000 square miles of howling wilderness on the shores of Lake Superior." Like numerous fishermen, hunters, and hikers before him, Martin was attracted to the UP by its "magnificent waterfalls, great forests, high rough hills, long stretches of uninhabited country, abundant fish and game."

From his introduction to the region in the summer of 1940, when he selected it as a suitably remote site for a honeymoon, until Martin's death in 1987, the reporter, freelance writer, diplomat, and Democratic presidential speechwriter found himself drawn, again and again, by the UP's quirky charms. As he warned would-be tourists: "You will have to do nearly everything for yourself. The region is not geared to make your visit painless." The lack of modern conveniences and the clannishness of the locals could be maddening, he pointed out in *Call It North Country* (tattered, well-thumbed copies of which can still be found on bookshelves in many UP cabins), but if an outsider adjusted his thinking and fit into the region's ways, he could find "no better vacation spot."

## JOHN BARTLOW MARTIN

**Born: August 4, 1915, in Hamilton, Ohio**

**Died: January 3, 1987, in Highland Park, Illinois**

**Forms: Oratory, Biography, Nonfiction, Journalism**

**Recommended Works: *Call It North Country* (1944), *Indiana: An Interpretation* (1947), *Butcher's Dozen and Other Murders* (1950), *Break Down the Walls* (1954), *Adlai Stevenson of Illinois* (1976), *It Seems Like Only Yesterday: Memoirs of Writing, Presidential Politics, and the Diplomatic Life* (1986)**

The UP, however, became more than just a regular tourist stop for Martin. In January 1964 Martin and his wife, Fran, purchased a 180-acre site outside of Herman, Michigan. Not far from the water's edge on their property they discovered the ruins of an old trapper's shack, which they used as a temporary shelter. They constructed a camp (as cabins are known in the region) on top of a high, granite cliff sixty feet above the lake. Enormous white pines towered over the hemlocks located on the cliff, sheltering and shading the cabin.

Martin oversaw the construction (by Finnish carpenters) of a thirty-by-thirty-foot log cabin with a large living room, kitchen, bedroom, indoor bathroom, and enormous fireplace built out of fifty tons of native rock. As Martin's son Dan noted, his father and mother loved "the wildlife, the remoteness, the sense that they were in touch with nature." His family remembered that Martin did not believe in either trimming branches or cutting down trees on his land, even if doing so might improve the view of the lake from the cabin. "If you want to see the lake," Martin insisted, "go get in the boat and see it."

During his family's summer stays Martin fished, tried his hand at carpentry, did some writing, and relaxed in a sauna that later featured the front page of *The New York Times* announcing the resignation from the presidency of his longtime political foil Richard Nixon. "No television, no telephone, once a week to town for mail," he said of his routine. The cabin also became a sanctuary for Martin, a place where he could retreat to when tragedy struck, as it often did in the 1960s, as when his friend Robert F. Kennedy fell to an assassin's bullet in June 1968. At night, Martin, when troubled, could look up and see the Milky Way, appearing like "a white river," with every star "blazing" as he witnessed "man's satellites slowly tracking across the firmament."

I decided while working on a biography of Martin that I needed to visit his Upper Peninsula retreat to get a better sense of what this wild place had meant to him. Martin's daughter, Cindy Coleman, graciously offered to show me the cabin on a visit I made in September 2013, just before it was shuttered for the upcoming winter. I knew I was in the Upper Peninsula when, upon stepping out of the truck to open a gate so we could proceed along a rugged former logging road to the cabin, a large black fly saw its opportunity and delivered a vicious bite to the back of my neck. The spot still hurt when we passed a small, wooden sign with white letters affixed to a tree near the road that read: "J. B. Martin / Smith Lake."

Reaching the end of the road, I could barely make out Martin's cabin, nestled as it was among the trees. Although I did not stay long enough to hear coyotes howling in the night as Martin had done, I sat on the screen porch attached to the cabin, enjoying its dark wood floor; sturdy beams; and simple, rustic furnishings. Relaxing in one of the wooden chairs, I was stunned, at first, to see that, with Martin's death, there now was a clear view to the lake through the trees. Watching the waves from the porch as the wind rustled the branches of the nearby trees, I reflected that Martin had made all the right choices when it came to his cabin's location, but maybe, just maybe, had been wrong about the lake view.

# NORBERT BLEI

## Al Johnson's Swedish Restaurant
## Sister Bay, Wisconsin

*By Jenna Goldsmith*

Before Americans were obsessed with the Swedish practice of *fika*, Norbert Blei was perfecting it at Al Johnson's Swedish Restaurant and Butik in Sister Bay, Wisconsin.

"I *must* go to Al Johnson's for coffee . . . for conversation, camaraderie, my late morning break," Blei declares in his 2002 essay "Counter Culture." But it had snowed all night in Sister Bay, so much so that the road from Blei's home to his beloved coffee counter at Al Johnson's was impassable.

Blei's destination sits at the bottom of a hill, the focal point of Sister Bay, which is itself a hub of the scenic Door Peninsula. The restaurant, which began as a humble operation—just breakfast and dinner, cooked, served, and bussed by Al Johnson himself—is now a bustling terminus for locals and vacationers alike. It is not uncommon for diners to sit down for a meal of Pytt I Panna (Swedish hash) a full two hours after putting their name on the waiting list. Servers dress in traditional Swedish dirndls just as they did a half century ago, and the food is served on dishes from Porsgrunn, Norway. During the summer months, there are goats on the roof.

No matter how many times I visit Al's, I never stray from my usual short stack of Swedish pancakes, Swedish meatballs, and lingonberries (and lots of coffee). Though he has been gone for nearly seven years, I inevitably find myself staring at the coffee counter nestled in the restaurant's northeast corner, hoping to catch a glimpse of Norbert. I like to picture him there, hunched over a cup of coffee and a folded-over *Door County Advocate*, or his manuscript in progress, knowing full well that if he were *actually* there, I wouldn't have the gumption to approach him and risk interrupting his beloved *fika*. Still, I play this hologram game. I ask my mom to describe to me for the hundredth time my eccentric distant cousin Chuck Clemensen, another counter sitter, who Norbert called "Wall Street Charley." "Well, Chuck was tighter than the bark on a tree," my mom would remind me. "He died with the first nickel he ever earned, and he claimed to know the original recipe of Coca-Cola because he worked as a chemist for the company." Chuck frequently *fika*-ed alongside Norbert and Al. I imagine they spoke about Door County's rapid transformation, its influx of vacationers, and their shared history as native Chicagoans.

## NORBERT BLEI

**Born: August 23, 1935, in Chicago, Illinois**

**Died: April 23, 2013, in Sister Bay, Wisconsin**

**Forms: Nonfiction, Novels, Poetry, Journalism**

**Recommended Works: *The Hour of the Sunshine Now* (1978), *Door Way: The People in the Landscape* (1981), *Neighborhood* (1987), *Chi Town* (1990), *Winter Book* (2002)**

Though I never met Norbert, I feel that we are kindred spirits, tied together not just by our mutual Chuck but by our alma mater (Illinois State University), our vocations as writers, and our love of counter culture. As of late, I can't help but relate to the ambivalent Norbert of "Counter Culture," sitting in his warm, safe home, debating whether or not to brave the elements for *fika* at Al's. Before the COVID-19 pandemic, my own writing practice relied heavily on a coffee counter down the street from my apartment in Bend, Oregon. This practice, along with many others, was completely upended. And though I think of myself as flexible—professional enough that I can work anywhere—my writing life has suffered. I find myself wondering how Norbert would have fared without the respite of the safe, welcoming coffee counter at Al's.

Norbert eventually made it to Al's coffee counter that snowy February day. Did I ever really doubt him? Even February in Wisconsin is no match for *fikasugen*.

# ALDO LEOPOLD

## The Leopold Shack
## Baraboo, Wisconsin

*By Marc Seals*

I am not a Midwestern native—I was raised in the woods and swamps of north Florida, far from the Driftless Area of Wisconsin (where I now live). As a result, I was not familiar with Aldo Leopold or his work when I moved to Baraboo sixteen years ago. Soon after arriving, I picked up a copy of Leopold's *A Sand County Almanac and Sketches Here and There*, and I had not finished many pages before realizing that literature lost a fine nature poet when Leopold decided to dedicate his career to forestry. For example, Leopold writes, "One swallow does not make a summer, but one skein of geese, cleaving the murk of a March thaw, is the spring." And, "There are two spiritual dangers in not owning a farm. One is the danger of supposing that breakfast comes from the grocery, and the other that heat comes from the furnace." And don't get me started about the chapter where Leopold remembers watching the green fire fade from the eyes of a dying old wolf.

## ALDO LEOPOLD

**Born: January 11, 1887, in Burlington, Iowa**

**Died: April 21, 1948, in Baraboo, Wisconsin**

**Forms: Nature Writing, Nonfiction, Philosophy**

**Recommended Works: *Game Management* (1933), *A Sand County Almanac* (1949), *Round River: From the Journals of Aldo Leopold* (1953), *The River of the Mother of God and Other Essays* (1991)**

Leopold's *A Sand County Almanac*, published the year after he died in 1948, has been recognized as a foundational text in the field of environmental ethics for over fifty years. It has been ten years since I finally made the pilgrimage to the Leopold shack, riding my 1973 Peugeot road bike to Leopold's farm just outside of Baraboo. I dismounted and peered in the windows, where I could see bunk beds, a stone fireplace, the rustic kitchen—calling it "simple" would be an extreme understatement. Regardless, I knew that I was standing on sacred ground. This might seem an odd pronouncement, given the fact that the shack is a converted chicken coop (since no other building on the property was worth salvaging), but hear me out.

Leopold purchased the ruined farm on the shore of the Wisconsin River in 1935 for a mere eight dollars an acre to use the land as a sort of laboratory—he wanted to restore the natural forest and prairies. The experience helped him finalize what he terms the "land ethic." Leopold calls for a new relationship between humanity and nature, writing, "In short, a land ethic changes the role of *Homo sapiens* from conqueror of the land community to plain member and citizen of it. It implies respect for his fellow-members." He demonstrated this respect in his efforts to restore the property to its natural state. Leopold and his family planted over forty thousand trees on their frequent retreats from Madison, and the land is unrecognizable today. This "sand county" farm was not much good for farming, but it makes a great forest and prairie.

*A Sand County Almanac* is a memoir, a journal, a philosophical treatise, and more. Leopold honed his environmental philosophy on this property, and that's why it's sacred. There are not many chicken coops that helped give rise to a system of ethics. Beyond that, I struggle to convey what the shack means. I built a birdhouse replica of the shack last winter, and it turned out so nicely that the Aldo Leopold Foundation has supplied me with wood from trees planted by Aldo Leopold so that I can make birdhouses as a fundraiser for the foundation. I've taken literature classes to the shack just after we finished reading *A Sand County Almanac*, where I was able to witness the wonder on the faces of students who drank water from the original pump. I have driven out to the shack with Noah, my biology professor friend, on a ten-degree January day; we stood on the shore of the Wisconsin River and read our favorite passages to each other (for as long as we could take the cold). And I rarely cycle past without stopping in for a visit.

The Aldo Leopold Foundation, located in a wonderful visitor's center just down the road, is continuing Leopold's work, restoring the surrounding prairies to their original state. In short, every visit to the shack—and every rereading of *A Sand County Almanac*—feeds my soul.

# AUGUST DERLETH

## Rail Bridge
## Sauk City, Wisconsin

*By Kassie Jo Baron*

Sauk City, Wisconsin, is best known for being the home of the first Culver's. Then probably for the annual Cow Chip Festival, where residents spend Labor Day weekend seeing who can throw dried cow poop the farthest. Then, finally, for author August Derleth, who was born in Sauk City in 1909.

Growing up I knew almost nothing about Derleth. We were told he was kind of the Mark Twain meets Henry David Thoreau of Wisconsin. We never read his work in public school, even though the locations were, quite literally, in our backyards; instead, we fell asleep on our assigned copies of *A Sand County Almanac*.

But what I do know of him was that, as an eight-year-old, I would hold my bowl of orange slices in the back of my mom's car as we crossed August Derleth Bridge over the Wisconsin River and passed Derleth's state historical marker on my way to soccer games at August Derleth Park. On other days, we'd head to Leystra's, a local restaurant, and pass the massive pie case to head into "Augie's Room," where we could enjoy our slices surrounded by Derleth memorabilia.

About a half mile downstream from the August Derleth Bridge stood a disused pony truss railroad bridge that was built in 1901. One of Derleth's portraits shows him walking across this bridge, a part of his regular route sauntering around the town he dubbed Walden West. "It was a good place to be alone," he wrote. "I could meditate on any subject I chose. . . . How many poems came into being in that place! How much my view of Sac Prairie was expanded there!"

## AUGUST DERLETH

**Born: February 24, 1909, in Sauk City, Wisconsin**

**Died: July 4, 1971, in Sauk City, Wisconsin**

**Genres: Novels, Short Stories, Poetry, History, Biography**

**Recommended Works: *The Sac Prairie Saga* (1935–53), *The Solar Pons Series* (1945–73), *The Ghost of Black Hawk Island* (1961), *The Trail of Cthulhu* (1962)**

By the time of my own childhood, the brown trusses were out of place and certainly out of time. In 2002, much to the delight of certain pyromaniacal children (I will not say if I was among them), the center portion of the bridge was demolished. In 2018 the remainder of the bridge was taken down, but I wasn't there to see if it exploded. The spot is now the trailhead for the Great Sauk Trail, a bike path that runs through town. A chain-link fence erected in the same rusted brown of the bridge is now all that prevents visitors from stepping out onto the remaining span, which juts precipitously over the rush of the river twenty-some feet below. Wisconsin & Southern Railroad's "No Trespassing" sign stands in front of extra trusses strewn haphazardly—if such a thing is possible—across the sun-bleached wood of the tracks.

It wasn't until I started my PhD program at the University of Iowa that I discovered Derleth might not just be a hometown boy after all. During a standard icebreaker, a professor shocked me by saying, "Isn't that where August Derleth, the Lovecraft guy, is from?" I promptly went home and fell down an eldritch rabbit hole. It never occurred to me that Derleth did anything more than write a book about a mystery on Mosquito Island (which you can see if you look upstream from August Derleth Bridge).

Outside of Sauk City, Derleth is best known as H. P. Lovecraft's publisher and the founder of Arkham House, a publishing company specializing in weird fiction that is still located in Sauk City but is now all but defunct. A minor scandal arose when Derleth published stories as a "posthumous collaborator" with Lovecraft, viewed by others as an inappropriate imposition into the mythos. And Derleth's scandals didn't end there. In 1951 he was engaged to sixteen-year-old Sandra Evelyn Winters. In 1953 Derleth told a reporter from *The Rhinelander Daily News*, "We hope to be married Easter Monday—that's April 6. . . . I'll be 44 on Feb. 24 and Sandy will be 18 on March 1." Residents certainly raised eyebrows, but they weren't scandalized enough for me to hear this vital piece of hometown gossip until 2021, four years after I'd left the state.

Leystra's restaurant closed in 2017, after thirty years, marking the end of Augie's Room. Two years later Sauk City completed construction of a splash pad and playground in what used to be August Derleth Park. The park was creatively renamed Riverfront Park, and the formerly rustic sign at the entrance replaced with a significantly larger sign featuring cartoon turtles and racoons who have, I am convinced, murderous impulses in their fiberglass hearts. During construction the state historical marker was taken down.

These signs now decorate the walls of the August Derleth Society, currently in the building where I used to take tap-dancing lessons. I visited the society for the first time earlier this year. "The only thing left is the bridge," I joked with Jon Caflisch, the society's treasurer, a man so passionate about Derleth he convinced me to join, even though, until then, I had never read any Derleth (it's only twenty-five dollars per year, and I get the newsletter now). Jon pointed to the green "August Derleth Bridge" sign hanging just over a bookshelf filled with Derleth hardcovers. The bridge, it seems, doesn't have a name anymore.

Derleth's legacy was a fixture in the Sauk City of my childhood, even though no one I knew could tell you a single thing about him. Piece by piece that legacy evaporated, replaced with Culver's relics and those Lovecraftian wildlife statues. I'm not saying there's a conspiracy to erase Derleth from the region he wrote so fondly about, but I'm not *not* saying that either. If you're passing near Sauk City, make some time to visit the August Derleth Society because, as Jon told me, "we might not be here much longer."

# LORINE NIEDECKER

## River Cabin
## Blackhawk Island, Wisconsin

*By Shanley Wells-Rau*

> I was the solitary plover
> a pencil
>     for a wing-bone
> —Lorine Niedecker, "Paean to Place"

What more solitary place than a small off-grid cabin on an island that's not really an island jutting into a lake that's not really a lake. The cabin was a writing sanctuary for Lorine Niedecker, said to be America's greatest unknown poet, who will forever be linked to Blackhawk Island in southeast Wisconsin.

Look at Blackhawk Island on a map, and you'll see it's actually more of a peninsula that points into what is called Lake Koshkonong, an open-water area that is really just the Rock River being messy all over its flood plain. The river likes to outstretch itself and, in its flood-prone ways, created a recreational haven for boaters and fishers.

Placed less than one hundred feet from the Rock River, Niedecker's cabin was bought as a kit from a catalog and assembled by her father in 1946. He sited it closer to the road than the river in hopes of preventing displacement during the regular floods of spring. Elevated on concrete feet, the twenty-by-twenty-foot one-room house hovers over four cement steps. The front and only door faces east, away from the river, as if to shrug off the idea of annual flooding. This one room contained Niedecker's life: bed, books, table, typewriter, sink, pencils, handheld magnifying glass. With no running water, she hauled buckets as needed from her parents' house across the road. That was the house she grew up in. The house she needed to escape.

## LORINE NIEDECKER

**Born: May 12, 1903, in Fort Atkinson, Wisconsin**

**Died: December 31, 1970, in Fort Atkinson, Wisconsin**

**Forms: Poetry**

**Recommended Works: *New Goose* (1946), *North Central* (1968), *My Life by Water: Collected Poems 1936–1968* (1970), *Collected Works* (2002)**

Her father, a congenial carp seiner and fisherman's guide who was inept with finances, was carrying on an affair with a married neighbor close in age to his daughter. This neighbor and her husband were milking Henry Niedecker of property and money. Her mother, Daisy, had lost her hearing after her only child's birth and turned her head away from her husband. Her "big blind ears" couldn't hear what her eyes couldn't see. A lifetime of fighting flood mud, "buckled floors," and increasing poverty seem to have settled around her like a mourning shawl.

Niedecker left the area a few times—for college, until the family's finances made her quit (early 1920s), for artistic and romantic companionship with a fellow poet in New York City (early 1930s), for work as a writer and research editor for the Works Progress Administration in Madison (1938–42), and finally for Milwaukee (1963) when she married a man who lived and worked there. But that spit of land brought her back after each exodus. Once married, Niedecker and her husband, Al Millen, returned to the river every weekend, eventually building a cottage at the riverside, just steps from her cabin. They moved into the cottage for good in 1968 when Millen retired. Niedecker lived there until her death on December 31, 1970.

In the opening lines of her autobiographical poem "Paean to Place," Niedecker submerges herself deep inside a location she said she "never seemed to really get away from."

> Fish<br>
>     fowl<br>
>         flood<br>
>     Water lily mud<br>
> My life
>
> in the leaves and on water<br>
> My mother and I<br>
>                 born
>
> in swale and swamp and sworn<br>
> to water

Painted green when built, the cabin today is chocolate brown. Sturdy wood, unfinished inside. A brass plaque by the door shines with the lines: "New-sawed / clean-smelling house / sweet cedar pink / flesh tint / I love you." Her signature is embossed below. When I visited, it was hot and dry. The riverside window was open, allowing a breeze to push stifling July heat into the plywood corners. A lovely space. I could see myself writing there. I told myself I could even manage life with "becky," as she called her outhouse.

It's not hard to imagine the constant cleanup from the river's yearly ice melt and flooding. Tall maples and willows accustomed to watery life block the sun over a dirt yard that would easily become muddy with rain. The only access to sunshine seemed to be on the riverbank or in a boat on the river itself. The tree canopy jittered with life, a "noise-storm" as Niedecker once wrote to a friend. I looked to see what birds were holding conference, hoping to meet one of the famous plovers so linked to her work. I saw none. Just movement, shadows, and chittering, and I thought of her technique to overcome her own failing eyesight by memorizing birdsong. She could see birds as they took flight. Sitting still, they were invisible to her except through their calls and conversations with one another.

I grew in green
slide and slant
    of shore and shade

Neighbors saw her walking, always walking, stopping to peer in close at some flowering plant. She bent in—nose distance—to see past her own bad eyesight. Before her marriage to Millen, she worked as a hospital janitor in Fort Atkinson. Her failing eyes required that she work with her body, no longer able to serve as a librarian's assistant as she had in in the late 1920s or a magazine proofreader as in the late 1940s. Her eyesight wouldn't allow her to drive. If a ride wasn't available, she walked the four miles to work. Four miles home again.

Out-of-place electric guitar riffs float past underbrush the afternoon of my visit. Someone is listening to Led Zeppelin's "Kashmir," seemingly not at peace with the sounds of birdsong or tree breeze. The blaring music makes me think of Niedecker's struggle with disrespectful vacationers and rude neighbors. She persisted in centering poetry inside her hardworking life in a community slowly turning blue-collar loud. Her neighbors didn't know she was writing her way into the poetry canon.

The current owners are descendants of the couple who bought the property from Millen's estate in 1986. They kindly allow poets on pilgrimage, and they seem to care lovingly for the property. As I walked to the river to meet it up close, the owner appeared with a genial greeting. He asked if I'd noticed the 1959 flood marks on the wall inside the cabin. I hadn't. Eagerly, he guided me back to Niedecker's "sweet cedar pink" to show me that and other details. After friendly conversation, I decided to head back to town. I didn't need to meet the river up close. I've already met it many times in her poetry.

# CHICAGOLAND

# LISEL MUELLER

## 27240 N. Longwood Dr.
## Forest Haven, Ilinois

*By Jenny Mueller*

"Our trees are aspens, but people / mistake them for birches"—so begins Lisel Mueller's "Another Version," set in 1970s Midwestern suburbia. This proves to be a territory of error. After mistaking the aspens, which spread along the southern edge of the property where Lisel and Paul Mueller had lived nearly twenty years, their visitors romanticize the couple "as characters / in a Russian novel, Kitty and Levin / living contentedly in the country." My parents surely matched Tolstoy's Kitty and Levin in the strength and longevity of their marriage.

But not all happy families feel happy. Nor, by the end of the 70s, did we live in the "country" anymore, even though the guests still think so, gazing out with pleasure on the scene.

> Our friends from the city watch the birds
> and rabbits feeding together
> on top of the deep, white snow.
> (We have Russian winters in Illinois,
> but no sleigh bells, possums instead of wolves,
> no trusted servants to do our work.)

## LISEL MUELLER

**Born: February 8, 1924, in Hamburg, Germany**

**Died: February 21, 2020, in Chicago, Illinois**

**Forms: Poetry, Translation**

**Recommended Works: *The Private Life* (1975), *The Need to Hold Still* (1980), *Second Language* (1986), *Waving from Shore* (1989), *Alive Together: New and Selected Poems* (1996)**

The city friends came from Chicago and its neighbor-city, Evanston. My parents had moved from Evanston in the late 1950s, buying one acre in Lake County, to Chicago's north. There they built one of the first houses in "Forest Haven," a tiny subdivision near the interstate. The house stood at the dead end of one of the subdivision's five streets, in a northwest corner lot separated by barbed wire from a farm that bordered all of Forest Haven's north end as well as our portion of its west. In my childhood, in the 1960s, I gazed west through the wire at the edge of the backyard, looking past the small cattle herd that grazed in the sunset, toward the dark line of woods where the pasture ended and my sight ran out. Past that lay the railroad, another small new subdivision, and the Des Plaines River. Contrails burned their courses over me, arrowing back and forth from O'Hare—newly opened to passenger traffic, half an hour down the interstate.

In those early days, it *was* almost country around the house where Lisel Mueller's poems were born. She came to this writing late in life—already forty-one when her first book was published in 1965. By 1997, when her selected poems won the Pulitzer, she had already nearly stopped writing. Glaucoma diminished her ability to read, and she could no longer drive. One day she found my father at the kitchen table, trying and failing to write his own name. He was losing his language to Lewy Body Dementia. She sold the house and moved them to a complex in Chicago five minutes' walk from both groceries and my father's nursing unit. She never wrote another book of poetry.

In "Another Version" we seem to be at the comfortable end of the '70s American lyric, with its quiet voice, personal sorrows, nature ready-to-hand for muted epiphanies. While the city slickers admire the peaceable kingdom outside a contented country home, an old man is dying inside. "He is my father," Mueller writes,

> he lets go of life in such slow motion,
> year after year, that the grief
> is stuck inside me, a poisoned apple
> that won't go up or down.

But "like the three sisters" in Chekhov's play, "we rarely speak / of what keeps us awake at night."

> like them, we complain about things
> that don't really matter and talk
> of our pleasures and of the future:
> we tell each other the willows
> are early this year, hazy with green.

"Another Version" begins with the visitors' error and ends with their hosts' secrecy. The misunderstandings pile up like northern Illinois snow. Russian allusions mask a German story. The old man was Fritz Neumann, who first arrived in Illinois as a political refugee. As a child in Nazi Germany, Lisel was forced to keep quiet about her father, whose known leftism had marked him as an enemy, someone against whom her schoolmates and neighbors should inform. Neumann, too, kept quiet when at home, but often he was far away. For much of the 1930s he took ill-paying temporary teaching work in France and Italy, while his wife raised two daughters alone in Hamburg. In 1937 luck landed him a scholarship to study at a teacher's college near Evanston. His wife and children joined him in the US in 1939, ending the years in which Lisel clamped her lips tight to suppress her fears—the child's terror that her parents might disappear, made very real by her father's two arrests. Now Lisel became a Midwesterner. She lived all her adult life in Indiana and Illinois. She wrote often of her own luck. But she never lost her night fears, and when an interviewer asked if she considered the Midwest home, she dodged the question, answering, "Let me say what countless other displaced persons must have said: I am more at home here than anywhere."

Her father remained on the move: from teaching job to teaching job in America, then returning to his native Hamburg after the death of his wife in the 1950s. Remarried unhappily, he kept traveling, taking steamships across the Atlantic for long US visits. One night in the 1970s he touched down at O'Hare and never left. A stroke had stricken him with aphasia. He retained, however, a teacher's memory for history: treaties, battles, empires, republics.

But how many people understood that there were non-Jewish German political refugees? In my experience, the old man who came to die with us represented little-known history that always puzzles Americans, even now. My mother sometimes invoked a more famous poet, Brecht, as a shorthand. In poems about her parents, she borrowed Brecht's description of European exiles "changing countries more often than shoes," and she quoted Brecht's sorrow at talk of small pleasures in terrible times, his despair that a casual "talk about trees is almost a crime / since it means being silent about so much evil."

Undoubtedly, Lisel Mueller talked about trees: aspens and willows, the great maple that still stands at an edge of the front yard—if I can trust the internet. But I can't, of course, since the house is currently listed on Zillow as "uninhabitable." On my laptop, I can see that the windows are boarded in the upstairs room that became my mother's study, from which we saw the long views north and west. In that study she wrote the books for which she won awards, poems that were popularized on the radio by the era's voice of the Midwest, Garrison Keillor. The Poetry Foundation praises her work "for its attentiveness to quiet moments of domestic drama, and its ability to speak to the experiences of family and semirural life." Happy families in suburban nature, quietly sad, the great luck of a long, loving marriage. But she also wrote, almost always, of displaced persons, and in a journal she commented, "My preoccupation with history marks me as outside the mainstream of American poetry. No matter how long I've lived and written here, that has not changed and will not change."

In "Another Version," when the daughter can't speak of her father, whose life was determined by history, she talks about trees instead. Her poem makes the pain of such evasion its point.

Suburbia is full of oscillations, migrations. My father, who worked in the city, drove back and forth for years on ever more crowded roads. As the subdivisions multiplied along them, our yard filled up with deer, displaced from the cleared woods. My mother likened them to "refugees," "risking death on the road / to reach us, their dispossessors." My sister and I moved to Chicago—which made us into the city visitors gazing out on the aspens, itching to return to urban streets. There, we were sure, our authentic lives waited.

But some things never change. In 2020, reviewing an anthology of poems responding to the pandemic, *The New York Times* took furious aim against its "tepid" contents' resort to natural imagery. There were too many poems "about flowers. Or birds. Or trees." *The New Yorker*'s founding editor, Harold Ross, had been "wise to rage against tree poems," the critic complained. And perhaps the book really was tepid. But what an astonishing charge! As if we could still see no urgency in trees. As if we still believed that trees crowded out our witness of history, not the other way around. As if we hadn't all learned to pronounce a new urbane word, *Anthropocene,* to slip inside our poems. As if grief, the poisoned apple in my throat, were only for childhood and not for aspens, "country," snow.

# SANDRA CISNEROS

## 1525 N. Campbell Ave.
## Chicago, Illinois

*By Olga L. Herrera*

I grew up in the 1970s and 1980s in the Little Village neighborhood on the southwest side of Chicago. At the time, the area was in transition between Eastern Europeans leaving for the suburbs ahead of the incoming Mexican immigrant families who bought up the neighborhood's turn-of-the-century working-class homes. If I had read *The House on Mango Street* when it was published in 1984, I would have been convinced that Sandra Cisneros was writing about Little Village. That's how real it felt, with versions of Lucy and Rachel from Texas living down the street and Cathy Queen of Cats who is moving away because, she says, "the neighborhood is getting bad."

*The House on Mango Street*, however, was based on Cisneros's childhood in Humboldt Park on the near north side of the city in the 1960s. Even though our two neighborhoods felt similar, they have distinct characters. A tiled archway over the eastern end of the neighborhood symbolizes Little Village's Mexican identity, while in Humboldt Park, enormous metal Puerto Rican flags arch over a diverse mix of eateries on Division Street, including a Mexican taqueria and a Colombian café. Recently, gentrification has been changing the demographics and character of Humboldt Park more swiftly, making a significant change on Cisneros's old street.

## SANDRA CISNEROS

**Born: December 20, 1954, in Chicago, Illinois**

**Died: —**

**Forms: Novels, Poetry, Short Stories**

**Recommended Works: *The House on Mango Street* (1984), *Woman Hollering Creek and Other Stories* (1991), *Loose Woman* (1994), *Caramelo* (2002)**

*The House on Mango Street* was partly inspired by her memories of the house her family bought at 1525 North Campbell Avenue when she was a young girl. If you do an online image search for the "real" house on Mango Street, you will find images of a red-brick two-story house with a flat roof and a small front yard bordered by a black wrought-iron fence. It looks just as Esperanza describes. But it's not a picture of the original house.

At a symposium I attended in 2017, Cisneros explained that this image had circulated for years but was, in fact, a photograph of the house directly across the street. The red house in the picture is 1524 North Campbell Avenue, and it is a mirror image of her house, with the front door on the reverse side. Her childhood home had been demolished in the early 2000s, and a new condominium building was constructed in its place in 2005. You couldn't see her original home anymore, she said, but the one across the street would give you a good idea of what it looked like.

These two houses tell the story of gentrification in Humboldt Park. One is a modest two-story house with painted brick, a metal awning, and narrow windows. The other is a sleek three-story building with large windows that open to balconies on each floor, with a garden level below. Located between two larger, older apartment buildings, it bears elements of their style, but because the footprint of the plot belonged to that smaller house, the new building at 1525 North Campbell is wedged into the space, with the northern exterior wall angled away to make room for a narrow gangway. Ceilings have swept upward, and bay windows and a new floor have sprouted. It has an attenuated look, seeming to both belong and not belong.

The differences represent not only changes in architecture but also in affordability and the families who can live in this building. Gentrification reverses the mid-century trend of white flight to the suburbs. Now wealthy families move in, and less affluent immigrants and families of color have fewer chances to live in this culturally significant neighborhood. In a city notorious for segregation, the Humboldt Park neighborhood has been home to a diverse community that includes Mexican Americans, Puerto Ricans, Eastern Europeans, and African Americans. *The House on Mango Street* brings that rare diversity to life. Since the mid-1990s, residents have fought to preserve the neighborhood's character by organizing around issues of affordable housing, community development, and park use. Now, when I walk over to Division Street in Humboldt Park and see El Paisano Tacos across from Nellie's Puerto Rican restaurant, I see that the community has held on to those cultural differences that make this a special place.

# GWENDOLYN BROOKS

## South Side Community Art Center
## Chicago, Illinois

*By Angie Chatman*

The building at 4724 South Evans Avenue was located a block south of Cottage Grove, one of the main thoroughfares through the Bronzeville neighborhood of Chicago. The three-flat building, now demolished, initially housed four generations of my family.

The oldest generation—my great-grandfather Ernest Hezekiah Fambro, along with his two sons Curtis and Timothy, his wife, Nellie, and her mother, Amelia Beasley Ball—had moved to Chicago from DeKalb County, Georgia, in 1916. This was early in the Great Migration of African Americans from the agrarian South to the industrial North of the United States, which continued through the 1960s.

## GWENDOLYN BROOKS

**Born: June 7, 1917, in Topeka, Kansas**

**Died: December 3, 2000, in Chicago, Illinois**

**Forms: Poetry, Novels, Autobiography**

**Recommended Works: *A Street in Bronzeville* (1945), *Annie Allen* (1949), *Maud Martha* (1953), *The Bean Eaters* (1960)**

My relatives weren't the only Negroes to settle in Bronzeville. Gwendolyn Brooks and her family also migrated to Chicago in response to lynchings and other forms of racial unrest in Topeka, Kansas, as well as for economic opportunities. Brooks lived in other places after her literary successes brought more lucrative teaching assignments, but those were temporary addresses. Chicago was home. This is obvious from the title of her first book of poetry, *A Street in Bronzeville,* published in 1945, as well as *Bronzeville Boys and Girls*, published in 1956.

Due to national and local laws mandating segregated housing, at its peak three hundred thousand Negroes lived in Bronzeville, in the area between 39th and 51st Streets from Cottage Grove to Halsted (until the Dan Ryan Expressway was built in 1961 and cut the western boundary line of the neighborhood to State Street). Dr. Daniel Hale Williams performed the first open-heart surgery at Provident Hospital, the first African American owned and operated hospital in the country. Loraine Hansberry's 1959 stage play, *A Raisin in the Sun*, was based on her family's experience living in and attempting to move away from Bronzeville.

Once on a Saturday morning my mother took us to the South Side Community Art Center, a three-story brick building on Michigan Avenue. We were going to hear Mrs. Brooks, who was then the first African American Poet Laureate of the state of Illinois, read her poems. My younger siblings and I sat on the linoleum floor on mats of woven fabric, fans moving the air like a barge on the Chicago River. Mrs. Brooks's voice rose above the hum, like that of the soloist in the choir. I don't remember what poems she read, only that I recognized the tenor of the words. Her poetry had the same rhythm and cadence of conversations among my relatives during a backyard cookout in the sunshine.

My mother had promised we'd stop for ice cream after the reading. She took a detour on the way and pulled over in front of 4724 South Evans. Stairs led up to the entrance. Every apartment had the same layout: an open living room, three bedrooms, one bathroom, and a kitchen. There was a small yard in the back. My siblings and I were dismayed that a family of six shared one bathroom.

I never lived in that building on 47th and Evans; it's now an empty lot. For my mother, though, it was the telescope she used to focus on fond memories of carefree days with her three older sisters: days full of hopscotch, double-Dutch jump rope, roller skating to the Hall Branch library—a mile and a half away—and movies at the Regal Theater. Ms. Brooks also uses her experiences in Bronzeville as a lens with which she can zoom in and out not only to comment on the quotidian activities of Black folk but also to display how dysfunctional racist practices are for both Black people and white people.

I have not lived in Chicago for over twenty-five years. Yet as the Black Lives Matter movement grew from Minneapolis to Chicago to cover the globe, I turned my telescope toward home. It occurs to me—each time there's another murder of a Black man/woman/child by police, and as people of color face a disproportionate impact from COVID-19—that "We die soon." Too soon.

I turn also to Brooks's *Annie Allen*, published in 1949, especially a poem entitled "Beverly Hills, Chicago," about a drive through Beverly, a then all-white neighborhood on the South Side:

> Nobody is furious. Nobody hates these people.
> At least nobody driving by in this car.
> It is only natural, however, that it should occur to us
> How much more fortunate they are than we are.

# RICHARD WRIGHT

## 4831 S. Vincennes Ave.
## Chicago, Illinois

*By Joseph S. Pete*

Powell's Books used to have a few locations in Chicago, none anywhere near as large as the fabled city block full of books in Portland. Now only its venerable Hyde Park bookstore remains, but I fondly remember the Lincoln Park Powell's with its distinguished rows of dark wood bookshelves soaring up to the ceiling, the rarefied upper shelves reachable only by sliding ladder. It had the hallowed air of some centuries-old university library. It's where, as a pock-faced and perpetually despondent teenager, I first obtained a copy of Richard Wright's *Native Son* (1940), which swiftly became one of my favorite and most reread books.

Fran Lebowitz said at a recent talk at the Auditorium Theatre in Chicago that literature should be a window and not a mirror. I found Wright's *Native Son* to be both. It was a mirror in that I hailed from heavily industrialized and culturally similar Northwest Indiana just outside the familiar South Side landscapes he described. As a troubled youth, I could also relate strongly to Bigger Thomas's alienation and desperate sense of doomed hopelessness. And Mary Dalton's rebellious dalliance with communism spoke to my burgeoning political consciousness. I was delving deeper and deeper into reading serious literature, and *Native Son* had more recognizable touchstones than the nineteenth-century British and Russian classics I was devouring around that time. It just clicked for me.

## RICHARD WRIGHT

**Born: September 4, 1908, in Roxie, Mississippi**

**Died: November 28, 1960, in Paris, France**

**Forms: Novels, Short Stories, Memoir, Essays, Poetry**

**Recommended Works: *Uncle Tom's Children* (1938), *Native Son* (1940), *How "Bigger" Was Born; Notes of a Native Son* (1940), *Black Boy* (1945)**

But it was also a window into the African American experience that I could never fully know, and that intrigued me. I had started to see the white flight, abandonment, and segregation that split greater Chicagoland asunder as the great defining original sin that corrupted the area. Highways came to divide white and minority neighborhoods in both Chicago and the Calumet Region. I went to high school about a block south of Gary (when it was still the murder capital of the United States), where as many as thirteen thousand vacant buildings have rotted in shameful testament to people's unwillingness to live next door to people who look different. The sins of our forefathers scarred the landscape with blight, boarded-up storefronts, and rubble-strewn buildings with collapsed roofs. *Native Son* explores racial discrimination that sadly remains just as relevant as ever. A recent HBO adaptation, instead of putting Bigger through a show trial, modernized his plight by having Bigger gunned down extrajudicially by trigger-happy police.

Wright grew up in Jim Crow Mississippi and moved, as a young adult, to Chicago's South Side, his family following the Great Migration from the South to the more prosperous industrialized cities of the North. He spent the most time in one place on the second story of a row house in Bronzeville, a largely residential neighborhood flanking Grand Boulevard (now called Dr. Martin Luther King Jr. Drive). He lived with family in a two-story building with a cream-colored brick facade, bay windows, a tiny patch of lawn, and an entrance with stone stairs and relatively unembellished Greek pillars, the most modest home in a strip of taller and more architecturally extravagant houses. Today the home is privately owned, and no tours are offered, but you can admire the solid masonry of the stone-and-brick exterior and enduring handiwork of craftsmen from 1893, when it was built.

Wright lived on that densely populated stretch of South Vincennes Avenue in his early twenties, working as a postal clerk until the Great Depression cost him that position. He went on to bounce around the city, working a series of unskilled jobs, but spent that formative period in the Black metropolis that produced many intellectuals, artists, and musicians, such as Gwendolyn Brooks, Louis Armstrong, Ida B. Wells, and Sam Cooke.

During his downtime, Wright studied great authors and started to pursue his literary ambitions. He contributed to the area's vibrant culture, founding the South Side Writers Group and the literary journal *Left Front* as he started to publish his own poetry. He also began his first novel, *Lawd Today!*, which he finished in 1935 but wasn't published until after his death decades later.

There's not much to see now on the quiet residential street other than a plaque designating the house as a Chicago Landmark, but the modest appearance of the abode that helped nurture Wright to greatness is the point. Ninety years after he lived and started writing there, the neighborhood continues to hum with culture. There's the Harold Washington Cultural Center, the Southside Community Art Center, Room 43, the Bronzeville Art District Trolley Tour, and the Bronzeville Walk of Fame, among many other points of interest.

Though just south of the glittering skyscrapers of the Loop, the majority-Black Bronzeville often gets as overlooked as it was when Wright lived there from 1929 to 1932. In *Native Son* Mary Dalton tells Bigger, "I've been to England, France and Mexico, but I don't know how people live ten blocks from me. We know so little about each other." Even today, many suburbanites and recent Big Ten grads transplanted to the North Side have never set foot in the rather genteel neighborhood. I frequently attend White Sox games just across the highway, but the ballpark feels a world away. The divisions that doom young men like Bigger Thomas still stand today in great sweeping corridors of concrete and ingrained prejudice.

# HUGO MARTINEZ-SERROS

## South Chicago City Dump
## Chicago, Illinois

*By Emiliano Aguilar Jr.*

Chicago's South Side is littered with the remains of its industrial past. From the facade of the former US Steel South Works to sites bustling with activity, such as the Pullman National Monument. I grew up in the shadow of Chicago, over the state line in the appropriately named East Chicago, Indiana. My hometown and much of Northwest Indiana, often referred to as "Da Region," looked more like Chicago and shared more of its history than other parts of Indiana. We even have our own ruins, such as the abandoned warehouse of the Edward Valve Company, the half-scraped ruins of Cleveland Cliffs (formerly ArcelorMittal and before that Inland Steel), and the ever-shrinking Marktown.

This world comes alive in the short stories of Hugo Martinez-Serros, whose family arrived to work in the region's steel industry. Like them, tens of thousands of people arrived on the South Side to labor arduously in often unsafe environments. Ethnic Mexicans arrived as *solos,* single men, ahead of their families. These pioneers paved the way for their families and extended networks.

## HUGO MARTINEZ-SERROS

**Born: September 25, 1931, in Chicago, Illinois**

**Died: —**

**Forms: Short Stories**

**Recommended Works: *The Last Laugh and Other Stories* (1988), *Steeling Chicago: South Side Stories* (2014)**

In "Distillation," first published in *The Last Laugh and Other Stories* (1988), Martinez-Serros recalls a family drive from the family's home on the South Side to a municipal dump across the neighborhood. Recalling the weekly Saturday drive southward from their home through alleys crossing 86th, 89th, and 95th Streets, Martinez-Serros describes the final destination vividly: "Before us was the city dump—a great raw sore on the landscape; a leprous tract oozing flames, smoldering; hellish grounds columned in smoke, grown tumid across years." The narrator, along with his family, sifts through the trash, looking for items to salvage. Together they search for items to sell and for discarded produce as a means to survive during the Depression.

As clichéd as it might be, what is one person's trash if not another person's treasure? I first read Hugo Martinez-Serros after picking it up from the free box at the Purdue University Northwest library. While the book had seen better days, it showed clear signs of love: dogears, a weathered spine, yellowed pages, scribblings from an earlier reader, and a fair amount of shelf-wear. Salvaging this copy from among discarded textbooks and novels, I discovered Depression-era South Chicago. While familiar to me in my work as a historian, thanks to scholars like Gabriela F. Arredondo and Michael Innis-Jiménez, the world Martinez-Serros described differed greatly from the region I knew as a lifelong resident.

Northwest Indiana and Chicago's South Side are part of the Rust Belt. Once an industrial sprawl of hundreds of thousands of jobs manufacturing hundreds of items, the region began to decline in the 1970s and 1980s. However, the Rust Belt is not simply a ruin—some vestigial piece of our shared past. For decades, cities have worked to revitalize their communities and, in some cases, evoke their industrial heritage. In the 1990s Northwest Indiana communities turned to the gaming industry and lakefront casinos to supplant the loss of manufacturing jobs.

These revitalization plans did not exclude piles of trash. In the 1990s the City of Chicago contracted landscape architect Dick Nugent to design the Harborside International Golf Center on top of the 225 acres that formerly held solid waste, incinerator ash, wastewater sludge, and construction debris. Childhood searches for scrap to sell or for barely expired food were replaced by golfers scouring the rough for balls that went astray. In high school I played on one such dump turned golf course as a part of my varsity team. Like Martinez-Serros and his family sifted through the refuse and remains at the municipal dump, I, too, scavenged through the former dump, though I was only looking for wayward golf balls. These carefully designed courses of bright green fairways are nestled among industrial complexes. On clear days, you can see the iconic Chicago skyline.

The region's residents turned heaping piles of trash into a site of recreation and frustration. While the narrator retold stories of joyful and almost play-like salvaging, this was coupled with the frustration and fear of his brother falling into a pile of trash. This joy and fear of garbage-diving became replaced with the joy of a long drive and the frustration of a mixed putt. However, the presence of the golf course for recreation is a mixed bag. While many praise the efforts of turning trash into treasure, changes to the Chicagoland landscape are not limited to trash heaps. In some cases, rich historical sites, such as those on the Calumet Heritage Area's Critical Calumet list, are under threat of removal in the name of progress. While some residents are content with this change, others view it as a loss of the shared heritage and history of the area. Although many deride the area, which still suffers from the harmful legacy of environmental injustice, those of us who remain continue to chip off the rust and show that Da Region is a vibrant home.

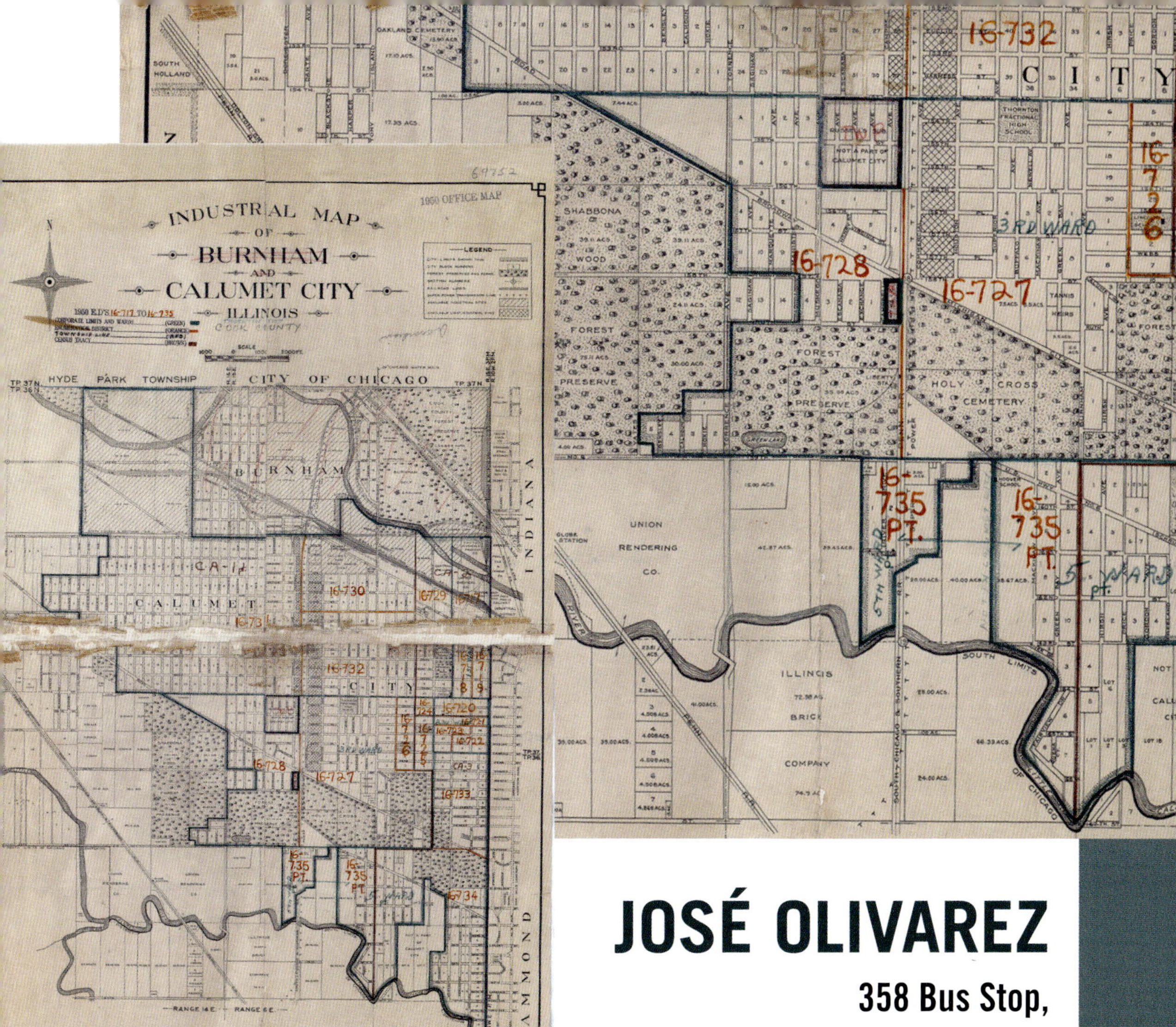


# JOSÉ OLIVAREZ

## 358 Bus Stop, Torrence Ave. & Pulaski Rd. Calumet City, Illinois

*By Ava Tomasula y Garcia*

> forgive my geography, it's true i'm obsessed
> with maps—
> —José Olivarez, "Wherever I Am, That Land is Chicago"

The Calumet Region coheres into shape and sense through the totalizing language of maps. The grid through which reality has been arranged here for over two hundred years are that of longitude, latitude, scale, treaty boundary, *x-marks-the-spot*. Isn't that the work that maps do, after all? They make the real, real. Chart, fix, occupy, extract. They make the given world seem inevitable.

## JOSÉ OLIVAREZ

**Born: February 14, 1988, in Calumet City, Illinois**

**Died: —**

**Forms: Poetry**

**Recommended Works: *Citizen Illegal* (2018), *The BreakBeat Poets*, vol. 4, *LatiNext* (2020, edited with Felicia Chavez and Willie Perdomo), *Por Siempre* (2023, with Antonio Salazar), *Promises of Gold* (2023)**

I've been looking at these maps for a long time, trying to understand how *land* becomes *resource* and then gets thrown away. How people continue to live on it and love it.

José Olivarez is a poet from Calumet City, the city that takes its name from this Region. I think he gets it. His images always seem to return home to the Region. This is true even when he's battling, word by word, the terms of that return: this is one of the most segregated and polluted areas in the lands now called the United States. Looking at the maps, the Calumet Region emerges as a total sacrifice zone; a waste dump for centuries of capitalism; an overdetermined and overburdened ninety-ish-square miles stretching from South Chicago through Northwest Indiana along the southern shore of Lake Michigan.

A hard place to call home. Even harder not to go back to the map to describe it; harder still not to get trapped by the dense tangle of border lines and scale markers and RxR crossings which would choke you. To not feel like there's no way out of the world its representations would have you believe are inevitable.

Blueprints to the city-size steel mills, past and present. Hazardous waste containment sites marked out on a grid. So-called early settlement maps of Indiana and Illinois show how the Potawatomi Nation was rounded up and cornered by gunpoint. How Menominee himself refused to sell Neshnabé land, even after he was viciously detained by settler militia men. See how quickly land speculation is mapped into reality in the wake of the Trail of Tears: limestone quarries marked out, coal veins sought, railroad lines laid down.

Chicago booms into existence on the map, literally constructed from the "raw materials" of the cleared Calumet: water, wood, limestone, coal, sand for cement, and clay for bricks. The world's first refrigerated train cars, carrying meat from the Chicago stockyards across the country, cooled by ice cut from Calumet lakes and rivers and running the rail lines that crisscross the Region today. Plat maps showing how houses butt up against the Standard Oil refinery, now BP.

My family's history of living and working around the Region walks in lockstep with a history of illness: cancer and dementia from so much pollution, from day-in-and-day-out drinking in the soils and waters that industry has determined must be wasted for bigger profits. It seems like illness is hard baked into what it means to be from here, and for me, so is leaving. When Olivarez writes, "i needed to believe suffering was honorable," the line hits hard.

Yet what I love most about Olivarez's work is that, while always being grounded in place, he doesn't write about the *map*. He doesn't "mistake the map for the territory," as Sylvia Wynter put it. This poetry doesn't go around, in Olivarez's words, "pretending the bones / are the real thing." He's after life, not its flattening. When I take the bus up Torrence

Avenue through Cal City—past the train lines, past the scrap metal yard, past the recycler plant—I'm riding through territory that exceeds those bones. The land doesn't give up. Look one way and you see intermodals speeding by on miles of burned-out rail lines. Look the other way, and you see sand cranes and egrets burst out of the dune grass. A cloud of starlings flits through the sunset. Marsh water floods the road. Heavy industry mixes with the watery, oh-so-alive earth.

Olivarez finds the little cracks in the totality. His images of life in Calumet City mix with my own memories, peeling themselves off the map: Olivarez in "Cal City Winter," as a kid on another frozen winter morning, "jumping up & down at the bus stop / trying to warm up." My own memories, waiting in the car for Berta to get off work at the Burger King at River Oaks Mall, breath curling in the December air. Biting into a gordita from Loli's, steaming hot down my throat. Springtime bugs gliding back and forth on the Little Cal River, weaving a gossamer haze, summer heat shimmering, a thousand mirages. People always say that we have the prettiest sunsets and then joke that it is because of the pollution. The road the car snakes along was once the shore of an ancient lake, was taken over by settler stagecoaches, was a sand mining pit, was paved over for scrap trucks to traverse. You settle into place.

This is what no map will ever show but sometimes a poem does: the way individual lives layer up moments of anger, pain, and love—how these emotions sediment themselves into place as tracks that others, whom you will never meet, will walk. This is what living in the Calumet Region means, too. Olivarez's poetry has become my map to the Cal Region. Not a map as in *chart, fix, occupy, extract.* A map as in "i'm always out south / of somewhere. i know the sun rises / in Lake Michigan & sets out west."

With it, I'm trying to navigate those questions that I haven't been able to figure out for my own life: "I want to learn what the birds know—/ to love a home when it is abundant / & to leave when the love stops."

Olivarez's map is a question in answer to my questions. Where does a person begin and the place they're from end? Can you ever leave a home? Can a home ever cease to be that—can it be ground out, like a cigarette butt on a cold winter morning? When you leave, do your memories go with you? Or do some of them stay behind, settling into the landscape?

Surely, some mark of the love a place gave you and that you gave back stays in the soil. Surely.

# JEAN SHEPHERD

## 2907 Cleveland Street
## Hammond, Indiana

*By Samuel Love*

"Ours was not a genteel neighborhood," Jean Shepherd wrote of Hohman, his fictional Northwest Indiana hometown. The opening story from his 1971 book *Wanda Hickey's Night of Golden Memories and Other Disasters* describes a community "nestled picturesquely between the looming steel mills and the verminously aromatic oil refineries and encircled by a colorful conglomerate of city dumps and fetid rivers." Whoever wrote the back cover copy for the 2000 Broadway Books trade paperback apparently didn't read that part, describing the collection as a "beloved, bestselling classic of humorous and nostalgic Americana."

The association of nostalgia with Shepherd's work has long puzzled but not surprised me, especially in the light of the 1983 film *A Christmas Story*, which is based on parts of his 1966 novel *In God We Trust: All Others Pay Cash*. He is the author of arguably the quintessential modern American Christmas tale, but much of the bite of his work has been lost in the process of transcribing and adapting for viewing audiences the narratives that originated on late night radio in New York City in the 1950s. His stories first saw print in *Playboy* and *The Village Voice* in the 1960s, were adapted for public television in the 1970s, and finally, for Hollywood in the 1980s.

Shepherd always insisted that his books were novels, not memoirs or collections of short stories. He also insisted that his literary works were fictional, that Hohman was a "mythical place," a composite of all of the region's industrial communities. Yet his description of fictional Hohman accurately describes the geography of his actual boyhood neighborhood in Hammond, Indiana. The Indiana Harbor steel mills and the Standard Oil refinery were just a few miles upwind. Even closer was the polluted Grand Calumet River. To the south were the brackish waters of the Little Calumet. And to the east, the Gary City Dump.

## JEAN SHEPHERD

**Born: July 26, 1921, in Chicago, Illinois**

**Died: October 16, 1999, in Fort Myers, Florida**

**Forms: Short Stories, Screenplays, Radio**

**Recommended Works: *In God We Trust: All Others Pay Cash* (1966), *Wanda Hickey's Night of Golden Memories: And Other Disasters* (1971), *A Fistful of Fig Newtons* (1981)**

Jean Shepherd was born in Chicago in 1921 but grew up in Hammond, where the main street is Hohman Avenue. His family lived on Cleveland Street on the southeast side of town, in the Hessville neighborhood, near families named Schwartz, Flickinger, and even Bumpus. His books and films contain the typical disclaimers about "resemblance to individuals living or dead," yet he often used the names of real people for his popular "kiddom" stories.

Of the two houses on Cleveland Street that the Shepherds called home, the one at 2907 has the strongest claim as "The Jean Shepherd Boyhood Home"—on February 18, 1939, a seventeen-year-old Jean etched his name in the attic rafters. The current owners have lived there since the late 1970s, raising a family and growing to tolerate the curious people who wander by and photograph the exterior—provided the curious don't linger around too long or violate the family's privacy. When Shepherd's younger brother Randy arrived in a limousine and asked to see the inside, they turned him away. They had no idea who he or Jean Shepherd were.

The nearest thing to a public Shepherd monument is the House from *A Christmas Story* museum in Cleveland, opened in 2006 in the home used for the film's exterior shots. It is a more appropriate celebration of the cultural phenomenon and ultimately the creativity of Jean Shepherd. Better to celebrate his talent as a fiction writer than perpetrate fictions about his life for tourists. Shepherd's real-life father abandoned the family. And Shepherd himself eagerly left Indiana after his World War II service. "People ask me if I miss Hammond," he told a crowd at the county library in 1984. "Do you miss the cold sores you had last week?"

Shepherd's relationship with the region is often mischaracterized as love-hate. I don't think there was hate from either side. Even before the film, his hometown began embracing the man and his myths. Shepherd made regular public visits in the last three decades of his life. And we have continued to remember him since his death in 1999. On the south end of Hessville is the Jean Shepherd Community Center, opened in 2003. Local theatre companies stage adaptations of *A Christmas Story* during the holiday season, and the nearby Indiana Welcome Center hosts an annual exhibit called A Christmas Story Comes Home.

Perhaps what some people mistake for nostalgia was Shepherd's refusal to pander to his audience by mocking his hometown and the people there. "Never make fun of anything," he frequently reminded his audience, "unless you love it."

# LEW WALLACE

## Grand Kankakee Marsh
## Porter County, Indiana

*By Matthew A. Werner*

Indiana once had one of the greatest natural habitats in North America: the Grand Kankakee Marsh. Author Lew Wallace loved it so much he kept a houseboat on its thruway, the Kankakee River. It was his respite. Then, in the name of progress, men obliterated the marsh and ruined the river.

Of the Kankakee, Wallace wrote, "Never in all my world travels have I seen a more perfect spot, nor a more tantalizing river." He grew up near the Wabash River. During the Mexican War, Wallace swam the Rio Grande. As a Civil War general, he met the Mississippi. While US minister to the Ottoman Empire, he saw the Rhine, Danube, and Nile Rivers. As New Mexico Territory governor, he crossed the Pecos and the Sante Fe. The man had seen some rivers.

The Kankakee River meandered 250 miles through two thousand oxbows from South Bend, Indiana, to Momence, Illinois. North and south of this stretch lay one million acres of marshland—half of which flooded permanently and half that did so with the changing seasons. Sand dunes that served as islands interspersed the flat, peaty marsh. The landscape included tall grass, cattails, oak trees, and giant sycamores. Wild apple trees, walnut trees, wild rice, strawberries, blackberries, and raspberries grew in abundance.

## LEW WALLACE

**Born: April 10, 1827, in Brookville, Indiana**

**Died: February 15, 1905, in Crawfordsville, Indiana**

**Forms: Novels, Drama, Biography**

**Recommended Works: *The Fair God; or, The Last of the 'Tzins: A Tale of the Conquest of Mexico* (1873), *Ben-Hur: A Tale of the Christ* (1880), *The Prince of India; or, Why Constantinople Fell* (1893)**

The wildlife habitat had few peers—beaver, mink, otters, opossums, cougars, wolves, bison, elk, and fox lived there. Folklore claimed you could walk across the marsh hopping from muskrat den to muskrat den. The bottom was full of mussels. Lunker bass, walleye, and pike thrived. Bees stuffed hollow trees with honey; bats made homes in others. It was a bird paradise—purple martins, Carolina parakeets, loons, trumpeter swans, egrets, and whooping cranes nested in the marsh. Bird populations were so great that visitors described flocks that darkened the sky.

Local Potawatomi people lived with the marsh, using its abundance of mammals, birds, fish, and plants to provide food and medicine. The Grand Kankakee Marsh was a natural food pantry.

The United States government forced out the Potawatomi in the 1830s. As a result of the Swamp Land Act of 1850, Indiana carved the marsh into squares and sold it to speculators and settlers. It was said that the marsh was "the only place you could buy land by the gallon." Many men sought to conquer the marsh and drain its water. Others, like Lew Wallace, enjoyed the marsh's magnificence.

By the time Wallace arrived in the Grand Kankakee Marsh in 1858, it was a hunter, trapper, and sportsman's destination. Gun and hunt clubs that catered to wealthy men flourished on the sand islands and banks of the Kankakee River.

Wallace returned again and again over forty-three years. He bought a lumber barge and converted it into a houseboat aptly named The Thing. It moored one hundred yards south of Collier Lodge at Baum's Bridge. With his friend, Ira Brainard, Wallace modified the vessel and created fixtures from neighbors' unwanted furniture. The floating cabin was ten feet by thirty-seven feet. It had three sections (sleeping quarter, kitchen, and living room) and was topped with a framework of iron pipe and canvas. Early Porter County historian Hubert Skinner said, "There have been many boats on the Kankakee, but none ever attracted more attention than the queer barge he devised." From the living room, Wallace likely wrote parts of *Ben-Hur*, *The Prince of India*, and his autobiography.

During his visits, Wallace fished, tinkered with his boat, and visited with the people of the Grand Kankakee Marsh. He stopped at various lodges and hunting clubs along the river. "River rats, trappers, guides, pushers, and just ordinary home folks accepted him for his friendliness and his interest in the Kankakee," wrote Skinner.

For a brief period during the Civil War, General Wallace was shelved. With no soldiers to lead, he retreated to the Kankakee to fish, think, and write before he was called back to battle where he served through the end of the war.

Viewed as a land of financial opportunity, profiteers plundered the Grand Kankakee Marsh. Railroad boxcars carted away the marsh's splendors. Businessmen killed swans for down, egrets for fancy hats, muskrats and mink for fur, cattails for furniture stuffing, and mussels for pearls and buttons. Frogs and waterfowl were killed by the thousands and served in Chicago and New York City restaurants.

To drain the water, men dug ditch upon ditch, but the marsh remained. Then men blasted a mile of limestone ledge on the river bottom in Illinois. The marsh retreated, but only a little. In 1902 steam dredges began straightening the bends and curves of the Kankakee River and doomed the marsh.

Wallace last visited the Grand Kankakee Marsh in 1904. He died in 1905. In 1922 dredges bypassed the final bend of the Kankakee, turning its 250 miles of meandering river into a 90-mile-long ditch. Ninety-nine percent of the marsh drained away. Finally, the Grand Kankakee succumbed to its killers.

Loggers removed trees for lumber. In its wake, men planted rows of corn. The United States migratory bird population declined by one-fifth. No more duck, geese, cattails, or frog legs shipped out. The hunt clubs vacated. The Kankakee River no longer flowed where Wallace moored The Thing.

Today you cannot jump from muskrat den to muskrat den. Fox dens have been plowed. You won't find mussels. There is no wild rice to harvest. Loons do not come here. Flocks of birds do not darken the sky. The marsh tries to reclaim its territory when heavy rains flood the corn fields, but the water stubbornly drains.

It would be kind to say the men who drained the Grand Kankakee Marsh did not know what they were doing. They knew. They called it progress. Men murdered that perfect spot, that tantalizing river that Lew Wallace loved. Had Wallace lived to see its death, he would have died of a broken heart.

# MICHAEL MARTONE

## US Highway 30
## LaPorte County, Indiana

*By Dawn Burns*

> My main interest is in making the ordinary strange and wonderful.
> —Michael Martone

On my basement wall, above a small writing desk, hangs a three-piece canvas print of Northern Indiana farmland with US Highway 30 in the background. The picture's not much to look at, yet when I found this triptych of ordinariness in a Lansing, Michigan, thrift store, I was overcome with wonder, feeling I knew the exact location—4494 West US Highway 30, Hanna, Indiana, 46340—an address as precise as my memories are approximate. An address to which I could mail a postcard because it once was my home.

Growing up I watched all manner of vehicles drive by the intersection of US 30 and County Road 450 West from my upstairs bedroom window. Traffic sped by in both directions as eternally as bread slices fall away from the giant Sunbeam loaf at 350 Pearl Street in Fort Wayne, the city ninety-two miles east, where extended family lived and where Michael Martone was born on August 22, 1955, in St. Joe Hospital, one week shy of eighteen years before me and, as he notes in *Brooding* (2018), in "the same year as . . . the commencement of the Interstate Highway System."

## MICHAEL MARTONE

**Born: August 22, 1955, in Fort Wayne, Indiana**

**Died: —**

**Forms: Short Stories, Essays, Creative Nonfiction**

**Recommended Works: *Fort Wayne Is Seventh on Hitler's List* (1990), *The Flatness and Other Landscapes* (1999), *The Blue Guide to Indiana* (2001), *Winesburg, Indiana* (2015, edited with Bryan Furuness), *The Complete Writings of Art Smith, the Bird Boy of Fort Wayne* (2020)**

Michael Martone in fours, like the four squared corners of a county township, like how Indiana looks flying over, like he writes in "The Flatness" (2000), a grid inscribed into the skin of the Midwest which "transmits in fields and waves," which "is a place of sense":

| | |
|---|---|
| Michael Martone whose parents were Tony and Patty, whose brother is Tim, who grew up both in his mother's freshman English class at Central High School and in Fort Wayne's North Highlands neighborhood, a "truly high ground in a flat land . . . where all the tv and radio towers are," he told me. | Michael Martone who, across from his maternal grandparents' home at 1811 Poinsette Drive, played baseball and went sledding in Hamilton Park—a trash pit before it became a park—where, in summer, he says, such artifacts as "old bottles, screws and nails, cans, batteries" would emerge at his feet. |
| Michael Martone who was declared "Bard of Fort Wayne, Indiana" on June 1, 2020, a day forever marked as Michael Martone Day, the proof existing on a proclamation stamped with an official gold seal and signed by Mayor Thomas C. Henry. | Michael Martone who read, every year, Edith Hamilton's *Mythologies*, whose childhood addresses were once 1730 Spring Street and then 1812 Clover Lane and who makes mythologies out of Fort Wayne, Indiana, and himself. |

Growing up in Hanna, I knew no Michael Martone. Michael Martone's whereabouts were no concern of mine. When I watched traffic, not once did I conjure a writer from Indiana who wrote about Indiana. Instead, I asked myself four questions: "Who are the people driving by? Where are they coming from? Where are they going? What if they break down?" Sometimes cars did break down, and my dad would help. As travelers sat around our kitchen table, I'd hear the answers to my questions. I liked finding out these facts; I also liked daydreaming my own fictions.

I would not meet Michael Martone until 1997 (or was it 1998?) when he visited my Notre Dame MFA cohort of creative writers. By then I no longer lived on US 30, and we did not meet because of unforeseen car trouble. Though I bought his 1990 collection, *Fort Wayne Is Seventh on Hitler's List,* I would not fully read it for another twenty years, concerned I might be influenced. Still, simply by publishing a book with Fort Wayne in the title, he'd given me permission to write about Indiana.

No doubt I've got my facts wrong about my thrifted picture. I would not stake my Hoosier credibility on the highway being US 30 any more than I would on the landscape being Northern Indiana. About "the flatness," Michael Martone writes, "They are thinking about Northern Ohio, about Indiana, about the long stretch through Illinois and on into Iowa. It is flat." My picture could be from any of these states, or none. Who am I to say?

What I've long loved about Michael Martone—about all the Michael Martones—is how his writing both secures and blurs, for he makes Fort Wayne and all of Indiana as real-and-not-real as Art Smith, "bird boy of Fort Wayne," whom I can read about both on the Smithsonian's website and in *The Complete Writings of Art Smith, the Bird Boy of Fort Wayne* (2020).

In Michael Martone's mythologies, Dan Quayle will always be out snipe hunting, Jacques Derrida will always be eating an Awful Big, Awful Good pork tenderloin at a Winesburg café, and mayonnaise will always be pumped through the Trans-Indiana Mayonnaise Pipeline.

To his mythologies, I add my own. Dawn Burns, in fours:

| | |
|---|---|
| My great-aunt Mary who once babysat Dan Quayle saying he'd been a good boy as we stood with my grandmother holding Bush-Quayle '92 signs outside the Huntington County Courthouse, waiting for the vice-president to appear to his hometown crowd. | My dad buying Penguin Point pork tenderloins as we drove through Warsaw, heading home late at night on US 30, needing the comfort of deep-fried breaded pork, shredded cabbage, mayo, and a slice of cheese on a plain white bun. |
| My mom preferring Miracle Whip to mayonnaise for everything—in deviled eggs, coleslaw, and potato salad, on cold meat and fried egg sandwiches—and who's to say where Miracle Whip comes from? | What do these details say about my family's particular variation of Hoosierness? Or mine? Do my stories fit on the Indiana grid? What unevenness do I layer onto the topography? |

Of all Michael Martone's work, *Winesburg, Indiana,* a 2015 anthology featuring stories by more than two dozen Indiana authors, best illustrates how we patchwork our mythologies together but, like a highway mirage on a hundred-degree day, can never arrive at the places we seek.

When I asked Michael Martone if he'd ever driven from Fort Wayne to Chicago, he said he'd driven "many times up the old Lincoln Highway 30 that parallels the old Pennsy RR to see White Sox games and the art museum and Science and Industry Museum." "That," he said, "is why I put Winesburg, Indiana, near there near Columbia City."

Funny to find out at last the happenstance of how Michael Martone came to place Winesburg smackdab in familiar family territory for me, my eight sets of aunts, uncles, and cousins radiating out across Indiana from my two sets of grandparents—Burns and Tschantz—in Whitley County, my own nuclear family of four the satellite flung out farthest to that rental home at the corner of US 30 and 450 West where a postcard can no longer go, the abandoned house long gone, burned for firefighting practice by the Hanna Township Volunteer Fire Department in 2008.

I imagine my childhood home ablaze, black smoke rolling across all four lanes of traffic, every passerby slowing to notice, only I was not there to watch them from my second story window. I wonder if Michael Martone's childhood homes still stand. I could find out by asking, but I haven't. Maybe one day when visiting friends who live near Winesburg I will drive the extra twenty miles to Fort Wayne and find out.

I do not write much at my basement writing desk below the three canvases that, put together, show the height of summer in maybe-Indiana on maybe-US 30. I thought I would, and I've tried, but most often I choose my second-floor home office where, if I stand and look out the window, I can view the fence separating my small yard from the backsides of Eastside Lansing businesses and the parking lot that packs full on the weekends for the bars and live music. From my window's angle, I cannot see the Everybody Reads bookstore from where I ordered Michael Martone's *Plain Air: Sketches from Winesburg, Indiana* (2022) from my good friend Scott, but it comforts me to know the bookstore lives beyond my sight.

I like the idea that I wrote this sitting in my basement where the picture transported me away from the sound of the washing machine, the smell of litterboxes, the sight of cinderblock walls surrounding me on three sides. I like the idea, but I don't like to sit too long where dampness might settle into my skin, unlike the skin of Indiana where mildew blooms white, strange, and wonderful across the landscape of the ordinary.

# BONNIE JO CAMPBELL

## H House
## Comstock, Michigan

*By Lisa DuRose*

The Kalamazoo River flows right through the center of Comstock, Michigan, behind the library and township hall and the twenty-four-hour gas station. Past Merrill Park, where people feed bread to ducks. It floods every spring, drowning the playground equipment. Comstock was never on my must-see list, but Bonnie Jo Campbell convinced me otherwise.

As Bonnie and I trudged through the late spring mud, twisting through tall oaks and cherry trees, we arrived at the site of Bonnie's childhood home, where her mother, Susanna Campbell, greeted us. Built in the shape of an H (to represent the first letter of Bonnie's maternal grandfather's last name, Herlihy), the house appeared like a spacious cabin, set in the deep woods. Once inside, we sat on an enormous worn couch, an occasional leaf poking out behind cushions, the artificial boundary between the outside and inside blurring in the springtime afternoon sun. The high ceilings and huge wooden beams accented the four-by-ten picture windows, one of which overlooked a creek. Susanna entertained us with stories about her house (an expansive ranch-style cottage built by her father in 1947), her animals (milk cows, horses, donkeys, pigs, goats, and chickens), and raising her five kids as a single mother. Stacks of magazines, books, and newspapers occupied a large portion of the room, which was warmed by tongue-and-groove wood paneling, a limestone brick chimney, and a woodburning stove. Susanna seemed to know everyone in Comstock—store owners, local contractors, township officials, the postmaster—her connections stretching as far as the creek beside her house.

While the rural aspects of Comstock felt unfamiliar to me, having grown up in a working-class urban neighborhood in Saint Paul, Susanna's stories rang true. That walking tour and Bonnie's deep connections to the place evoked a sense of home in me during a time of pervasive homesickness. I was attending graduate school at Western Michigan University in Kalamazoo, just a few miles west of Comstock, and when I arrived in August 1993, I couldn't have been more disappointed. Everything felt lackluster and limited—the restaurant choices, the bookstores, the queer community. I was a twenty-two-year-old snob from the Twin Cities who disguised my homesickness in the veil of cultural arrogance. And so it was easy for me to dismiss the appeal of a place like Comstock. I suppose I just needed the right tour guide.

## BONNIE JO CAMPBELL

**Born: September 14, 1962, in Kalamazoo, Michigan**

**Died: —**

**Forms: Short Stories, Novels, Poetry, Essays**

**Recommended Works: *Women and Other Animals* (1999), *American Salvage* (2009), *Love Letters to Sons of Bitches* (2009), *Once Upon a River* (2011), *Mothers, Tell Your Daughters* (2015), *The Waters* (2024)**

One day in 1995, in the hallway outside my office, Bonnie appeared—a six-foot tower of cheerfulness and good humor. She struck a deep contrast to the rest of our graduate-student flock panicking over workshops and papers and commiserating about difficult students. Bonnie had just abandoned her sensible plan to complete a PhD in mathematics and—with the encouragement of her mathematics professor—decided to pursue her lifelong passion to write. She had already shed her doubt and misery, crying over mathematical proofs. Now here she was, confidently landing back on the familiar soil of southwest Michigan. Bonnie would spend the next three years in Western's MFA program, transforming family stories, town legends, and her razor-sharp observations on Comstock into her first major publication: *Women and Other Animals* (1999), a collection praised by *Publishers Weekly* for its portrayal of "misfits in middle America's economic and social fringe with subtle irony, rich imagery and loving familiarity, describing domestic worlds where Martha Stewart would fear to tread."

Getting a glimpse into Comstock—its modest, sometimes dilapidated homes, occasional dirt roads, ponds, woodlands, and railroad tracks—and meeting the formidable Susanna, any observer could see that the spark and material for Bonnie's writing lay right in front of her, ready for her to harness. A passage from her 2011 novel *Once Upon a River* demonstrates how carefully she depicts the impact of local industry on the rural beauty of southwest Michigan: "They all fished the snags at the edge of the river for bluegills, sunfish and rock bass, though they avoided the area just downstream of the Murray Metal Fabricating plant, where a drainpipe released a mixture of wastewater, machine oil, and solvents into the river—some of the fish there had strange tumors, bubbled flesh around their lips, a fraying at their gills. On certain windy days, the clay-colored smoke from the shop wafted along the river, reached them on their screen porches, and even when they closed their windows, the smoke entered their houses through the floorboards and the gaps around their doors."

Decades since her first publication, Bonnie has remained steadfast in her devotion to write accurately and lovingly about places like Comstock and the people who occupy these rural spaces. Her novels and short story collections, including the National Book Award finalist *American Salvage* (2009) are inspired by Comstock's landscape and industry. And nearly every character she has crafted, including those from her most recent novel, *The Waters* (2024), emerges from a rural Michigan terrain.

On a recent trip to Comstock, I would have astonished my twenty-two-year-old self: nostalgia washed over me. I arrived in late spring into the lush green Michigan landscape, lodging at the Campbell homestead, guarded by donkeys Jack and Don Quixote. The presence of Susanna Campbell, who died of cancer in September 2020, still presides. "H House," as Bonnie now calls it, has undergone some major cleaning and restoration. She hopes to transform the house, and its eight-acre lot, into a retreat for writers, musicians, and artists. A few yards from the house, just under a patch of pawpaw trees, Bonnie has set two memorial stones, one for Susanna and one for Susanna's sister, Joanna, who died in 2019. "She loved & was loved & she read a lot of books" is inscribed on Susanna's stone—so fitting for a mother who inspired a writer who sings the songs of Comstock and its people.

# SOJOURNER TRUTH

## Harmonia Cemetery
## Battle Creek, Michigan

*By Jeffrey Insko*

In the heart of downtown Battle Creek, Michigan, near the bank of the Kalamazoo River, stands a memorial statue of the abolitionist activist and orator Sojourner Truth. Twelve feet tall, bespectacled, and beshawled, Truth towers over an oversize lectern, presumably addressing an enrapt audience, her right hand resting on a Bible. Dedicated in 1999, the monument commemorates the twenty-seven years—the last twenty-seven years of her life—Truth spent in Battle Creek, much of it just across the river from the memorial site in the home on College Street that she bought in 1867.

But if you were to travel six miles downriver to Bedford Township, you might find, not far from the river's southern bank and perched on a hill at the edge of what is now an industrial park, Harmonia Cemetery, the last remaining vestige of the short-lived utopian community Truth joined when she first moved to Michigan in 1857. A year earlier, Truth had visited Battle Creek from her home in Northampton, Massachusetts, for the annual meeting of the Progressive Friends in Michigan, a group of dissident Quakers devoted to abolition, women's rights, and Spiritualism. Truth had been introduced to Spiritualism—the belief that the living could communicate with the dead—through her friends the radical reformers Isaac and Emily Post. During the first half of the 1850s, Truth attended other yearly meetings of Progressive Friends (sometimes called the Friends of Universal Human Progress) in New York and Pennsylvania, as well as séances and various antislavery gatherings with many of the period's leading reformers and social and religious dissenters.

## SOJOURNER TRUTH

**Born: 1797, in Swartekill, New York**

**Died: November 26, 1883, in Battle Creek, Michigan**

**Forms: Autobiography, Oratory**

**Recommended Works: *The Narrative of Sojourner Truth* (1850), "Ain't I a Woman?" (1851)**

The precise circumstances that caused Truth to decide to join the Progressive Friends in Michigan remain unknown. Well before the move, she had already earned renown and respect among abolitionists for her powerful speeches, sharp wit, and fierce activism; so it's easy to see why her Western friends would have been eager to have her join them. What's more, her time with the Northampton Association of Education and Industry, a mixed-race communitarian experiment she had joined in 1843, had accustomed her to living among like-minded radicals and troublemakers. Whatever her reasons, she sold her Northampton property and paid $400 for a lot and house in the fledgling village situated just south of the river, where the Hicksite Quaker Reynolds Cornell had purchased some 230 acres of land in 1850. Later, in 1855, he platted and parceled 140 of those acres into one-acre lots and incorporated the Village of Harmonia. Its name derived from the 1850 Swedenborgian philosophical tract *The Great Harmonia*, dictated, so the story goes, by the prominent Spiritualist Andrew Jackson Davis while entranced.

By 1855 the Battle Creek area was already a progressive haven, a welcoming home for the religiously and politically unorthodox, and a central hub for Western abolitionism. Cornell was active in the state's antislavery society. The city's first antislavery newspaper, *The Signal of Liberty*, launched in 1841, followed by the even more boisterously abolitionist paper, *The Michigan Liberty Press,* which ran from 1848 to 1849, when it was destroyed by fire. Battle Creek was also a station on the Underground Railroad, where so-called stationmasters like Erastus and Sarah Hussey—and Truth herself—assisted freedom seekers on their journeys from enslavement. It was home, too, to a small but thriving free Black community.

As for Harmonia, too little is recorded of its history, although we know the community was biracial, socially lively (it was rumored to be a bastion of free love!), and included, along with a store and a blacksmith shop, a seminary called the Bedford Institute, probably conducted according to Spiritualist tenets and run by Cornell's son Hiram. Census records indicate that Truth's grandson Samuel Banks attended the school for at least one year in 1859. Vibrant though it may have been, the community remained small; as late as 1873 it appears that relatively few of the original lots were occupied with houses. Even worse, a tornado swept through the village in 1862, destroying much of it and shearing the top two floors off the four-story school. The next year the Cornells moved away from Michigan, and Truth appears to have moved from Harmonia about the same time, though she left the house to her daughter Sophia, who lived there with her family for another thirty years. In 1867 Truth purchased and moved into the house on College Street.

Other than a handful of headstones, almost all visible traces of Harmonia have long since been erased, overwhelmed by the twin forces of empire and industrialization. During the First World War, the land of utopian dreams was converted into a military training ground named, unfortunately, for the Michigan native and disgraced army general George Armstrong Custer; the schoolhouse itself was converted, literally, into a gun school. Today, Fort Custer remains a National Guard training center. The rest of the area hosts an industrial park populated mainly by facilities that produce automotive parts. Earlier this year, when a local historian set out to pinpoint the precise location of Truth's Harmonia residence, plat maps revealed that the site is now the recycling center at a thermal manufacturing plant.

At the bottom of the hill, the Kalamazoo River has been for centuries the life-giving artery of the region for indigenous peoples, settlers, and utopians alike, but it has suffered from decades of industrial pollution, not least the million gallons of diluted bitumen that gushed into the river after an oil pipeline burst just upriver from Battle Creek in 2010. Four years and a billion dollars' worth of cleanup after the spill improved the condition of the river considerably, but a significant amount of unrecoverable oil still remains. West of Battle Creek, areas of the river remain contaminated with the long-ago banned industrial chemicals polychlorinated biphenyls, or PCBs. Ongoing mitigation efforts at those sites have been severely hampered recently by a botched dam drawdown in 2021 that released hundreds of thousands of cubic yards of sludge and sediment, smothering fish spawning habitats and creating massive mudflats. The river suffers still.

How many times, one wonders, must Truth and her comrades have crossed that unspoiled river, planning for justice? Even more terribly, perhaps, the route taken by that same pipeline as it traverses the state on its way to petrochemical refineries in Ontario uncannily follows the pathway to freedom taken by hundreds of the formerly enslaved, who were seeking refuge, not toxins, on the other side of the border. Underground transport today portends ecocide and planetary destruction rather than freedom. Which is to say that now, as much as then, we need Sojourner Truth's expansive vision of justice. We also need more of the courage she displayed in pursuit of it.

# JIM HARRISON

## Mixed Coniferous Forest
## Osceola County, Michigan

*By Camden Burd*

"What we think of our hometown is our first substantial map of the world," Jim Harrison wrote in his 2002 memoir, *Off to the Side*. A hometown takes the misshapen clay of a person and molds them, stands them up, and positions them in some vague direction. For Harrison, that was Reed City, Michigan—a rural town in Osceola County, situated in the northern portion of the state's lower peninsula—where his family lived for much of his childhood. It was there, in a region defined by poor soil, long winters, and geographic isolation, where Harrison would cultivate the literary perspective that informed his essays, poetry, and novels.

There was nothing romantic about life in central Michigan at the middle of the twentieth century. It was rural, not wild, and definitely not idyllic. Hardship abounded. Harrison remembered ever-present poverty, in his family and with others. "Fate has never ladled out hardship very evenly," he wrote. "Symmetry, balance, ultimate fairness seem to be abstractions remote to our occasionally naked sense of reality, as startling as walking out of a crisp and idealized civics class at a country school and into a lavish party of congressman and lobbyists." He recalled eating at friends' homes—minimal meals that included catsup sandwiches or a plate of beans. It is no wonder that his boyhood heroes included Eugene V. Debs and Walter Reuther.

## JIM HARRISON

**Born: December 11, 1937, in Grayling, Michigan**

**Died: March 26, 2016, in Patagonia, Arizona**

**Forms: Poetry, Novels, Memoir**

**Recommended Works: *Legends of the Fall* (1979), *Dalva* (1988), *The Road Home* (1998), *Jim Harrison Complete Poems* (2021), *True North* (2004)**

But Harrison did not conflate sympathy with sentimentalism. He never waxed nostalgically about the inherent values of his neighbors. Poor residents of rural Michigan—like their wealthy counterparts—could steal, lust, and lie too. Reed City also exposed a young Harrison to the tragic throughline of humanity. After a childhood accident involving a feuding neighbor and a glass bottle, he lost vision in his left eye. The accident, and a subsequent failed surgery, left him in a severe state of depression that would come and go throughout his life. Years later, his father and sister were killed in a car accident while driving on a Michigan highway. For Harrison, the human experience was defined by hardship—which was not shared equally.

The environments of northern Michigan provided temporary respite from his own depression and the realities of rural life. Amid the scattered forests and fields surrounding Reed City, Harrison found a landscape that absorbed him. "The natural world would always be there to save me from suffocating in my human problems." He believed that wandering the woods, studying birds, fishing, and a general curiosity for the natural world could "lift you out of your self-sunken mudbath, the violent mixture of hormones, injuries, melancholy, and dreams of a future you not only couldn't touch but could scarcely see." It is important to note that Harrison rarely framed such excursions as an antidote to the modern world. His conception of nature did not fit the simplistic framework of civilization versus wilderness—a dichotomy he believed mostly spoke to upper- and middle-class men who invented the concept to bolster their own ideas of masculinity. "There is nothing quite so fatuous as a man self-consciously trying to act manly," he writes in *Off to the Side.* Harrison immersed himself in the natural world for one simple reason: "Because that's how I grew up."

After several fits and starts Harrison received undergraduate and graduate degrees from Michigan State University. He worked in publishing for a short time in Boston and later received an offer to teach at SUNY Stony Brook. But he couldn't shake the landscapes of his youth and, after two years of teaching, moved back to Michigan, first to Kingsley and then to a farm in Leelanau County. He regularly visited a small, remote cabin near Grand Marais. In *Off to the Side* he notes that these places "would appear nondescript and scrubby to those who favor the cordillera of the Rockies but to me it was homeground, similar to the terrain around Reed City where I had grown up." Grand mountain ranges seemed almost vain to the writer, who preferred a bedraggled forest on sandy soil. The excursion into the natural world was not about summits or vistas. It was about losing oneself in the commonplace environments he knew near Reed City.

Settled in northern Michigan and connected to the landscapes of his youth, Harrison found literary momentum. He wrote his first novel, *Wolf: A False Memoir*, in 1971 and quickly followed with *A Good Day to Die* (1973), *Farmer* (1976), and *Warlock* (1981). The author preferred to focus on characters of unassuming backgrounds: bad farmers, lazy detectives, floundering professionals—nearly all of whom suffered from a life crisis or deep depression. All his characters were flawed. Most were unlikeable.

Harrison's protagonists were poor, and those who weren't carried traits that signaled to readers the politics that Harrison had carried since childhood. The protagonist in *True North* (2004), David, spends his life rebuking his family's legacy—lumber barons who clear-cut the forest of Michigan's Upper Peninsula during the region's mining boom. He despises his inherited wealth, disowns his father (a sexual predator), and commits his entire life to researching his family's environmental destruction. It is mostly a solo project, a type of penance for inheriting the family name. Over the course of several decades, David stews, guilty and ashamed. He only finds temporary relief by staying in an austere cabin in the dense northern woods where he can take regular walks and escape his own "self-sunken mudbath." In *True North,* as in many of his other works, these woods are the landscapes where Harrison's characters find brief sanctum.

The author's own relationship to Michigan's rural landscapes can be seen through his characters. In short, they wander in the woods to cope with their own traumas. The forests and fields, like those near Harrison's boyhood home, helped to lift the cognitive baggage of life. As he noted in *Off to the Side*, the landscape could "draw away your poisons to the point that your curiosity takes over and 'you,' the accumulation of wounds and concomitant despair, no longer exist."

The place consumes you so that your mind can't. Exploring Harrison's boyhood landscapes, I couldn't help but feel the scenic humility. Osceola County's forests and prairies never stuck me as particularly iconic or overwhelmingly picturesque. However, while meandering through the brush, tall grasses, and stilted pine, I found that time had been distorted, my consciousness muted. And in my own navigation of these landscapes, I also came to understand how they had been foundational in shaping Harrison's "map of the world."

# ROBERT HAYDEN

## Paradise Valley
## Detroit, Michigan

*By Ayesha K. Hardison*

Robert Hayden's poems are artifacts from a long-gone yet storied neighborhood in Detroit. He grew up in Paradise Valley, the near east side commercial district adjacent to the more residential community called Black Bottom (named originally for its rich soil). Similarly, Hayden's biography is a palimpsest for the lost and resistive. Born Asa Bundy Sheffey in 1913, he discovered, at forty years old, his parents William and Sue Ellen Hayden neither adopted him nor legally changed his name when they committed to foster him. In the poem "Names," he writes, "You don't exist—" a problem his narrator struggles to resolve: "As ghost, double, alter ego then?" Hayden's old neighborhood, like his representation of it, has an analogously complicated history.

Once a mixed-race community with Jewish, German, and Italian households living alongside African American families, Paradise Valley was one of few areas where Southern migrants could move in Detroit, and in the 1920s it became a Black enclave. With over three hundred Black-owned businesses, including medical offices, retail shops, hotels, restaurants,

## ROBERT HAYDEN

**Born: August 4, 1913, in Detroit, Michigan**

**Died: February 25, 1980, in Ann Arbor, Michigan**

**Forms: Poetry, Essays**

**Recommended Works: *Heart-Shape in the Dust* (1940), *Figure of Time* (1955), *A Ballad of Remembrance* (1962), *Words in the Morning Time* (1970), *Collected Poems* (1985)**

and nightclubs, the district was the center of Black economic fortitude in the ensuing decades. Throughout the 1930s, the Haydens lived on St. Antoine, Beacon, and Napoleon Streets as well as East Vernor Highway. While these streets still exist, waves of urban development have altered their geography.

By the late 1940s Detroit initiated its urban renewal by demolishing old, dilapidated housing and, later, constructing the Chrysler Freeway, the northbound section of I-75 and I-375, to accommodate autoworkers who followed manufacturing to the suburbs. The interstate was completed in 1964, destroying Hastings Street, a major Black Bottom and Paradise Valley thoroughfare, and sounding the neighborhoods' death knell. Since the early 2000s Ford Field and its parking lots have supplanted some of this landscape, including the corner of Beacon and St. Antoine where the Haydens once lived.

Other landmarks mapping Hayden's career are distinguished by historic property, new construction, and everything in-between. Falcon Press, which published Hayden's inaugural collection, *Heart-Shape in the Dust* (1940), was located at 268 Eliot Street, the home of Louis E. Martin. Editor of the *Michigan Chronicle*, Martin founded the Black weekly newspaper in a one-room office on St. Antoine in 1936 and hired Hayden to join the newsroom stationed in his dining room. Presently, a 5,663-square-foot vacant lot sits there, flanked by a Georgian Colonial built in 1900 and contemporary brick condos. The empty space marks the publisher's absence in the neighborhood now called Brush Park.

Hayden's poems about the city, then, are artistic signs outlining historic negative space. Paradise Valley is source material for his Depression-era poems, such as "Sunflowers: Beaubien Street" and "Bacchanal." In the latter, published in *Negro Caravan* (1941), Hayden's blues-infused narrator laments his lost factory job and bemoans his lover seduced by "one of these Hasting studs." Finally, in the fifth poem from "Elegies for Paradise Valley," published in his last collection, *American Journal* (1978), Hayden invokes the disappeared people of the neighborhood:

> Where's Nora, with her laugh, her comic flair,
> stagestruck Nora waiting for her chance?
> Where's fast Iola, who so loved to dance
> she left her sickbed one last time to whirl
> in silver at The Palace till she fell?

Hayden also inquires about the "mad," "snuffdipping," "defeated," "shellshocked," "taunted," and those who passed for white, "who cursing crossed the color line." He concludes with the repeated line, "Let vanished rooms, let dead streets tell."

Old street names memorialize such corporeal absence but obscure it with their new orientations. As Hayden elucidates in a 1978 documentary, "I had Beacon Street in mind when I wrote the poem, 'Dead Streets' because there are no people there now." Hayden's *Heart-Shape in the Dust* is an elegy for the neighborhood, too, as it eponymously documents Falcon Press's ephemerality. Paradise Valley is a metonym for the people celebrated in Hayden's poems, like Phillis Wheatley, Frederick Douglass, Bessie Smith, and Malik ElShabazz. In turn, Detroit's ongoing transition—from suburban expansion and deindustrialization to corporate returns and economic recovery—give added meaning to his compositions. "How clearly you / materialize," he promises in the fourth elegy to Paradise Valley, "before the eye / of memory—"

Note: Except where noted, all poems cited from *Robert Hayden: Collected Poems* (1996) were edited by Frederick Glaysher. This essay's literary and cultural history draws on the work of Melba Joyce Boyd, Frank Rashid, Ronald Walcott, and the Detroit Historical Society.

# PAUL VASEY

## Ambassador Bridge
## Michigan—Ontario Border

*By Ramya Swayamprakash*

I grew up in India. I have now lived in the United States, and in Michigan, for almost a decade. But I cannot claim to be from Michigan or India—it is hard to call a place your home when your connection to it is defined by a temperamental piece of paper. Emotionally and geographically, I feel like a vagabond, without a place to root me. As much as I feel that lack of place, my entire adult life has been guided by rivers. I have followed them to their sources high in the Himalayas, chanced upon some of their most magical beginnings in Tibet, and written about their entrapment in peninsular India. I grew up listening to stories about these rivers. Rivers have been home, intellectually.

Yet when it came to the river that I have written and thought about for the past decade, I did not know of it until I met it. The first time I flew over the Detroit River, in 2013, was the first time I even heard of it. Growing up in India, I was familiar with New York and San Francisco. Much of the Midwest was a blob, with the Great Lakes at its center. At the time, Detroit was just beginning to be in the news because of its financial situation. When the captain announced we were flying over the Detroit River, I did a double take

## PAUL VASEY

**Born: April 15, 1947, in Southampton, England**

**Died: —**

**Forms: Memoir, Novels, Nonfiction**

**Recommended Works: *A Troublesome Boy* (2007), *The River: A Memoir of Life in the Border Cities* (2011)**

and wondered whether this was a chicken and egg situation—which came first, the river or the city. The answer, as I was soon to find out, was inconsequential.

The larger story has always been how this river strait has become what author Paul Vasey calls "a fabric" of our lives, a part of "our vocabulary." I was recommended Vasey's 2013 memoir *The River: A Memoir of Life in the Border Cities* by one of my dissertation advisors, and I read it during the summer of 2017 when I was in Windsor, Ontario, finishing up archival research for my dissertation. In the shadow of its more famous neighbor, Windsor was an interesting vantage point to be researching from and reading about. I used *The River* as a sort of guide to walk the city and get to know it better. The Detroit River looms large in Vasey's imagination in ways that I had not factored until I read the book and walked the city myself. The river was as much a wayfinding device as it was the edge of theater—you could watch an entire city go by on the other side if you sat long enough. There was a rootedness to the river that I had not yet found on the other side of the river and border. I spent a wonderous afternoon speaking with retired ship captains at the Marsh Collection in Amherstburg, understanding the river and specifically the infrastructures that I would then spend half a decade writing about—and that I continue to gush about.

The river was everywhere and never too far that summer in Windsor. The air was muggy and humid, and winds blew little or no smoke from Zug Island. It reminded me of summers long ago, in Bombay, a lifetime and half a world away. That summer, as I kayaked across from Walkerville to Peche Island, it was breathtaking. The summer sun lit up the water into a magical shade of blue, and the ruins of Hiram Walker's mansion seemed to come alive. If you squinted enough, you'd experience some time travel. From the main shipping channel on the other side of the island, the familiar but jarring sound of a massive laker—a ship that plies the Great Lakes—might wake you up from your reverie, just in time to head back to the mainland and across the border.

These memories are perhaps just my rose-tinted glasses, but as I remember it the river seemed more open—more welcoming—on the Canadian side. A decade ago, it was also just easier to get to the Detroit River from the Canadian bank and sit by it, watching it, just as Vasey did, "rolling past with ducks and gulls on its back, the ocean on its mind." It was a centering experience. As trucks crawled by on Ambassador Bridge, standing under it at Assumption Park, I would gaze at the Michigan Central Station.

Walking under Ambassador Bridge along the riverfront trail, near some maintenance workers, I spotted a laker. This is the park where Vasey talks about the history of Jesuits landing along the southern bank of the river. On that summer day, as I looked onto Assumption Church and the bridge, Vasey's descriptions of the park swam in my head. It was, however, the people of Windsor whose descriptions really occupied my mind. Vasey paints Windsor with the love of an insider-outsider, a feeling I understand deeply.

My biased view of the river may have been filtered by the political border, which while silent and unproblematic for most North Americans, remains an anxiety-inducing experience for immigrants and those individuals with "weak" passports like mine. Taking a day trip to Windsor was a thrill, not least because I was crossing into another country with ease. I was even welcomed with a smile! Crossing back into the US was a lot scarier. For those of us with weak passports, borders are real, and as much as I enjoyed *The River,* I found myself jealous of the author's obliviousness to the barrier. I wanted to feel that obliviousness for a minute.

I do not quite know how to explain my relationship with this river. It is unremarkable on the surface, but every time I am near, it feels like home. While I may never be oblivious to the border, the river has never judged me for the misfortunes of geography. Standing on its banks, geological time rolling by while I try and write about humans, I feel humbled, mesmerized by everything this body of water—which flushes every twenty hours or so—has seen. I have spent a decade trying to understand and tell these stories. These tales and their river have grounded and sustained me. As a person, I am very much a work in progress, but this river and everything it does are the closest thing I have to a "home," at least one rooted in place.

Taking my toddler to meet the river last spring was a special homecoming, my worlds colliding in the best possible way. Yet when my toddler asked to go to the Canadian bank where the parks looked cooler, I had to say no. My child holds a stronger passport than I do. The border that was immaterial to my child was very much visible to me, with a weak passport in my back pocket. If we crossed over, my toddler could return at the drop of a hat, but I could not. One does not need a wall to see the border divide everywhere—you just need to carry a weak passport.

As I was writing this, stuck in Canada awaiting my passport with a US visa stamp, sometimes my toddler would wistfully ask for their passport to cross the border "home" to go shop at Target, since the Great White North lacks that convenience. For the first time in their life, the border has become visible. As a parent I feel guilty about taking away their obliviousness. As a scholar, I hope this will enable more careful attention to and, someday, abolition of borders, at least in our minds. Either way, we will wait, gazing at the sun-kissed waters of the Great Lakes, thinking about making homes.

Note: For further reading on "passportism," the discrimination against people holding passports from certain countries and its uncritical acceptance by citizens of wealthier nations, see Shahnaz Habib, *Airplane Mode: An Irreverent History of Travel* (2023).

# PHILIP LEVINE

## Belle Isle
## Waawiiyaatanong

*By Daniel A. Lockhart*

I've come to the river, as one does frequently in Waawiiyaatanong, in the closing weeks of winter. The land has begun to wake up from the snow and the river itself contains patchworks of ice, a south sliding quilt of the lakes above us. The air is thick with fog, giving the world an evenness of white and gray. Punctuated by the restless patterns of geese and swans rejoicing over the return of open water. Across from where I stand, separated by the Fleming Channel of the Detroit River, is the jewel of an urban park, Belle Isle. I am reminded of the island and the city across the water from us nearly hourly, as the clarion tower sings out its song across the water and the city streets between. What is before me in this moment is that spirit made real. A near translucent moment of a city in the clouds, an island at its heart.

To think, this is the same restless river in which, in his poem "Belle Isle, 1949," Levine and his Polish high school girl were baptized "in the brine / of car parts, dead fish, stolen bicycles, / melted snow." The river of industrial stove making, the river before the monumental decline of the great Horatio Algerian city, the river that is hardly visible past the row of phantom trees that make up the horizon that used to be, and still is, the island anchor of Levine's poem. Today, even the vision of the opposite bank is gone, and the river is a nexus of dull light. Sharp edges of fluorescent modern Detroit, and Windsor for that matter, are absent. I have loved the constellation of skyscraper lights that dominate us here. Even in daylight they are gone. But here, alone, I am smudged by the warming mist of snow as the spring sun finds its way in.

## PHILIP LEVINE

**Born: January 10, 1928, in Detroit, Michigan**

**Died: February 14, 2015, in Fresno, California**

**Forms: Poetry, Essays**

**Recommended Works: *The Names of the Lost* (1976), *Ashes: Poems Old and New* (1979), *What Work Is* (1991), *The Simple Truth* (1994), *The Bread of Time: Toward an Autobiography* (1994), *The Misery* (1999)**

Is this the perfect calm of the water between city and island? "Turning at last to see no island at all / but a perfect calm dark as far as there was sight." Before me, that darkness chased away and the river sheened as if it had never known of the Griffon, a burning Rouge River, the gore of Bloody Run. This river is a different river than Levine's—more ancient, freed from ore haulers, the shadow of stoves, the traffic of Jefferson. Freed, at least temporarily, between shipping seasons. Across the river there are certainly drums. A passing car on the island's ring road, hidden in the dense fog bank hovering above shore. There is no possibility of touching the river beyond. Signs warn of its threat on the metal fence that separates us. Alone. There is no woman, there is no warmth of another in all of this. The river is changed. And it is light now. And I find myself lost in thoughts of the warmth of a lover's breath upon my skin. Taken by the heavy cold in the air around me, I understand that each time is of itself. The spirit lives on. But the impermanence of the world allows, at best, for anchors in our memories. We no longer build stoves. Few of us swim in the river. The water is undisturbed as it passes before me, its surface defiant and purposeful like sturgeon skin. And the world is the white of an elder's hair; wèlathakèt returned. And it is quiet, while the river slides by in her earliest stages of waking in this, the earliest hours of spring. Moving us, in silence, "back where we came from."

TONI MORRISON

## TONI MORRISON

Born: February 18, 1931, in Lorain, Ohio

Died: August 5, 2019, in New York, New York

Forms: Novels, Essays, Drama, Children's Literature

Recommended Works: *The Bluest Eye* (1970), *Sula* (1973), *Song of Solomon* (1977), *Tar Baby* (1981), *Beloved* (1987), *Playing in the Dark: Whiteness and the Literary Imagination* (1992), *Paradise* (1998), *A Mercy* (2008), *What Moves at the Margin: Selected Nonfiction* (2008), *Home* (2012), *The Source of Self-Regard: Selected Essays, Speeches, and Meditations* (2019)

# TONI MORRISON

## Childhood Home
## Lorain, Ohio

*By Tara L. Conley*

> This region (Lorain, Elyria, Oberlin) is not like it was when I lived here, but in a way it doesn't matter because home is a memory and companions and/or friends who share the memory. But equally important as the memory and place and people of one's personal home is the very idea of home. What do we mean when we say "home"?
> —Toni Morrison, *The Source of Self Regard*

In astronomy, there's an idea that describes how displacement and difference observed in a perceived object depends on the viewpoint, the location from which the object is observed. Parallax, from the Greek word *parallaxis* (meaning *change*), is a multidimensional way of seeing. In literature, and by extension film, parallax is a device sometimes used to tell a story about a single event, place, or person through the perspective of multiple characters. James Joyce's *Ulysses* (1920) employs parallax, as does Netflix's *Kaleidoscope* (2023) and *Knives Out* (2020–2022), and David Fincher's 2014 psychological thriller, *Gone Girl*.

In my classroom, when I discuss the idea of social difference, I hold up a marker. I ask students to describe exactly what they see from their vantage point. Each description is slightly different: "It's plastic and round," one student says. "It's hard to see from where I sit," says another. The story of the marker, as told by my students, contains multitudes. The point of this exercise is to show how perceived differences depend on perception and to demonstrate how the relationship between subject and object is mediated. Perception is never truly unidirectional, and is instead affected by our memory, ways of knowing and being, and sense of place and environment. We don't so much observe objects *out there* as we become affected by the experience of seeing.

I've been thinking a lot about parallax lately as I revisit previous writings on Toni Morrison, fellow Ohioan and Lorain County native. During the summer of 2019 I published a piece for *CityLab/Bloomberg* about visiting Toni Morrison's childhood home in Lorain a few days after she passed. My article was among others published at the time that highlighted Morrison's legacy as a Pulitzer Prize–winning novelist and cherished luminary on the Black American experience. I took a different approach, writing instead about the shape of borders, real and imagined, that make up the regional landscape both Morrison and I call home.

In *The Source of Self Regard* (2019), when Morrison asks, "What do we mean when we say 'home'?" I think about our shared home region of Lorain County, the shape of its borders, and the houses that hold memories of growing up during eras of radical social and political transformation. Born mid-February 1931, during the Great Depression, Morrison's early life in Lorain was marked by an era of cataclysmic economic downfall. Born on the first day of February in 1981, amid an economic recession, my early life in Elyria was marked by the rise of neoliberal economic reforms and New Right political movements. Despite the half-century gap between us, underlined by different eras of social and political strife, Morrison and I belong to a shared ancestral line of Black American travelers who migrated to Ohio, seeking an escape from the south—what sociologist Karida L. Brown calls "the battered womb of the Civil War."

The decades spanning roughly 1910 to 1970 transformed Ohio's landscapes. During this historical period, known as the Great Migration, Black people left the South to seek opportunities in Midwestern cities like Elyria and Lorain. Once bustling, the region gradually decayed as industries left, businesses shut down, and economic progress stalled. For many, including my own family members, this fostered a visceral sense of being stuck in time. Amid the circumstances, Black people were especially vulnerable to the repercussions of these changes and subject to racial resentment as social institutions crumbled around them.

Even the Black River, a natural tributary that flows into Lake Erie and connects Elyria and Lorain, was once a thriving center of commerce. As time passed, however, it became known for its polluted and treacherous waters that claimed the lives of those who ventured too close to its shores. The story of the Black River became a parable of the sower—once vibrant and then weathered by time, reflecting the place and dispositions of the people surrounding it.

Black travelers have always been keenly aware of landscapes that bend and close in on us. We also recognize when it's time to leave. Morrison understood this too. She left Lorain in 1949 to attend Howard University in Washington, DC, and soon realized the price Black Americans pay when leaving home. During an interview with Colette Dowling in 1979 Morrison said, "If black people are going to succeed in this culture, they must always leave." She continued:

> Once you leave home, the things that feed you are not available to you anymore, the *life* is not available to you anymore. . . . So you really have to cut yourself off.

I left Ohio at a young age, but unlike Morrison I returned to live, teach, and make stories about home. One of those stories is my documentary film, called *Dry Bones*, about Ike Maxwell and the summer of 1975 when Elyria erupted in protest after Ike's brother, nineteen-year-old Daryl Lee Maxwell, was shot and killed by a White police officer. Regardless of where I lived geographically, I always remained tied to northeast Ohio. The reason I returned isn't merely rooted in having been born and raised in Lorain County; rather, it's the region's story of social difference that draws me back.

In 2019, when I returned home to Lorain County, I noticed how neighborhood symbols and historical landmarks came to represent racial and social division. For example, while driving toward Toni Morrison's former childhood home—a modest, two-story, pale-blue colonial at the corner of Elyria Avenue and East 23rd Street—it was difficult to miss the house across the street, a large "Trump 2020" banner waving on the porch. It stood as a clear and intentional symbol of White racist attitudes and beliefs in one of Lorain County's most heavily populated Black cities. It also served as a reminder that, within shared landscapes, disparate realities exist. Four miles away, in Elyria, sits the YWCA building, a historical landmark located across the street from my childhood home. When I learned Daryl Lee Maxwell was arrested in the YWCA parking lot during the summer of 1975, bleak visions emerged of a young man I never knew heading toward the end of his life. Less than one month after Daryl Lee was arrested in the YWCA parking lot, a White police officer named Michael Killean shot and killed him outside a local bar, igniting a three-day protest and uprising. These moments, separated by time and space and imbued with rememory, reveal the legacy of White power in America, persisting through its symbols of supremacy and authoritarian acts of violence.

Morrison's childhood home in Lorain and mine in Elyria provide vantage points to reflect on the perpetual shadow of racial subjugation in our shared home region. Through a contemporary political symbol of White resentment and a nearby historical landmark of a haunting past, the answer to Morrison's question about home crystalizes for me; home isn't merely a broken place of shared memories or a place where Black travelers come and go. Home reveals a way of seeing, with searing clarity, Black people's enduring resilience across cruel landscapes.

# TONI MORRISON

## Lakeview Park
## Lorain, Ohio

*By Ashley Burge*

As a teenager I entered what Toni Morrison calls her narrative "village" through her first book, *The Bluest Eye* (1970), and I was pleased to see three young Black girls traverse the familiar experiences of home life while prodding the unfamiliar territory of adolescence. I found much comfort in these girls' fantasies and fears, and I wept, as I still do, over their tragedies. I was also entranced by the way Morrison framed her beautifully tragic characters in picturesque settings of nature and growth and beauty. Any serious Morrison reader is well attuned to her complex and intriguing characters, sparse but rich prose, and "unspeakable" thematic materials. I remember sprawling on my bed admiring these Black girls amid golden-brown autumn leaves or tight red rosebuds. To me, these snapshots of nature were a buffer to the hopelessly tragic story that would soon unfold.

In *The Bluest Eye*, Morrison uses the backdrop of Lorain, Ohio, her midwestern hometown, to illuminate the traumas inflicted on young Black girls and women in the 1940s. Specifically, she represents the Edenic Lakeview Park, with its beautiful rose gardens, situated among the pristine beachfronts on West Erie Avenue, as a pathway to cathartic revelation and renewal. For Morrison, nature and the natural world are a catalyst for survival; so the book's version of Lakeview, called Lake Shore Park, is an ideal space to anchor her vision.

Lakeview Park has become a landmark in Lorain County with its approximately 2,500 roses planted in a rotary wheel. The park sits on Lake Erie, its circular design symbolizing wholeness and rebirth. In a more just world, it would be the ideal space for Morrison's tragic protagonists to transcend the confines of intersectional oppression. But in 1940s Lorain, Ohio, spaces such as these were inaccessible to the three Black girls who epitomize themes of victimhood and survival in Middle America. In *The Bluest Eye*, these girls, Claudia, Fredia, and Pecola, are accosted by the traumas of racism, sexism, and classism well before they have escaped the naive joy and confusion of adolescence. The tragic character Pecola does not understand or question her obsessive desire for blue eyes, but she is awestruck when the green-eyed "high-yellow dream child" Maureen Peal enchants teachers, parents, and students. Portrayed as a type of Persephone embodied in Morrison's season-themed narrative, Maureen disrupts the equilibrium of the girls' identities and symbolizes the overwhelming otherness of Black girlhood in America. In these young girls' experiences with racism and sexism, Morrison interrogates the worst possible scenarios for those who are othered, marginalized, and dismissed, and she indicts the communities that are complicit in their annihilation.

In many ways, *The Bluest Eye* is an autobiographical rendering of Morrison's own othered identity in the small Midwestern industrial town of Lorain, Ohio. Morrison adamantly affirmed her Midwestern roots throughout her career. In conversation with Collette Dowling she said, "Everything I write starts there. . . . Whether I end up there is another question, but that's the place where I start. . . . It's my beginning, my 'thing,' and I have distorted it, piled things on, I have done whatever it is that writers do to places, and made it my own. So it is mine now." Even while claiming the Midwest as her own, she confessed to Robert Stepto, "I know that I never felt like an American or an Ohioan or even a Lorainite."

Morrison's allegiance to the Midwest shows in her ability to carve out the validity of Black identity in a region that often silences diverse voices. Morrison's family faced such disenfranchisement. Before relocating to the Midwest for better opportunities, they had deep roots in the South, with her mother being from Alabama and her father from Georgia. She often recounts the story of eighty-eight acres of land that were legally taken from her Native American maternal great-grandmother to show how white supremacy and systematic oppression renders land inaccessible to Black and brown people.

Morrison emphasizes this extension of day-to-day oppression in *The Bluest Eye* as she traces the growth and then disintegration of Pecola's character. Before a pivotal scene in which Pecola is rejected by her mother and humiliated in front of the little white girl who her mother cares for, Morrison details the natural beauty of the white neighborhood that these young girls cannot access:

> We reached Lake Shore Park, a city park laid out with rosebuds, fountains, bowling greens, picnic tables. It was empty now, but sweetly expectant of clean, white, well-behaved children and parents who would play there above the lake in summer before half-running, half stumbling down the slope to the welcoming water. Black people were not allowed in the park, and so it filled our dreams.

Here Morrison embosses the fictionalized Lake Shore Park onto Lorain's own Lakeview Park, with its lush rose gardens, manicured lawns, and picturesque lakeside. The tragedy of its beauty is that these young Black girls in 1940s Lorain are denied access to the dream of smelling those rosebuds, playing on those lawns, or frolicking on that lakeside. They are shut out from its beauty in nature and, therefore, alienated from their community, which adds to the despair that leads to Pecola's demise.

When I reflect on my first immersion into *The Bluest Eye* as a teenager, I realize that my delight in Morrison's poetic rendering of nature points to the reclamation of spaces that have been historically inaccessible to the Black community. Within that legalized denial enacted prior to the 1960s there was not only the unspoken denial of the ecstasy of nature but also the disenfranchisement of property, wealth, and mobility that still plagues Black Americans today. I was not personally denied access to Lorain's natural enclaves, but the tragic narrative of denial was a tangible specter that haunted my hometown of Birmingham, Alabama, even in my adolescence.

These are, perhaps, the sentiments that were impressed on me as I empathized with Claudia, Frieda, and Pecola. And these are, perhaps, the sentiments that many Black Americans must navigate as they encounter the traumas connected to public parks and natural resources in America. It would not be difficult to surmise that Morrison incorporates the tragic denial of Lake Shore Park in her narrative because her desire to access its beauty and nature also dominated her own dreams as a child. However, Morrison's novels never persist in the tragic or linger too long in despair. At their core, they are about healing that can lead to survival and subjectivity. In *The Bluest Eye*, Morrison took the pang of rejection and adorned the park with flourish and meaning and gravitas and three little Black girls whose voices would have otherwise been silenced. Now, Lakeview Park is forever hers, and through her reclamation, it becomes ours.

# TONI MORRISON

## *Cleveland Is the Reason* mural
## Cleveland, Ohio

*By Monique Wingard*

In the tapestry of life, sometimes the threads that pull us away are the same ones that guide us back home. In 2013 the job market in Cleveland had left me feeling shut out, unwanted, unworthy. I hit the road for a job in Chicago, in pursuit of a better life. After ten years away I came back to be closer to home. When I returned, while walking through downtown Cleveland, a striking mural caught my eye. There, prominently displayed on the side of a building at 334 Euclid Avenue, alongside LeBron James and Tracy Chapman, was the face of Toni Morrison—Nobel laureate, Pulitzer Prize winner, and Ohio's own literary giant.

As I stood before Morrison's portrait on that Euclid Avenue wall, it was her smile that ignited my renewed sense of purpose and belonging. The mural, commissioned by Browns player Myles Garrett and created by Glen Infante, welcomes visitors near the Destination Cleveland convention center, and it now serves as a powerful reminder of Morrison's legacy and the potential within every Black woman from Ohio to persevere in the face of adversity.

After nearly a decade away, I felt a surge of emotions as I stood before Morrison's mural. The vibrant colors and bold lines captured not just her likeness but her spirit—unapologetic, fierce, and inspiring. As I gazed at the mural with my mother by my side, I was struck by a sense of homecoming and responsibility. Morrison's watchful eyes seemed to ask, "What will you contribute to our shared legacy?"

This mural takes on even greater significance in light of recent statistics. In 2020 Bloomberg CityLab published a report analyzing Black women's quality of life (based on health, education, and economic factors) in forty-two US cities. Shockingly, Cleveland—with its nearly 50 percent Black population—ranked dead last. This statistic is sobering, but it's crucial to understand its context. While the label of "worst city for Black women" holds some truth, it also leaves room for change and renaissance. It should prompt us to demand that Black women and organizations in Cleveland remember their power and responsibility to advocate relentlessly for each other and for a better life in the city.

Morrison once told an audience of college students, "The function of freedom is to free someone else." Her words resonate powerfully, encapsulating the responsibility we have as Black women in Ohio—to lift as we climb, to create opportunities for those who come after us, and to transform our communities. The mural reminds us of this responsibility. It challenges us to stand up, be counted, and hold ourselves and our community accountable. It urges us to be persistent in our pursuit to change Cleveland and uplift the entire state of Ohio.

As we look upon Morrison's face on that Euclid Avenue wall, we must ask ourselves, How can we embody her spirit of unapologetic Blackness and unwavering determination? How can we weave our own threads into Morrison's tapestry of Black womanhood?

We can start by:

1. Supporting and uplifting other Black women in our communities
2. Advocating for policies that address the disparities highlighted in the CityLab report
3. Creating and supporting spaces for Black women to thrive in business, arts, and education
4. Mentoring young Black girls, ensuring they see the potential within themselves

The Toni Morrison mural in downtown Cleveland is more than just a beautiful piece of art. It's a beacon of hope and a call to action. The mural, which is entitled "Cleveland is the Reason," was created by artist Glen Infante in April 2021 to remind the world that he and others are proud of the people who have shaped the city. The mural reminds us of the power of imagery, our words, our actions, and our unity. As Black women in Ohio, we have a responsibility to change the narrative, to rewrite Cleveland's story, and to continue the work that Morrison began. Let us stand tall, speak boldly, and act with purpose, knowing that we carry within us the same strength and resilience that Morrison embodied. By doing so, we honor her legacy and create a better future for all Black women in Cleveland and beyond. As Morrison would have done if she were still with us, let us be relentless in our pursuit of justice, equality, and empowerment for Black women in our city and our state.

My exodus in 2013 was born of necessity and hope—a pursuit of better opportunities in a job market that seemed to have no place for me. At the time, I couldn't have known about the harsh realities that would later be quantified when CityLab named Cleveland the worst city for Black women. Yet as I stood before Toni Morrison's vibrant visage on that Euclid Avenue wall, I felt a renewed sense of purpose and belonging, despite the sobering statistics that had emerged during my absence. Chicago had been great, and DC okay, but neither quite felt like home. There's a unique rhythm in Ohio that resonates in the souls of those born there, whether in my birth city of Dayton or my adopted home of Cleveland. It's a cadence of perseverance, a melody of pride, and a harmony of shared identity that calls us back, no matter how far we roam.

Now, as I gaze up at Morrison's unwavering eyes and electric smile, I feel a surge of determination. This has been more than a homecoming; it is a reclamation. A reclamation of my place in this city, of my identity as an Ohioan, and of my responsibility to weave new threads of hope and opportunity for others into the tapestry of Cleveland's future and beyond.

The city has changed since 2013, and so have I, but one thing is certain—I am home, ready to stand firm and forge a new path in the state that shaped me and Toni Morrison. Armed with the knowledge and experiences gained during my time away and inspired by Morrison's unapologetic celebration of Black womanhood, I'm determined to be a beacon for young Ohio women—our future leaders. My mission is clear: to ignite a fierce pride in their Ohio roots, a pride so deep that it becomes an unshakeable foundation built by trailblazing Black women like Congresswoman Stephanie Tubbs Jones, activist Mary B. Talbert, philanthropist Dr. Zelma Watson George, and educator Louise Troy.

Together, we'll rewrite Cleveland's story, just as Morrison rewrote the narrative of Black women in literature. We'll transform this city into a place where Black women not only survive but thrive, where every young girl can see herself reflected in the success stories around her. This is our home, our legacy, and our future—and we will make it shine with the brilliance of every young woman who dares to dream here, carrying forward the torch that Morrison and countless other Ohio daughters lit for us all.

# TONI MORRISON

## Thayer Hall
## West Point, New York

*By Trivius G. Caldwell*

Born Chloe Wofford on February 18, 1931, in Lorain, Ohio, Toni Morrison was the second of four children and a precocious reader. She attended Howard University in 1949 and, later, taught there for seven years. In 1965, following the birth of her second son, Morrison moved to Syracuse, New York, to work for Random House. There she edited work by African American writers Angela Davis, Gayl Jones, and many others. Morrison's oeuvre is replete with aspects of African American vernacular and themes of race, gender, and sexuality. Her tenth novel, *Home* (2012), is a departure from much of her ephemeral work and centers around a male protagonist, a war veteran. Portraying Frank Money as a man grappling with profound troubles and trauma who embarks on a journey back home after the Korean War, underscores the significance of delving into complex notions of *home* while reevaluating the concept of family. It seems odd that Frank Money and cadets at the United States Military Academy at West Point might have something in common, yet the tragedy of war is but one way of straying from home.

The academy is nestled in the Hudson River Valley, north of bustling New York City. The old fortress, West Point, is home to almost 4,300 cadets from across our nation and territories. They represent the best of us as they prepare to lead our nation's sons and daughters. The Cadet Corps calls the academy home, and along the Hudson river, they prepare to defend liberty. In the spring the sun peaks over the adjacent mountain range, toying with cadets as they scuttle to classes under the final chill of winter. On the clearest day, the cityscape of the Big Apple appears like a distant mirage.

Sometimes cadets travel by train toward the city's glow. Unbeknownst to them, the river flowing broadside of their locomotive was also home to perhaps the greatest literary genius of our time, Toni Morrison. She too called a portion of the Hudson's bank home. Morrison lived in the village Grand View on the Hudson, a quiet place to write while staring into the river's reflection of that passing train. Her novels—including classics like *The Bluest Eye* (1970) and *Beloved* (1987)—represent the reality of the American African interior by depicting an Africanist presence in America's soul. Teaching at West Point, I often admired cadets as they reflected on their future military service while gazing into that same soothing water. The Hudson River is more than just a canal to the Big Apple; it is an artery of the imagination.

Follow that river north and the gothic architecture of Thayer Hall emerges from the rolling hills of the Hudson highlands. Thayer Hall stands as a testament to both history and transformation. Originally conceived as the Riding Hall for the horses, this architectural gem proudly showcases the Gothic Revival style, mirroring the grandeur seen in other structures at West Point from the same era. Its robust exterior, crafted from gneiss masonry in random ashlar coursing, is accentuated by limestone parapets, window and door surrounds, and elegant belt courses. Granite additions, particularly at the bridges leading to the building's west side, further enhance its stately presence.

On March 22, 2013, Toni Morrison shuttled a short distance north to lecture to the plebe (freshman) class in the Roscoe Robinson Jr. auditorium in Thayer Hall. Her work on depicting the totality of our American experience is all too familiar to cadets—those charged with reading *Home* as they reflect on the inner turmoil and implications of their service—especially given the experiences of Morrison's protagonist Frank Money.

The acoustics in the auditorium transformed her writing into a symphony, harmonizing the rustle of a thousand pages turning simultaneously with the mellifluous cadence of Morrison's *jazzing* voice. At once, the soundscape transformed the room into both canvas and cave, capturing the collective breath of anticipation and the energy of a captivated audience as cadets immersed themselves in Morrison's literary imagination. The ethereal fusion of turning pages, coupled with Morrison's voice resonating in the air, created a transcendent experience wherein the written and spoken word converged with an almost orchestral precision, inviting listeners to navigate her narrative. The auditorium, alive with the resonance of storytelling, became a sanctuary where the magic of literature unfolded in a captivating and immersive symphony. After all, Morrison makes fiction an oral art form. She is a master of manipulating sound by employing jazz characteristics in her writing.

Interestingly, that auditorium is named after a St. Louis native who ascended the military hierarchy to become the first African American four-star general in the United States Army. The auditorium—formerly known "South Aud"—served as a lecture facility for the Corps of Cadets long before the 1958 commemoration of the auditorium for General Robinson, who is emblematic of the pride that motivates cadets to serve in times of war. However, the purpose of renaming it demonstrates the same exigence motivating Morrison's fiction—belonging.

The Cultural Affairs Seminar, a cohort of cadets of color at West Point, petitioned for the auditorium's name change because they were not satisfied with their lack of reflection in the gothic stone. Like others seeking to join the Long Gray Line to defend freedom, they wanted to be represented at the historic military mainstay. As with Morrison's depiction of the Korean War veteran Frank Money—not to mention Shadrack, Paul D, and the Harlem Hellfighters in other novels—the cadets were willing to scratch the calcified scab of national history by using voice and action to assert their place.

Long landscapes like the Hudson River, the stone Riding Hall, and the auditorium and its acoustic flair served as the setting for the writer's tutelage. Everyone awaited her voice, loud like the silence itself, signaling a legacy and ghosts of the past. On the hallowed grounds of West Point, she whispered Frank Money's thoughts: "I only remembered the horses. They were so beautiful. So brutal. And they stood like men."

# TONI MORRISON

## Chesapeake Bay
## Northeast Maryland

*By Alice Sundman*

We are driving southward on I-95, toward Washington, DC. I am trying to take in the landscape around us, a landscape I have never seen before but that I still, somehow, *know* in my mind. Here, in the midst of gray concrete and endless numbers of cars, I finally get a few glimpses of parts of Chesapeake Bay, of patches of verdant vegetation—and of a landscape in which Jacob Vaark, a character in Toni Morrison's 2008 novel, *A Mercy*, makes his way toward the slaveholder D'Ortega's plantation in Maryland in the late 1600s.

For someone who grew up on a small island in the Baltic Sea, the enormous highway and the great distances are quite a contrast to my childhood windblown pines, low cliffs of red granite, and thousands of tiny islands in the archipelago of the Åland Islands of Finland. I am used to short distances ideal for cycling, to walking in the forest, to picking berries, to going for a swim in calm, shallow bays—to experiencing the place concretely, through my body, and thus getting a sense of actually being in the landscape.

In the car on the highway, I am at a distance from everything. I can see water, trees, parts of the ground. . . . But how does it feel to actually be there, in the place?

In *A Mercy*, Jacob is traveling by boat, on foot, and on horseback. Having sailed down the river into Chesapeake Bay, he is now struggling with the water, the sand, and the mud as he tries to find his way through the fog toward land:

> The man moved through the surf, stepping carefully over pebbles and sand to shore. Fog, Atlantic and reeking of plant life, blanketed the bay and slowed him. He could see his boots sloshing but not his satchel nor his hands. When the surf was behind him and his soles sank in mud, he turned to wave to the sloopmen, but because the mast had disappeared in the fog he could not tell whether they remained anchored or risked sailing on.

For Jacob the place evokes a sense of chaos, but this is due to political skirmishes and shifting territorial claims rather than the landscape itself, whose Indigenous inhabitants give him a sense of stability and of life lived in accordance with nature and the land.

Seeing the vastness of the landscape and the long distances of seemingly interminable highways, I wonder how Morrison managed to create the sense of immediate bodily experience of the landscape that Jacob experiences. For even if she most likely knew this place far better than I do, her experience from the late 1900s and early 2000s differs considerably from Jacob's seventheenth-century ditto.

Perhaps part of the answer can be found in her archived manuscripts, the Toni Morrison Papers, at Princeton University Library. It is well known that Morrison did thorough research for her novels. She studied reports and books of facts, and she used places she had visited or lived in as inspiration for her fictional places. But how did she create this particular fictional landscape through which Jacob is traveling? Her archived research material for the novel includes information about Native American place names and their relation to topographical features, which most likely informed her writing. Facts about and descriptions of actual places thus form part of her creation of the fictional landscape. But more important, I think, are two crucial skills: her crafting and her imagination.

Early drafts I studied in the archive suggest that the landscape in this passage was not a priority at the beginning of her writing process; in these drafts, she focuses on sketching the contours of Jacob as a greedy settler. In later and more elaborate versions, the landscape is gradually given a greater role as she develops it into a thematic feature that becomes part of a human–place relation, which also allows her to develop Jacob into a more complex character. In her final, published version of this passage, as in other textual moments involving other characters in the novel, human–landscape interactions are *crafted* into complex thematic features that enrich both setting and character.

In her essay "The Site of Memory" Morrison comments on the significance of imagination for her writing: "Memories and recollections won't give me total access to the unwritten interior life of these people. Only the act of the imagination can help me." In addition to her drafting and crafting the landscape, she *imagined* Jacob walking in these regions in 1682. Her imagination enables her to create a story that invites the reader to feel a closeness to the place, despite the chronological, and sometimes geographical, distance. She invites us to experience the place along with a seventeenth-century settler: "He took delight in the journey. Breathing the air of a world so new, almost alarming in rawness and temptation, never failed to invigorate him. Once beyond the warm gold of the bay, he saw forests untouched since Noah, shorelines beautiful enough to bring tears, wild food for the taking."

In the car on the highway, I realize that despite the traffic, despite the concrete, despite the radically changed place, the landscape I see is also the one Jacob is sailing, walking, and riding through. This actual place, marked by the imprint of today's humans, is interwoven with the fictional place Jacob traverses in another century. Along with these watery landscapes, I see my childhood Baltic archipelago with its narrow fairways on which thousands upon thousands of vessels have sailed through the centuries—some out fishing between the islets, others on their way toward the world's oceans as part of a growing shipping industry—all on a sea that binds together the continents. In my mind and through my imagination, fed by my childhood island landscape, I can now experience this coexistence of times and places. For this, I thank Toni Morrison, whose drafting, crafting, and imagining made this amalgam of placescapes possible.

Just a Word in Your Ear

JUST SUPPOSE you were going to buy a new roof this year. You would expect to pay anywhere from $2.00 to $4.00 per hundred square feet, wouldn't you? Now, the interest on $3.00 at six per cent is 18 cents per year. So the cost of the new roof would be 18 cents per square per year, not counting repairs, cost of putting on, or anything.

Well, we have proven to thousands of cases that with ROOF-FIX you can keep the old roof in perfect condition at five cents per square per year. Think it over. It's a dollar and cents matter. Buy ROOF-FIX and keep the price of the new roof in your pocket. Catalog free. Write for it.

THE ANDERSON MFG. CO., Elyria, Ohio

# SHERWOOD ANDERSON

## The Old Topliff and Ely Plant
## Elyria, Ohio

*By Doug Sheldon*

Sherwood Anderson's desertion of everything Elyrian was the first literary myth I swallowed whole. A counselor and I were walking along the railroad tracks that divided the north and south sides of town and faced a U bend in the Black River that cradled a mostly empty lot scattered with construction debris and discarded rock (now the BASF chemical plant, oddly apropos to Elyria's industrial past). He asked me if I knew who Anderson was. Being twelve, I had no idea. He proceeded to tell me that Anderson walked these tracks out of town, wound up in Cleveland, and then moved to Chicago to become a writer. It engaged me in a swirl of wannabe masculinity that this man had burned down his life, hiked his way along the retreating wilderness of pre–World War One Ohio, and used Cleveland's cobweb of train tracks to migrate himself to Chicago, where men became writers.

## SHERWOOD ANDERSON

**Born: September 13, 1876, in Camden, Ohio**

**Died: March 8, 1941, in Colón, Panama**

**Forms: Short Stories, Novels, Poetry, Drama, Memoir**

**Recommended Works: *MidAmerican Chants* (1918), *Winesburg, Ohio* (1919), *Poor White* (1920), *The Triumph of the Egg* (1921), *A Story Teller's Story* (1922)**

Again, being that I was twelve, I am sure he left out that Anderson's migration was spurred by a mental breakdown, a wearying due to the drudgery of manufacturing or to the singularity of his marriage or to any number of other things Anderson was not particularly talented at.

The tracks follow the river and then diverge from it as you move west. In the nineties, when I was walking with my counselor, Elyria's past lay along them like a graveyard of iron rods and crumbled limestone. The town's industrial self-sufficiency was long dead by the time I heard of Sherwood Anderson. Years before my birth, it became a bedroom community where people commuted to jobs in Cleveland. We knew many people like Anderson in Elyria. People who desperation had broken and hope couldn't heal. I didn't know then I was looking at the bones of a hulking dragon, ghosts of smokestacks that puffed the Ohio sky with a soot and energy that furnished mail-order solutions to leaky roofs.

These products gave the Andersons status, money, and a house to be envied. Years later, his soon-to-be ex-wife told biographer Walter Rideout, "Roof-Fix carried us to Elyria." He employed many men, like himself, who were new locals, having moved to Elyria from the farming hinterlands with promises that it could be as big as Toledo or Cleveland. A 1910 advertisement listed the name of his factory as "The Old Topliff and Ely Plant"—even his business bore the name of the town's founder. He was Elyria's property. In the same year he processed paint, roof tar, and a few dozen other products that spilled their runoff through half-buried pipes and sludged their exhaust over the slate piled along the riverbanks.

For two more years shipments were packed into train cars with a monotony that burrowed itself into Anderson. Then came a fugue state, as Anderson's contemporaries called it. He just couldn't process his Elyrian life. On a seemingly normal Thanksgiving morning in 1912, Anderson mumbled something about wet feet to his secretary and wandered out of his office, through the doors of the snow-colored castle on the elbow of the Black River. He abandoned his life, choosing a route where no one he knew would look: the railroad tracks. An umbilical cord to his factory, the railroad disseminated Roof-Fix all over northern Ohio and beyond, routes he had likely reviewed dozens of times a year, mapping an unconscious escape route. He was found three days later in Cleveland, shoeless and babbling, half painted with mud. Writing, and possibly some undeclared trauma, had carried him out of my hometown and to the capital of the Midwest. Which it would do to me almost a century later.

Not much lasts a hundred years in my hometown. Any evidence of Anderson's thriving business in Elyria is buried under layers of soil and time, a palimpsest tinting the successes of this minimetropolis in faded sepia. It was as if the earth took revenge on Elyrians for amassing all that industrial weight and swallowed it out of spite. Elyria's problem wasn't that it burned him out but that it dry-rotted him. Even if you were president of the local business collective, as Anderson was, you weren't insulated from how a life of denied talent cracks the mind.

*Progress*, when I was abandoning Elyria, was a slang word for replacing unionized manufacturing careers with stock jobs at Walmart, of which we had three. My high school was collapsing under asbestos tiles and a lack of choices. You either went to the community college, worked fast food, or left town. I am sure there were more choices for wealthier kids, going to the top universities in the state or taking over their father's car dealership, but for a kid who watched the future of his town melt away as we all crawled toward the 2000s, it was enough to make you wonder what that mud on Anderson's legs felt like. I am not defending a person ditching all responsibilities at the feet of those left behind because you had to live your vision, but being an Elyrian, I get it.

# KURT VONNEGUT

## The Kurt Vonnegut Museum and Library
## Indianapolis, Indiana

*By Laura Beadling*

Like many, I found and loved Kurt Vonnegut somewhere in my miserable teenage years. *Slaughterhouse-Five* (1969) is now one of my favorite novels to teach, whether in Great American Books or Science Fiction Literature, and at least some of my students have had similar reactions. When the Kurt Vonnegut Library and Museum moved to its new location in downtown Indy, I knew I had to go, and late in December 2019, my husband and I packed up the dogs and headed west from Youngstown.

*Slaughterhouse-Five* showcases Vonnegut's finely tuned eye for evocative juxtapositions. Structurally, the book strings together short vignettes from across protagonist Billy Pilgrim's life, which is fitting given his assertion that he's "come unstuck in time," as the first page tells us. The narrative ping pongs between Billy's sad youth, his hellish experiences in World War II, his humdrum breakdowns in Illium, New York, and his domestic contentment as an exhibit in a Tralfamadorian zoo with porn star and fellow captive Montana Wildhack.

The trip from Youngstown to downtown Indy is also filled with jarring incongruities. After several hours of flat sameness on I-70 West, suddenly we were in the city. As we drove through downtown, we passed the gigantic blue, curved-glass Marriott Hotel and, a minute later, a small homeless encampment under an overpass. Less than five minutes later, we pulled into a spot just off Indiana Avenue, right outside the museum.

The most striking artifact inside the museum was the icebox from Vonnegut's childhood home. Such an incongruous object to include in a museum dedicated to a writer, especially a writer of science fiction and satire. It can't have been easy to install either. The giant thing, made of painted wood and a number of serious-looking metal fasteners, looked murderously heavy and was, also incongruously, topped by a jaunty toy Tralfamadorian. My eyes went back to it again and again.

## KURT VONNEGUT

**Born: November 11, 1922, in Indianapolis, Indiana**

**Died: April 11, 2007, in New York, New York**

**Forms: Novels, Short Stories, Drama, Nonfiction**

**Recommended Works: *The Sirens of Titan* (1959), *Cat's Cradle* (1963), *Slaughterhouse-Five* (1969), *Happy Birthday, Wanda June* (1970), *Breakfast of Champions* (1973)**

The museum building itself is lovely, brick with a second-floor patio and plenty of windows, situated in a lively neighborhood. I noticed that the Madame C. J. Walker Building was across the street, and so we took a walk around the area, one of Indy's six cultural districts. Although the Walker Building is closed on the weekends, we appreciated the beautiful details, including intricate art deco-esque terra-cotta ornaments depicting African art motifs. Both buildings sit quite near to Indy's Canal Walk, which is a pretty promenade alongside an old industrial canal that cuts through downtown.

The visit made me think about structures and organization. Given the lack of a chronologically coherent narrative, *Slaughterhouse-Five* relies on purposeful juxtapositions between the vignettes to create meaning. Museums are similar, deliberately placing objects to illuminate connections and disjunctions. City blocks can sometimes do the same, although not always intentionally. The placement of the museum on Indiana Avenue, once a thriving residential and commercial African American neighborhood, is an example. Although few of Vonnegut's characters were African American, he was an outspoken lover of jazz, and Indiana Avenue boasted over thirty-three jazz clubs at its height. Furthermore, each building offers different but important programming throughout the year. The Walker Legacy Center offers a wide variety of African American art, history, and cultural programs. Alongside its usual focus on banned books and freedom of speech, the Vonnegut Museum's particular focus this year is on civic engagement.

Whether inside the museum or throughout the city, these juxtapositions can be, like jazz, improvisational and surprising and beautiful. I'm sure Vonnegut would approve.

# BOOTH TARKINGTON

## North Meridian Street
## Indianapolis, Indiana

*By Wesley R. Bishop*

Booth Tarkington would still recognize his hometown of Indianapolis, Indiana, which he described in his novel *The Turmoil* as "a midland city in the heart of fair open country, a dirty and wonderful city nestling dingily in the fog of its own smoke."

Although Indianapolis has undergone significant changes since Tarkington grew up there more than a century ago, the spirit of the city, a spirit he often strove to capture in prose, is still very present. *The Turmoil*, first published in 1915, is not Tarkington's best-known work, but it makes a strong case for being the novel that best understands the urban sprawl of Indianapolis.

Even as I write this in the twenty-first century, Indianapolis is less a cohesive entity and more a conglomeration of different parts haphazardly tied together by long avenues that serve as borders for racial, geographic, and socioeconomic divisions.

These expansive streets—38th Street, Keystone Avenue, Massachusetts Avenue, Meridian Street—feel less like connections within the city and more like corridors racing somewhere else, kicking up smog from endless exhaust. Indianapolis is a place that aspires to sprawl.

Again, Tarkington's words feel familiar:

> The smoke [of Indianapolis] is like the bad breath of a giant panting for more and more riches. He gets them and pants fiercer, smelling and swelling prodigiously. He has a voice, a hoarse voice, hot and rapacious trained to one tune: 'Wealth! I will get Wealth I will make Wealth! I will sell Wealth for more Wealth! My house shall be dirty, my garment shall be dirty, and I will foul my neighbor so that he cannot be clean—but I will get Wealth!' . . . And yet it is not wealth that he is so greedy for: what the giant really wants is hasty riches. To get these he squanders wealth upon the four winds, for wealth is in the smoke.

## BOOTH TARKINGTON

**Born: July 29, 1869, in Indianapolis, Indiana**

**Died: May 19, 1946, in Indianapolis, Indiana**

**Forms: Novels, Drama, Short Stories, Nonfiction**

**Recommended Works: *Penrod* (1914), *The Magnificent Ambersons* (1918), *Alice Adams* (1921)**

I read *The Turmoil* during the long year of the COVID-19 lockdowns. It was a year of considerable unrest. COVID-19, the George Floyd protests, and the fallout from the final year of Trump's first presidency all swirled together, clogging the air, suffocating many in its path. It felt like monumental, terrifying history was being recorded on an hourly basis.

Yet the thing that most stood out to me as I read Tarkington from my apartment nestled next to the White River and 38th Street were the cries of the American nation for continued growth. Not just businesspeople, mind you, but school administrators and customers and politicians. All were demanding quick reopening, defying mask mandates, and adding another level of grime to an already perilous situation. These calls for "wealth"—much like we see in *The Turmoil*—happened while we could see the impacts of COVID-19. Air quality, smog or virus laced, be damned. Things needed to be open!

To stop economic activity—shopping, working, selling—was a metaphorical death, even if going forward meant an actual one.

Tarkington's acknowledgement of social issues often earned him notice from contemporary readers and critics. *The Turmoil* was followed by two other novels—*The Magnificent Ambersons* (1918) and *The Midlander* (1923)—which dealt with the issue of America's transition into a new industrial age. These novels all take place in a fictionalized Indianapolis, and ultimately, *The Turmoil*'s major characters conclude that despite the hurried rush of growth and development, the United States could (and probably would) continue to move forward culturally.

Today it reads as incredibly optimistic, but as I drove through the city over a hundred years after the book was written, I think Tarkington was correct. This is not an admission I expected to make.

Indianapolis and the United States have been violently remade in the process of industrialization. And just as Tarkington saw the rise of the industrial belt, current residents of the

Midwest's Rust Belt are watching the tail end of that process. From rise to fall, to remaking again, again, again.

Despite all of that, we still make art, we still think, we still strive for beauty and dignity.

As Tarkington notes, however, this is not a smooth process. The social classes that Tarkington discusses are still very much present in the city. The Indianapolis police department, a frequent subject of protests and calls for change, patrols the vast spread of the city.

At the height of the 2020 Black Lives Matter protests, marchers crossed 38th Street, a de facto border within the city that separates the city's working poor from its wealthiest, most privileged residents. Marchers breached that border, going so far as to stand outside the governor's mansion on North Meridian Street. I remember that night as my phone dinged with messages from friends and colleagues. Many in the city understood that a reckoning may have been about to begin, with the wealthy and sheltered forced to see the costs of inequality.

Yet the protesters, ringed by police, only chanted for a while and then turned away from the mansion and the rich denizens' homes and began the long trek back to the center of Indianapolis.

What lies in store for us, the subjects of this tumultuous age? It's impossible to say. Yet, like Tarkington's novel, I remain largely optimistic that despite whatever dirt- or pandemic-congested state waits for us, we will have (and must have) our ability to create meaningful representations of our existences—that, after all, is culture.

We continue to do it, and we must, even as the giants pant violently for wealth.

# HUNTER S. THOMPSON

## Churchill Downs
## Louisville, Kentucky

*By Charlie Cy*

In the spring of 1970, thirty-two-year-old writer Hunter S. Thompson returned to his hometown of Louisville to cover the ninety-sixth running of the Kentucky Derby for *Scanlan's Monthly*.

Less than seventy-two hours before the race, Thompson was over 1,300 miles from Churchill Downs in Aspen, Colorado, busy having, as he later recalled, "one of those long European dinners with lots of wine" with novelist Jim Salter. During the meal, Salter prompted Thompson, asking the Kentucky native if he planned on attending the upcoming derby. Intrigued, Thompson immediately phoned his editor, Warren Hinckle, in San Francisco at three thirty in the morning, shouting "I have a great idea, we must do the derby. It's the greatest spectacle the country can produce."

Straightaway, Hinckle endorsed the pitch and, within an hour, booked Thompson a ticket, wired expense money, and began the hunt for an artist to illustrate the event; Hunter loathed working with photographers, and so Hinckle arranged for British illustrator Ralph Steadman, already scheduled to fly to the states, to meet Thompson in Louisville.

## HUNTER S. THOMPSON

**Born: July 18, 1937, in Louisville, Kentucky**

**Died: February 20, 2005, in Woody Creek, Colorado**

**Forms: New Journalism, Novels, Memoir**

**Recommended Works: *The Rum Diary* (1960s/1998), *Hell's Angels* (1966), "The Kentucky Derby Is Decadent and Depraved" (1970), *Fear and Loathing in Las Vegas* (1971), *The Proud Highway: Saga of a Desperate Southern Gentleman, 1955–1967* (1997)**

What ensued was a frenzied 7,200-word, now-infamous, first-person account entitled "The Kentucky Derby is Decadent and Depraved." It was the genesis of gonzo journalism—a unique cocktail of "close to the bone" reporting with subjective, participatory and satirical narration.

The essay, alongside Steadman's apocalyptic sketches, mostly snubs the horse race, instead fixating on the local inhabitants and cultural milieu surrounding the derby's pageantry and debauchery:

> We hadn't seen that special kind of face that I felt we would need for a lead drawing. It was a face I'd seen a thousand times at every Derby I'd ever been to. I saw it, in my head, as the mask of the whiskey gentry—a pretentious mix of booze, failed dreams and a terminal identity crisis; the inevitable result of too much inbreeding in a closed and ignorant culture. . . . So the face I was trying to find in Churchill Downs that weekend was a symbol, in my own mind, of the whole doomed atavistic culture that makes the Kentucky Derby what it is.

Thompson's narrative is also set against a volatile national backdrop. He makes numerous references to Nixon's America. The falling stock market. Bombings in Cambodia. Interminable war in Vietnam. Antiwar protests that led to four students being killed by National Guard troops on the campus of Kent State, which occurred the Monday after the derby. And a racially fraught atmosphere in Louisville and across the country. There are multiple allusions to the Black Panthers, "white crazies," race riots, and a racial caste system.

I first read the piece in the summer of 2015, the same summer I first read Ralph Ellison's novel *Invisible Man*. Both struck like lightning. At the time I was living in the Bronx, blocks above the Harlem River and the northern tip of Manhattan; I was a nontraditional undergraduate student at Columbia University, studying African American studies and political science, hungry to write about America's racially divided working class.

I'd never read anything quite like Thompson's story. In many ways it had everything I'd been hunting for in a writer and mentor, especially for a white man born below the Mason-Dixon Line in the Jim Crow era.

Beyond the lean electric prose, comic hyperbole, and current of impending doom, Thompson's narrative provides an unvarnished insider's view of the social dynamics in Louisville and Churchill Downs.

As both a globe-trotting journalist and a native son who'd attended numerous derbies in the past, Thompson proves to be an expert tour guide. He not only captures the nuances of the town and track; he combats any romantic inclination to side with the local tribe and instead actively critiques the customs, class structure, and racial strata associated with his hometown's bankrupt bacchanal—from the Kentucky Colonels "in white linen suits vomiting in the urinals," to the governor, "a swinish neo-Nazi hack named Louis Nunn," seated in the "inner sanctum" alongside Barry Goldwater.

Better yet, he ultimately eschews self-righteousness for self-deprecation, turning the finger-pointing on himself in a moment of catharsis the morning after the derby as he discovers the hideous image in the mirror.

> There he was, by God—a puffy, drink ravaged, disease-ridden caricature . . . like an awful cartoon version of an old snapshot in some once-proud mother's family photo album. It was the face we'd been looking for—and it was of course, my own. Horrible. Horrible.

Thompson's takedown and insider-outsider perspective resonated with me on multiple levels. Though I was raised in Richmond, Virginia, once the capital of the Confederacy, I was born in Kentucky, like Thompson. I grew up with a remote connection to the derby, an intimate disdain for American aristocracy, and a contradictory subconscious need to fit in, which often manifested itself in grotesque bouts of drunken mayhem with my bourgeois peers.

The piece struck me so much that I sought assistance to produce something similar for my senior thesis that fall. I emailed a former literature professor, Dr. Farah Jasmine Griffin, the director of the Institute for Research in African American Studies, a long letter outlining my circuitous path into her formative seminar The Novels of Toni Morrison, to solicit her to be my thesis advisor.

She wrote back, "*Yes, I will advise your thesis. . . . You are a writer. Therefore, you MUST write.*" As a neophyte wannabe, her words felt like gasoline poured over a dying flame, validating a fragile dream I'd stoked to a point of exhaustion, a dream I feared bordered on delusion.

Unfortunately, I never quite captured what I wanted to say for my thesis, and in many ways, I'm still working on that essay today. Nevertheless, after graduating, I would, by happenstance, move from New York City to Louisville and attend my first derby in 2018 with my dear friend and flatmate Lisa Turner.

Like Thompson's, our plans were made in haste. It was a rainy, lazy Saturday. But with less than five hours to post, in an impromptu fit of spontaneity, we decided to foist ourselves up off the couch in Lisa's Old Louisville condo less than two miles from the track and attend the 144th Run for the Roses—the wettest derby on record, won by eventual Triple Crown winner Justify.

In three hours' time, we managed to purchase general admission tickets, hustle downtown to GQ Unlimited to procure proper attire, drive through Ali Baba Liquor Store and Smoke Shop for cigarettes and Old Forester (one bottle would be duct-taped to my calf, the other slugged beforehand), rendezvous with my amphetamine dealer (a mercurial young socialite-hipster I'd met on Tinder who'd first shown me around Louisville), get gussied up, drive to the fairgrounds, shuttle over to the track, enter Churchill's gates, and commandeer two mint juleps to sip, and stare at the sea of wildlife getting soaked in the rain with an hour to spare before the paddock judge commanded "riders up."

The key feat, though, was improving our station. We had nowhere to go but the infield, "that boiling sea of people across the track from the clubhouse," as Thompson put it. But Lisa was determined to upgrade. While I was on watch for the slightest sneer by fascist scum directed at her dark skin, which stood out like a pink flamingo, she herself was unfazed and preoccupied, busy eyeing one of the gatekeepers lackadaisically checking tickets to the lower-level bleachers along the homestretch.

The gatekeeper looked checked out, like he'd been there all week, as a slew of soused, ivory-faced beasts in ponchos were stampeding in and out of his narrow gate, shouting and slipping over each other on the soaked floors to get to the clogged bathrooms or pari-mutuel counters to put down bets.

We stood back to study the diabolical flow, while the attendant, anesthetized by the chaos, intermittently checked his phone. I was nervous about our prospects of getting through without being stopped. My veins pulsed with adrenaline and speed. Certain we were doomed, I studied Lisa's face. Moxie oozed from her eyes. Reassured, I followed her lead as she walked up to the man and glided past him with an arctic poise. We crab-walked down the aisle to open seats, just four rows back from the sloppy track, grinning like hyenas as the rain poured.

Minutes later the crowd, over 150,000 strong, undeterred by the elements, were welcomed to stand and sing "My Old Kentucky Home," our commonwealth's curious state song—a tragic minstrel tune turned derby tradition, bloated with misplaced nostalgia and sentimentality, a song I'd heard sung thoughtlessly since I was a child and had grown to despise like the monuments that lined my hometown.

Written by Stephen Foster in 1853, eight years before the Civil War, it was inspired by Harriet Beecher Stowe's *Uncle Tom's Cabin* and was often performed in the play based on her novel. Written from the perspective of a slave, the lyrics lament being sold downriver, away from a bucolic Kentucky plantation to a hostile land "where the sugar canes grow."

Kentucky banned *Uncle Tom's Cabin* from being performed in 1906. In 1928, however, the legislature enshrined "My Old Kentucky Home" as the state anthem. In a period rife with Lost Cause fervor and "Old South" reminiscences, the antislavery sentiment of Foster's tune was effaced, and it became instead a paean to the antebellum South. Over time it has been further sanitized; in 1986 the Kentucky General Assembly removed a racial slur from the lyrics, providing a path for the syrupy sweet chorus to be reinterpreted once again.

Standing in the rain next to my friend, dressed in a bow tie and suspenders with a bellyful of bourbon, aping the mask of the whiskey gentry, I could not help but sense in my bowels the decadence and depravity of the moment.

Half enthralled by the pomp and circumstance, too, I also could not help but feel a hint of shame as a willing participant in this "atavistic" ritual, as the bridled thoroughbreds made their way from the paddock to the starting gate, the crowd wistfully crooning a slave song.

# SARAH MORGAN BRYAN PIATT

## William Henry Harrison Tomb
## North Bend, Ohio

*By Sean E. Andres*

It's not hard to find something of historical significance in the Cincinnati area, but many people don't even think about North Bend. The town was founded by John Cleves Symmes, father-in-law of President William Henry Harrison, who swiftly and violently removed, swindled, and stole the land of the Indigenous peoples of the Northwest Territory, including those who had resided where North Bend now stands. As a child, too young to remember and appreciate the experience, I had visited Shawnee Lookout and the William Henry Harrison tomb with my family, and North Bend soon became a town I passed by on the way to the dentist.

But then in 2010, in my second year at Ball State University, I was introduced to little-known poet Sarah Morgan Bryan Piatt in an American Literature course. This was the beginning of a challenging hike up a steep hill. While working on an ongoing project on Cincinnati-area women's history, I delved into Piatt and, through a Piatt family member, began connecting to other researchers.

## SARAH MORGAN BRYAN PIATT

**Born: August 11, 1836, in Lexington, Kentucky**

**Died: December 22, 1919, in Caldwell, New Jersey**

**Forms: Poetry, Children's Literature**

**Recommended Works: *A Woman's Poems* (1871), *That New World, and Other Poems* (1877), *Dramatic Persons and Moods with Other New Poems* (1880), *Palace-Burner: The Selected Poetry of Sarah Piatt* (2001)**

Soon I was enveloped in Piatt's life and her work, which revealed her to be deeply sympathetic to Indigenous and enslaved peoples and grievously antiwar. Although the most famous woman in the Western world had fallen into obscurity after her death, I was able to uncover over twenty poems and a narrative from her youth to her late years. When I found out she had lived in North Bend, every time I passed by on the way to the dentist, I wondered whether random houses were hers. Then I learned that one of her houses was a half-mile up Mt. Nebo from Congress Green, where Harrison's tomb sits on what was believed to be a Native mound. As steamboats passed by, it was customary for them to fire a salute in his honor.

There, at the tomb, Piatt sings loud in my head with her sympathetic, sharp-tongued wit. I envision North Bend as she might have on her daily walks to the tomb with her husband and their children, spotting the wild rose, wild grape, and violets she documented in her poems. The river runs below, and I'm reminded of what the *Cincinnati Commercial* wrote about Piatt's writing, that it appears "sweet and peaceful" but proves to be like "the depths of a dark river," "shadowy and terrible."

Many people had drowned below that tomb and the Piatt family home, a weight Sarah carried with her. Still, without doubt, Piatt's "A President at Home" swells in me.

I pass'd a President's House today—
"A President, mamma, and what is that?"
Oh, it is a man who has to stay
Where bowing beggars hold out the hat
For something—a man who has to be
The Captain of every ship that we
Send with our darling flag to the sea—
The Colonel at home who has to command
Each marching regiment in the land.

This President now has a single room,
That is low and not much lighted, I fear;
Yet the butterflies play in the sun and gloom

Of his evergreen avenue, year by year;
And the childlike violets up the hill
Climb, faintly wayward, about him still;
And the bees blow by at the wind's wide will;
And the cruel river, that drowns men so,
Looks pretty enough in the shadows below.

Just one little fellow (named Robin) was there,
In a red Spring vest, and he let me pass
With that charming-careless, highbred air
Which comes of serving the great. In the grass
He sat, half-singing, with nothing to do
No, I did not see the President too:
His door was lock'd (what I say is true),
And he was asleep, and has been, it appears,
Like Rip Van Winkle, asleep for years!

The tomb, for me, is less about the Harrisons and more about the Piatts. It's hard not to think about her two children, here alluded to as "childlike violets up the hill," for they lie in unmarked graves beneath a tree somewhere on this "beautiful burial-hill" of grief, as Piatt refers to it in "Death Before Death."

The Piatts continued to keep North Bend historically relevant by placing emphasis on the tomb. Sarah's husband J. J. lobbied for it to become a national park, writing a bill that made its way to the congressional floor. When that failed, he intended to save the old-wood forest around the tomb by purchasing it and turning it into a park with proceeds from *The Hesperian Tree*, a book he edited, collecting work from Ohio and Indiana authors and artists, including William Henry Harrison's granddaughter, Betty Harrison Eaton, reflecting on life as a Harrison in North Bend. The book did not sell well. His attempts failed, and the forest was logged.

I certainly don't mourn the man in the tomb who violently swept through the Indigenous people of the Northwest Territory and lies in rest on top of their dead. However, I do grieve for the long-forgotten poet Sarah Piatt, who seems to try to atone for her predecessors' sins, seeking rebirth through the cruel river below.

# JOHN AUGUSTUS STONE

## Main Street
## Metamora, Indiana

*By Heather Chacón*

My first memory of Metamora, Indiana, is of being twelve and sitting on a wooden bench on the front porch of an old house turned shop with my friend Holly. It is December. Above us hang several pieces of artwork for sale, paintings of landscapes and animals on reclaimed barn wood done by a local artist. We are sipping hot chocolate with lots of whipped cream and laughing while her parents shop inside the crowded building, the laughter making what happened next all the more startling. A man suddenly grabs a painting off the wall above our heads and takes off running. He nearly makes it off the porch before being tackled, suddenly and fully, about the waist. Other people, whether patrons or employees we do not know, secure the painting. There are murmurs of "shoplifter" among the crowd, and eventually the store owner appears to loudly berate the man and ban him from the store. I do not remember any police being called, but the collective scorn from that crowd frightened me regardless.

Had I been more familiar with the history of Metamora, I would have also understood that the concepts embedded in this event—artistic ownership, community censure, thwarted commerce, repurposed materials as the start of mythos-building—were as much a part of this town's history as the nineteenth-century buildings and homespun atmosphere I loved.

## JOHN AUGUSTUS STONE

**Born: December 15, 1801, in Concord, Massachusetts**

**Died: June 1, 1834, in Philadelphia, Pennsylvania**

**Forms: Drama**

**Recommended Works: *Metamora; or, The Last of the Wampanoags* (1829), *Tancred, King of Sicily; or, The Archives of Palermo* (1831)**

You see, Metamora got its name from the play *Metamora; or, The Last of the Wampanoags* (1829), written by John Augustus Stone. Stone entered this play in a competition sponsored by one of the most—many say *the* most—prominent American actors of the nineteenth-century, Edwin Forrest. Keen to find a play he believed would be well suited to his style of acting and physical presence, as well as show that the young nation could produce works of literary and dramatic merit, Forrest offered $500 for the best original "tragedy, in five acts, of which the hero, or principal character, shall be an aboriginal of this country." From among the fourteen plays submitted, the Committee of Award (headed by William Cullen Bryant) chose Stone's.

Initially Stone was elated to win the prize and have his work performed by such an important thespian. This pleasure soon turned to worry and dismay, however, as *Metamora* became a meteoric success that helped establish Forrest's professional reputation and personal fortune without yielding such stability for its author. The play's popularity hinged, in part, on Forrest's acting talent, but it also gave the American people the opportunity to celebrate a uniquely "American" history.

While some brochures and websites mention that the town is named after a play, very few include any details of the play's plot or popularity. Set in 1600s New England, the melodrama tells the tale of Metamora, a fictional chief cast in the "noble Indian" mode, who eventually kills his wife to protect her from the terrors of settler colonialism and enslavement before himself being slain by white pioneers. Importantly, by 1829 New England was largely under the control of white settlers, thus allowing northeastern audiences watching Stone's play the chance to experience catharsis rather than fear of Native American retaliation. Yet Andrew Jackson's Indian Removal Act, passed in 1830, insured white Americans' interest in stories dramatizing the usurpation of Native American lands and the "disappearance" of their earlier inhabitants. The play became such a cultural phenomenon that it inspired the name of Metamora, Indiana, when the town was platted in 1838. This was not unique, as towns named Metamora can also be found in Michigan, Illinois, and Ohio—locations that had more recently been settled on the frontier.

Forrest performed *Metamora* to great acclaim until his death in 1872. The play spawned at least thirty-five additional "Indian" dramas, and Forrest made thousands by playing the role. Stone, meanwhile, never saw additional remuneration above his $500 prize money, unless you count the fact that Forrest bought Stone's headstone after Stone committed suicide by drowning in 1834. When Stone died, many whispered that Forrest's unwillingness to share the profits of *Metamora* contributed to Stone's melancholy. The scandal clung to Forrest for a while but ultimately did little to impact his popularity.

Today visitors to Metamora, Indiana, will find little evidence of why the town bears this name or the fact that it was established on land that used to be the home of Miami and Shawnee peoples. Instead, public memory centers largely on its identity as a "canal town." Metamora was established along the proposed route of Indiana's Whitewater Canal, an infrastructure project designed to transport raw materials from the state's interior to the Ohio River. Construction of the canal section in Metamora began in 1836 and was completed by 1847. Yet the canal was unfortunately prone to flooding due to the relatively low elevation of the surrounding land and its proximity to the Whitewater River. By the 1860s the railroad supplanted canal travel as the preferred means of transporting goods.

With this change, Metamora met challenges well known to much of the rural Midwest: declining populations, gradual shrinkage of family-owned farms, a dearth of well-paying jobs. A resourceful bunch, Metamora residents still used the canal to power several grist mills in the late nineteenth and early twentieth centuries, one of which still operates at the Whitewater Canal State Historic Site under the care of the Indiana State Museum. Their grits are extremely good, particularly on a summer day when you can watch them be freshly ground and placed directly in the bag.

In the last few years, interest in the town has risen somewhat, in part due to renewed interest in preserving historic architecture like Metamora's nineteenth-century shops and municipal buildings. The town's beautiful natural setting, affordability, and relative proximity to Cincinnati draw visitors who want to stroll around antique shops or take the family on a historic train or canal boat ride. It's a pity most visitors to Metamora's functioning wooden aqueduct, the only one still in existence in the United States, have no idea they're also visiting a town named after the "last of the Wampanoags."

Maybe it's time to make sure that this darker history is not also carried off into the night.

# HELEN HOOVEN SANTMYER

## Greene County Courthouse
## Xenia, Ohio

*By Jacob A. Bruggeman*

I first visited Xenia, Ohio, a small city in the state's southwestern corner, on a hot May afternoon in 2018. Headed north from Cincinnati on Interstate 71, smoke started rising out from under the hood of my 1999 Toyota Corolla. I pulled onto the highway's shoulder, popped the hood, and prepared to do battle with the Toyota's notoriously oil-burning engines. Equipped only with a container of 5W-30 motor oil, I realized that my modest mechanical knowhow was insufficient, and I called good ol' AAA.

## HELEN HOOVEN SANTMYER

**Born: November 25, 1895, in Cincinnati, Ohio**

**Died: February 21, 1986, in Xenia, Ohio**

**Forms: Novels, Memoir**

**Recommended Works: *Herbs and Apples* (1925), *The Fierce Dispute* (1929), *Ohio Town* (1962), *". . . And Ladies of the Club"* (1982)**

While waiting for the Triple-A guy, I saw a roadside sign pointing Xenia's way. Soon enough, I was riding shotgun in the tow truck as we rolled through the city and passed the Greene County Courthouse at 45 North Detroit Street. Built of Bedford stone in 1901–2, the Romanesque courthouse's soaring square clock tower has been a community touchstone in Xenia for more than half of the town's history.

Born in Cincinnati and raised in Xenia, novelist Helen Hooven Santmyer captures the courthouse's centrality in the opening passage of her memoir, *Ohio Town: A Portrait of Xenia* (1962). Santmyer acknowledges that, because so many similar structures are scattered "all along middle western roads," Xenia's visitors "must hardly give the courthouse a conscious thought." For the resident, however, the courthouse is distinct, familiar, and necessary:

> Along with the state of the weather and the time of day, there has always been in his mind a background consciousness of the tower with its four-faced clock, the goose-girl drinking fountain on the Main Street curb, the spread of lawn, and the trees in the square whose crests are stirred by winds higher than the roof.

*Ohio Town* proceeds with similarly rich descriptions of community life in chapters titled "Streets and Houses," "Church," "School," "The Railroad," and "There Were Fences," all focused on the rhythms of life in Xenia.

Founded in 1803, the same year Ohio was admitted to the Union, Xenia was an early testing ground for tribal relations and removal. In fact, in the early 1800s the Shawnee Indians called Old Chillicothe, a small village just north of Xenia, their home; Tecumseh, the famous and then-feared chief who organized a confederacy to stop settler colonialism, was born there. As time passed, the character of his ancestral lands changed as ploughs broke, railroads cut, and Main Streets sprung up on them.

Ohio communities like Xenia flourished as natives like Tecumseh were slain or forced further inland, and settlers began the long, frequently violent transformation of the region into what Xenia-born historian Arthur Schlesinger Sr. described as the Midwest's "valley of democracy."

From a young age, Santmyer cherished the products of that transformation: southwestern Ohio's communities and traditions. Enthused by Louisa May Alcott's *Little Women*, she dedicated herself to recording them in writing. After retiring as a librarian in Dayton in 1959, Santmyer published her two major critical and popular successes: *Ohio Town* and . . . *And the Ladies of the Club* (1982), a nearly 1,200-page epic telling of the story of generations of communal life in rural Ohio. Indeed, Santmyer's writing is a testament to the social dynamism of what might outwardly be described as a dull Midwestern town.

For Santmyer, the courthouse is a literary conduit for those intricacies: its enduring image "recall[s] the Saturday-night excitement of the past," when its "curb . . . was the center of noise and light and crowded movement." For Xenia's former residents, the courthouse remains the "the first vision to flash upon the inward eye," expanding into memories of "the courthouse as it was on quiet afternoons, when nothing moved in the length and breadth of the sun-blazing streets, and only a few persons were to be seen in open shop doors or on the benches under the elms."

To read Santmyer today is to revel in her satisfyingly efficient and life-affirming descriptions of midcentury Ohio life, whereby readers may access something of the joy and reverie once held common in its streets. At the same time, those celebrations also obscure the decidedly undemocratic origins of Ohio's settler communities: despite their virtues as sung by Santmyer and Schlesinger, towns like Xenia were built on stolen land. The extent to which Xenians—and indeed Ohioans—comprehend this erasure is unclear, but ignorance then is no justification for indifference now. To read Santmyer today, then, is to dwell in the tension between her wonderful rendering of Xenia's social and civic life and the true weight of its cost.

# ZITKÁLA-ŠÁ

## Earlham Hall
## Richmond, Indiana

*By Leah Abuan Milne*

I was a Midwest transplant, born and raised on the East Coast. Before I left home, friends joked about flatland and cornfields and voiced concerns about the fact that I was entering what they perceived to be a region of overwhelming whiteness. Culture shock, however, was nothing new to me. As the first in my immigrant family to attend college, I knew what it meant to feel unmoored, to walk into a room where no one resembled you.

My conference visit to Earlham College was an attempt to soften that dislocation. Books have always been my second home, so sitting in the Runyan Center listening to literary presentations, I was already more comfortable. A bonus? Zitkála-Šá went here in the 1890s. Having read her stories about being the only American Indian among over four hundred college students, I felt a kinship.

Earlham Residence Hall—where she stayed—was right next door. Bright leaves floated onto the campus quad where I stood before a sweeping redbrick building. Its entrance was framed by white columns, wooden benches, and painted Adirondacks. This was what the child in me imagined all college campuses looked like. Later I would learn that this tree-lined enclosure was called The Heart.

## ZITKÁLA-ŠÁ

**Born: February 22, 1876, on the Yankton Indian Reservation, Dakota Territory**

**Died: January 26, 1938, in Washington, DC**

**Forms: Short Stories, Memoir, Libretto**

**Recommended Works: *Old Indian Legends* (1901), *The Sun Dance Opera* (1913), *American Indian Stories* (1921)**

In "School Days of an Indian Girl," Zitkála-Šá—known to Earlhamites as Gertrude Simmons—writes about leaving her happy childhood on South Dakota's Yankton Reservation for White's Manual Labor Institute in Wabash, Indiana. Her introduction to education left her homesick; she was forced to cut her hair, adopt a new language and religion, and endure numerous abuses. One wouldn't blame her for leaving school entirely. And yet she went to college, much to the chagrin of her mother, who feared losing her daughter to "the white man's ways." If my visit was a modest attempt at self-encouragement, Zitkála-Šá's more permanent move to Earlham represented a willful assertion of a new life.

Gertrude's time at Earlham was lonely. She often isolated herself in her dorm room, and a classmate described her as "pleasant but somewhat distant." Nevertheless, she flourished, publishing poetry in the school newspaper and performing in recitals. Her speeches, however, were where she found her voice as an activist.

After winning Earlham's oratory contest, Gertrude was surprised when fellow freshmen celebrated by decorating the student parlor. *Maybe*, she thought, *my classmates aren't so bad.* But then, weeks later in the subsequent state-level competition, students from one university mocked her with racist epithets. Gertrude rallied. In her soft but determined voice, she lambasted America's prejudices, winning over all the judges save a Southerner offended by her position on slavery. She won second place.

I picture her afterward in The Heart, staring at Earlham Hall, those columns festooned in cream-and-yellow drapery in her honor. Like many of Gertrude's triumphs, this one was bittersweet. The humiliation of the night's racism lingered, and she rushed to her dorm room, questioning her decision to leave home.

Even as she became a student at the New England Conservatory of Music and a teacher at the infamous Carlisle Indian School, she would remember that night. Maybe she stared at the Stars and Stripes flying above the Hall's entrance and thought about how her speech referenced "our nation's flag" and "our common country," stubbornly and even hopefully insisting on a shared humanity that she knew was often denied. The image of her standing before Earlham Hall inspires me to contemplate my experiences in education, both alienating and invigorating, and the way that institutions can both fail us and uplift us. If Zitkála-Šá could make such resolute demands for equality after all she had experienced, I figure there's still hope for me.

# APPENDIX

## Chronological, by Author Birth

Sojourner Truth, 1797
John Augustus Stone, 1801
Elijah Lovejoy, 1802
Rachel, ca. 1814
Lew Wallace, 1827
Peter H. Clark, 1829
Mark Twain, 1835
Sarah Morgan Bryan Piatt, 1836
Kate Chopin, 1850
Edgar Lee Masters, 1868
Mary Hunter Austin, 1868
Booth Tarkington, 1869
Willa Cather, 1873
Zitkála-Šá, 1876
Sherwood Anderson, 1876
Henry Bellamann, 1882
Aldo Leopold, 1887
Thomas Hart Benton, 1889
John Joseph Mathews, 1894
Helen Hooven Santmyer, 1895
Mari Sandoz, 1896
F. Scott Fitzgerald, 1896
Meridel Le Sueur, 1900
Langston Hughes, 1902
Lorine Niedecker, 1903
Louis L'Amour, 1908
Richard Wright, 1908
August Derleth, 1909
Wright Morris, 1910
Tennessee Williams, 1911
Gordon Parks, 1912
Robert Hayden, 1913
R. A. Lafferty, 1914
John Bartlow Martin, 1915
Gwendolyn Brooks, 1917
James Emanuel, 1921
Jean Shepherd, 1921
Kurt Vonnegut, 1922
Lisel Mueller, 1924
William Gass, 1924
Malcolm X, 1925
Philip Levine, 1928
Maya Angelou, 1928
Toni Morrison, 1931
Hugo Martinez-Serros, 1931
Norbert Blei, 1935

Hunter S. Thompson, 1937
Jim Harrison, 1937
Ted Kooser, 1939
William Least Heat-Moon, 1939
James Tate, 1943
Paul Vasey, 1947
S. E. Hinton, 1948
Naomi Shihab Nye, 1952
Sandra Cisneros, 1954
Michael Martone, 1955
Kathleen Finneran, 1957
Bonnie Jo Campbell, 1962
Heid E. Erdrich, 1963
José Olivarez, 1988

## Type of Place

### *Homes*

Bonnie Jo Campbell
Willa Cather (Bladen)
Kate Chopin
Sandra Cisneros
Peter H. Clark
Kathleen Finneran
F. Scott Fitzgerald
William Gass
S. E. Hinton
R. A. Lafferty
Aldo Leopold
Meridel Le Sueur
John Bartlow Martin
Michael Martone
John Joseph Mathews
Wright Morris
Toni Morrison (Lorain)
Lisel Mueller
Lorine Niedecker
Jean Shepherd
Mark Twain (Elmira, Hannibal, Hartford, and London)
Tennessee Williams
Richard Wright
Malcolm X

### *Gravesites*

Willa Cather (Jaffrey)
Elijah Lovejoy
Edgar Lee Masters
Sarah Morgan Bryan Piatt
Mari Sandoz
Sojourner Truth

### *Parks and Natural Spaces*

Maya Angelou
Thomas Hart Benton
Willa Cather (Omaha and Taos)
Jim Harrison
Langston Hughes
Louis L'Amour
William Least Heat-Moon
Philip Levine
Hugo Martinez-Serros
Toni Morrison (Chesapeake Bay and Lorain)
Gordon Parks
Mark Twain (Hannibal and London)
Lew Wallace
Malcolm X

### *Institutions and Built Public Spaces*

Norbert Blei
Gwendolyn Brooks
Willa Cather (Chicago)
Mary Hunter Austin
James Emanuel
Heid E. Erdrich
Robert Hayden
Toni Morrison (Cleveland and West Point)
Naomi Shihab Nye
Rachel
Hunter S. Thompson
Kurt Vonnegut
Zitkála-Šá
Helen Hooven Santmyer

### *Infrastructure*

Sherwood Anderson
August Derleth
Ted Kooser
Michael Martone
Toni Morrison (Cleveland)
José Olivarez
John Augustus Stone
Booth Tarkington
James Tate
Paul Vasey

# CONTRIBUTORS

**Andy Oler** grew up in the Midwest and currently lives farther away from it than he would like. He is the author of *Old-Fashioned Modernism: Rural Masculinity and Midwestern Literature* (2019) and the editor of *Michigan Salvage: The Fiction of Bonnie Jo Campbell* (with Lisa DuRose and Ross K. Tangedal, 2023) and *Pieces of the Heartland: Representing Midwestern Places* (2018). He is departments editor at *The New Territory*, and his writing has appeared in such venues as *Hyped on Melancholy*, *Essay Daily*, *The Cleveland Review of Books*, and *Study the South*.

**Emiliano Aguilar Jr.** is a native of East Chicago, Indiana. Currently he is an assistant professor of history at the University of Notre Dame in South Bend. His manuscript in progress, *Building a Latino Machine: Caught Between Good Government Reform and Corrupt Political Machines*, explores the navigation of municipal and union politics by the ethnic Mexican and Puerto Rican community of East Chicago, Indiana. His writing has appeared in, among others, *Belt Magazine*, *Oxford Research Encyclopedia of American History*, *The Metropole*, and *Los Angeles Review of Books*.

**Sean E. Andres** is a marketer, writer, and former educator. As cofounder of public history project "Queens of Queen City" and a board member of Urbanist Media, the Cincinnati Observatory Center, and the Mac-A-Cheek Foundation for the Humanities, he partners with regional museums and communities to help preserve and empower the voices of historically marginalized populations, with a focus on women's history. He also performs on Stand-Up History, telling comedic stories of Cincinnati's past.

**Kassie Jo Baron** is an assistant professor of English at the University of Tennessee at Martin. She specializes in nineteenth-century American literature with particular interest in the literary representations of white, female New England mill operatives' bodies during the first US industrial revolution. She is a native of the Sauk Prairie area and a newly minted member of the August Derleth Society. She has never competed in the Wisconsin State Cow Chip Throw.

**Laura Beadling** was born and raised in Youngstown, Ohio, where she teaches literature, film, and screenwriting at Youngstown State University. She realizes now that she should have bought the plush toy Tralfamadorian on offer at the Vonnegut Museum's gift shop, as it would be a good addition to her office collection of tchotchkes.

**Wesley R. Bishop** is an assistant professor of American and public history at Jacksonville State University, Alabama. Prior to this he was an assistant professor of American history at Marian University in Indianapolis. He is the founding and managing editor of *North Meridian Press.*

**Marc Blanc** is a postdoctoral fellow in English at Washington University in St. Louis, where he earned his PhD. Growing up in the shadow of factory smokestacks in northeast Ohio fostered his passion for working-class literature of the industrial Midwest, which is the subject of his teaching and research. His other writings on the region's radical literary history have appeared in *Jacobin, Chicago Review, Belt Magazine, History News Network*, and *College Literature.*

**Ray E. Boomhower** is a senior editor at the *Indiana Historical Society Press*. He is also the author of more than a dozen books, including *John Bartlow Martin: A Voice for the Underdog, Richard Tregaskis: Reporting Under Fire from Guadalcanal to Vietnam*, and *The Ultimate Protest: Malcolm W. Browne, Thich Quang Duc, and the News Photograph That Stunned the World.*

**Jacob A. Bruggeman** is a PhD candidate in American history at Johns Hopkins University and an editor-at-large of the *Cleveland Review of Books.*

**Camden Burd** is assistant professor of history at Clemson University, where he researches and writes on topics related to the environmental history of the Midwest and Rust Belt. He is the author of *The Roots of Flower City: Horticulture, Empire, and the Remaking of Rochester, New York* (2024). His work has also appeared in *The Michigan Historical Review, IA: The Journal for the Society of Industrial Archaeology*, and several edited collections.

**Dr. Ashley Burge** is assistant professor of African American literature at Augustana College (Illinois), specializing in nineteenth- and twentieth-century African American literature. Her research and teaching emphasize Black feminism and ecocriticism as well as the intersections of race, gender, sexuality, and class. Her essays have appeared in the *North Carolina Literary Review*, the *Pennsylvania Communication Annual*, the *African American Encyclopedia of Culture*, and the critical anthology *Through Mama's Eyes*. Her current book project establishes a theoretical paradigm that transmutes trauma and fragmentation to wholeness and subjectivity in African American literature.

**Dawn Burns** is thoroughly Midwestern, having lived their whole life in Indiana, Ohio, and Michigan. Often their characters are Midwestern too, like Evangelina from Elkhart, Indiana, in *Evangelina Everyday* (2022), who may appear uncomplicated but has a rich inner life. Burns's MFA in creative writing from the University of Notre Dame prepared them for a lifetime of writing, creative community building, and teaching. Burns is founder of the SwampFire Retreat for Writers and Artists and a recipient of excellence awards from the

Society for the Study of Midwestern Literature and the Ohio Arts Council. An assistant professor at Michigan State University, Burns is committed to writing and storytelling as acts of personal and social change.

**Trivius G. Caldwell** is a native of Atlanta, Georgia. He is an active-duty army officer serving in the infantry branch and served as assistant professor of English at the United States Military Academy at West Point. Trivius has degrees from Tuskegee University, Auburn University, and the Command and General Staff College in Fort Leavenworth, Kansas. He is a PhD candidate in the Department of English at Duke University. His research interests include twentieth-century African American literature, sound studies, and hip-hop literature.

**Heather Chacón** is a proud native Hoosier and scholar of nineteenth-century American Literature. She is an assistant professor of English at Centre College in Danville, Kentucky, and previously taught at Greensboro College. When she isn't grading or in the archives, she enjoys being outside and visiting historic sites—beloved pastimes she first developed in Indiana.

**Angie Chatman** is a freelance writer and storyteller, born and raised on the South Side of Chicago. She has been nominated for a Pushcart Prize and won a Webby Award. Her short stories and essays can be found in or are forthcoming from *Iron Horse Literary Review*, *Taint Taint Taint*, *The Rumpus*, *Pangyrus*, *Hippocampus*, *Blood Orange Review*, *fwriction : review*, and elsewhere. Chatman received funding from the Kimbilio Center for Black Fiction, Ragdale, the Virginia Center for Creative Arts, and the Mass Cultural Council. An electrical engineer by degree, Chatman earned an MBA from MIT Sloan and an MFA in fiction and creative nonfiction from Queens University in Charlotte, North Carolina. She lives in the Dorchester neighborhood of Boston with her family.

**Christy Clark-Pujara** is professor of history in the Department of African American Studies at the University of Wisconsin—Madison. She is the author of *Dark Work: The Business of Slavery in Rhode Island* (2016), and her research focuses on the experiences of Black people in small towns and cities in northern and Midwestern colonies and states in British and French North America before the Civil War. Her current book project, *Black on the Midwestern Frontier: Contested Freedoms, 1725–1868*, examines how the practice of race-based slavery, Black settlement, and debates over abolition and Black rights shaped race relations in the Midwest.

**Tara L. Conley** is an interdisciplinary scholar and media-maker with established research and creative agendas. Her research and multimedia production engage scholarship and methods across media studies, feminist studies, Black studies, digital humanities, and science and technology studies.

**Naomi Crummey** is a professor of English at Blackburn College, where she teaches writing and literature. Her personal essays have appeared in *Prairie Fire*, *Kudzu House*, and *Grain*, and she coedited *The Wire in the College Classroom: Pedagogical Approaches in the Humanities* (2015, with Karen Dillon). A Canadian citizen, she lives in St. Louis, Missouri.

**Charlie Cy** is a freelance writer based in Louisville, Kentucky.

**Karen Dillon** is a professor of English at Blackburn College, where she teaches US literature and first-year writing. She has published two books: *The Wire in the College Classroom: Pedagogical Approaches in the Humanities* (2015, coedited with Naomi Crummey) and *The Spectacle of Twins in American Literature and Popular Culture* (2018). She is originally from Indianapolis, Indiana.

**Lisa DuRose** is coeditor of *Michigan Salvage: The Fiction of Bonnie Jo Campbell* (2023) and a faculty member at Inver Hills Community College, where she teaches in the English department. Despite earnest efforts to become a New Yorker in her twenties, she resides in St. Paul, Minnesota, just two miles from where she was born. She is writing a biography of Bonnie Jo Campbell.

**Alex Dzurick** is an educator and writer originally from Fulton, Missouri. He has published in *The New Territory*, *The Science Teacher*, and *Urban Environmental Education*. Currently living in the St. Louis area, Alex spends most of his time (when he's not teaching) writing quizbowl questions, solving crossword puzzles, and reading random Wikipedia articles.

**Taylor Fox** is a commerce editor at *Travel + Leisure*, where she tests and recommends travel products based on her travel and outdoor experiences. She earned an MFA in creative nonfiction from West Virginia Wesleyan University and holds three degrees from the University of Missouri: a master's in geography and two bachelor's degrees, in journalism and English. A former Peace Corps volunteer, she has spent her career learning and writing about cultures and hopes to continue sharing this passion with others. Fox has also been published in *The Dodo*, *Baroque Lifestyle*, *Missouri Life*, and the *Columbia Daily Tribune*.

**Caleb Freeman** is a writer and editor living in Halifax, Nova Scotia. He was born and raised in Tulsa, Oklahoma, and has been published in *Oklahoma Today*, *Visual Arts News*, and other publications.

**Conor Gearin** is a writer from St. Louis living in Omaha. His work has appeared in *The Best American Science and Nature Writing*, *The Atlantic*, *The Millions*, *New Scientist*, and *The New Territory*, where he is a contributing editor. He writes a newsletter called *Possum Notes.*

**Jenna Goldsmith** is a poet and writer living in Rockford, Illinois. She is the author of four poetry chapbooks, including *CRUSH*, winner of the 2022 Baltic Writing Residency Poetry Chapbook Contest, and *TITLE NINE*, which was published by *Press 254*, the teaching press of Illinois State University. She is the director of the low-residency MFA Program in Creative Writing at Oregon State University–Cascades. She was named poet laureate for the City of Rockford for 2023–25.

**Avery Gregurich** is a writer currently living and working in Marengo, Iowa. He was raised next to the Mississippi River and has never strayed too far from it.

**Aaron Hadlow** is a lawyer and writer. He lives in the Ozarks with his family.

**Ayesha K. Hardison** is a literary and cultural critic of African American fiction and representation. She is the Susan D. Gubar Chair and associate professor of English at Indiana University Bloomington. Her research and teaching explore questions of race, gender, genre, social politics, and historical memory. She is the author of *Writing through Jane Crow*, co-editor of the journal *Women, Gender, and Families of Color*, and director of the History of Black Writing project. She grew up in Inkster, Michigan.

**Susan Kumin Harris**'s studies of Twain's life and works incorporate many perspectives, from Twain's yearning to escape human time and space to his courtship days to his later anti-imperialism. Her most recent book, *Mark Twain, the World, and Me: Following the Equator, Then and Now* (2020), follows Twain on his journeys through Australia, India, and South Africa, exploring the cultural phenomena that he noticed (and those he ignored) and discussing her own relationship to one of America's most powerful writers.

**Michael Helsem** was born in Dallas in 1958. Shortly afterward, fish fell from the sky.

**Marina Henke** is a radio reporter and writer born and raised in St. Louis, Missouri. She now lives in Maine and works as a podcast producer and environmental journalist. Red brick, the River des Peres, and limestone bluffs are just a few of the reasons she dreams of returning home to make radio.

**Olga L. Herrera** is an associate professor in English at the University of St. Thomas in St. Paul, Minnesota. Her research and teaching interests include Latinx and Chicago literature, and she thinks that she will always be fascinated with the complexities and contradictions of cities.

**Ashley Howard** is an assistant professor of history and African American studies at the University of Iowa. A proud Omahan, her research interests include violence, social movements, and the Black Midwest. She is the author of *Midwest Unrest: 1960s Urban Rebellions and the Black Freedom Movement* (2025).

**Jeffrey Insko** is a professor of English at Oakland University in Michigan, where he teaches courses in nineteenth-century US literary history and culture and the environmental humanities. He is the author of *History, Abolition, and the Ever-Present Now in Antebellum American Writing* (2018) and the editor of the Norton Library edition of *Moby-Dick* (2023). He is currently writing a book about the Kalamazoo River oil spill.

**C. J. Janovy** grew up in Nebraska and lived on both coasts before settling in Kansas City. Her book *No Place Like Home: Lessons in Activism from LGBT Kansas* won the 2019 Stubbendieck Great Plains Distinguished Book Prize.

**Jacques Lamarre** is a playwright and a marketing specialist who consults for The Mark Twain House & Museum.

**Sheila Liming** is an associate professor at Champlain College and the author of three books: *What a Library Means to a Woman* (2020), *Office* (2020), and most recently, *Hanging Out* (2023). Her writing has appeared in venues like *The Atlantic*, *The New York Review of Books*,

*The Los Angeles Review of Books*, and *The Globe and Mail*. She lives, works, and plays the accordion (and bagpipes) in Burlington, Vermont.

**Daniel A. Lockhart** is the author of multiple collections of poetry and short fiction. He earned his MFA in creative writing from Indiana University, and his work has been a finalist for the Trillium Book Award, Raymond Souster Award, Indiana Author's Awards, First Nations Communities READ Award, and the ReLit Award. His writing has appeared widely throughout Turtle Island, including in *The Malahat Review*, *Grain*, *CV2*, *TriQuarterly*, *The Fiddlehead*, *Best Canadian Poetry*, *Best New Poetry from the Midwest*, and *Belt*. He is pùkuwànkoamimëns of the Moravian of the Thames First Nation. Lockhart currently resides at Waawiiyaatanong and Pelee Island.

**Samuel Love** is the editor of *The Gary Anthology* (2020) and lives in Gary, Indiana.

**Cindy Lovell** is a writer and educator. She teaches a course on *Tom Sawyer* for Quincy University, which is on the Illinois side of the Mississippi River. She is the former executive director of both The Mark Twain Boyhood Home & Museum (Hannibal, Missouri) and The Mark Twain House & Museum (Hartford, Connecticut). Cindy wrote the narrative for *Mark Twain: Words and Music*, a double-album benefit project for the Boyhood Home, featuring Jimmy Buffett as Huck Finn, Clint Eastwood as Mark Twain, and Garrison Keillor as narrator. GRAMMY Award–winner Carl Jackson produced the project, and performers included Brad Paisley, Sheryl Crow, Emmylou Harris, and other fans of Mark Twain.

**Matt Miller** serves as an associate professor of English at College of the Ozarks and tends a garden with his family in Branson, Missouri. His first collection of essays, entitled *Leaves of Healing: A Year in the Garden*, appeared in 2024. Find him online at matt-miller.org.

**Leah Abuan Milne** is an associate professor of multicultural American literature at the University of Indianapolis (UIndy). Her work focuses on contemporary ethnic American literature, especially African American and Asian American literature. She also studies postcolonial theory and women's and gender studies. She is the author of *Novel Subjects: Authorship as Radical Self-Care in Multiethnic American Narratives*, which won the Midwest Modern Language Association Book Prize in 2021.

**Jenny Mueller** lives in St. Louis. She is the author of two books of poetry, *State Park* and *Bonneville*. She is also the editor of *Moonie*, a posthumous e-book of poetry by Brian Young. She is the younger daughter and literary executor of Lisel Mueller. Unlike her mother, Jenny has been able to do years of coursework in creative writing, a privilege she tries to pass on to her students at McKendree University in Lebanon, Illinois.

**José Olivarez** is the son of Mexican immigrants, and the author of two collections of poems, including, most recently, *Promises of Gold*, which was long listed for the 2023 National Book Awards. His debut book of poems, *Citizen Illegal*, was a finalist for the PEN/Jean Stein Book Award and a winner of the 2018 Chicago Review of Books Poetry Prize. He coedited the poetry anthology *The BreakBeat Poets*, vol. 4, *LatiNEXT* (2020) with Felicia

Rose Chavez and Willie Perdomo and, alongside Antonio Salazar, published the hybrid book *Por Siempre* (2023).

**Devin Thomas O'Shea** is the author of *The Veiled Prophet* (forthcoming 2026). His writing is in *The Nation*, *Boulevard*, *Slate*, *Jacobin*, *Chicago Quarterly Review*, and elsewhere. He is represented by Erik Hane of Headwater Literary Management.

The descendent of steelworkers, **Joseph S. Pete** hails from the Calumet Region just outside Chicago, where the oil refinery flare stacks burn round the clock and the mills make clouds. An award-winning journalist, his writing and photography have appeared in more than one hundred journals, including *Proximity*, *Tipton Poetry Journal*, *O-Dark-Thirty*, *Line of Advance*, *As You Were*, *Chicago Literati*, *Blue Collar Review*, *The Rat's Ass Review*, *Euphemism*, *Jenny*, and *Vending Machine Press*.

**Christine Pivovar** is originally from Omaha and lives in Kansas City. She was a Durwood Fellow at the University of Missouri–Kansas City, where she earned her MFA in creative writing and media arts. She has reviewed books for *The Millions*, *The Rumpus*, and *The Kansas City Star*, and her creative work has been published in *The Prairie Schooner*, *The New Territory*, and *The Southeast Review*. She also works as a software product designer.

**Catherine Seiberling Pond** has written for *Old House Interiors*, *Victoria*, *Yankee*, *Literary Hub*, and *Rethink:Rural* (blog). She earned her master's in historic preservation studies from Boston University and has been a marketing specialist for the National Willa Cather Center in Red Cloud, Nebraska, since 2018—the centenary of *My Ántonia*. Most of the year, she works remotely from her farm in Kentucky, and she is writing a memoir about family farms and homeplaces.

**Mason Whitehorn Powell** is a writer and Brooklyn Law School graduate. Originally from Hominy, Oklahoma, he is an enrolled tribal member of the Osage Nation and lives in Rome, Italy.

**Jesse Raber** is an instructor at the Harvard Extension School and has also taught literature courses at several Chicago universities, including the School of the Art Institute of Chicago, Loyola University Chicago, and the University of Illinois Chicago. He is the cocreator of the Wintrust Chicago Gallery at the American Writers Museum and is currently working on a literary history of Chicago.

**Kit Salter** lived in twenty-two different places by the end of high school. He graduated from Oberlin College and took his master's and PhD at Berkeley. He is a professor emeritus of geography at the University of Missouri and taught for UCLA, the University of Oregon, and the National Geographic Society. He has been married to writer and geographer Cathy Lynn Salter for more than four decades.

**Joe Schiller** is an acquisitions editor at the University of Oklahoma Press. He is writing an environmental and labor history of rural deindustrialization in the Tri-State Mining District. He lives in Detroit Lakes, Minnesota.

**Marc Seals** is a professor of English at the Baraboo campus of the University of Wisconsin–Platteville, where he teaches courses in American literature, composition, and film. He has published articles and book chapters on authors such as Ernest Hemingway, Raymond Chandler, F. Scott Fitzgerald, Gwendolyn Brooks, Dashiell Hammett, and Zona Gale. A native of the Deep South, he has grown to love the Midwest.

**Matt Seybold** is an associate professor of American literature and Mark Twain studies at Elmira College. He is resident scholar at the Center for Mark Twain Studies, founding editor of their website, and executive producer and host of *The American Vandal Podcast*. He is coeditor of *The Routledge Companion to Literature and Economics* (2018, with Michelle Chihara) and a special issue of *American Literary History*, "Economics and Literary Studies in The New Gilded Age" (2019, with Gordon Hutner). His work has appeared in dozens of publications.

**Doug Sheldon** is a senior lecturer and English language learner specialist at the University of Illinois Chicago and president of the Sherwood Anderson Society. When not doing scholarly things, he can be found at his local watering hole or doing something lake related.

**Thomas Ruys Smith** is a professor of American literature and culture at the University of East Anglia in the United Kingdom. He is author and editor of a wide range of publications about the nineteenth century including, most recently, *Deep Water: The Mississippi River in the Age of Mark Twain* (2019) and *The Last Gift: The Christmas Stories of Mary E. Wilkins Freeman* (2023). He is currently writing a book about Mark Twain's relationship with London.

**Jason Stacy** grew up in Monee, Illinois. Since 2006 he has served as a professor of history and social science pedagogy at Southern Illinois University Edwardsville. His most recent book, *Spoon River America: Edgar Lee Masters and the Myth of the American Small Town*, was published by the University of Illinois Press in 2021.

**Sean Theodore Stewart** is a Pushcart Award and Best American Short Stories nominee. His stories have appeared in *The Arkansas International*, *December*, *Barrelhouse*, *Epiphany*, *The Normal School*, *Guesthouse*, *Salt Hill*, *The New Territory*, *Full House*, and *Bayou*. He holds an MFA from the University of Idaho, where he served as fiction editor of *Fugue*. He is originally from the Sandhills of Nebraska and now lives in Brooklyn with his wife, Samantha, and their pups, Ramona and Molly.

**Alice Sundman** was born on the Åland Islands of Finland and lives in Stockholm, Sweden. She is a literary scholar, currently working on a project exploring places of and between water and land in Anglophone literature. She is the author of *Toni Morrison and the Writing of Place* (2022).

**Ramya Swayamprakash** is a transnational and interdisciplinary environmental scholar of North America and South Asia. Broadly, Ramya's research—whether in India or North America—is premised on two central questions: What is nature? How does something become nature? She researches infrastructure creation, nature, and knowledge transfers in the nineteenth and twentieth centuries as well as between North America and South Asia.

Ramya's musings have been published in academic and public-facing avenues. She takes tea, dams, and dredging (not necessarily in that order) seriously.

**Ross K. Tangedal** is an associate professor of English and the director and publisher of the Cornerstone Press at the University of Wisconsin–Stevens Point. He is the author of *The Preface: American Authorship in the Twentieth Century* (2021) and editor of *Good Country: Ernest Hemingway and the American West* (2025), *Michigan Salvage: The Fiction of Bonnie Jo Campbell* (2023), and *Editing the Harlem Renaissance* (2021). He also serves as an associate volume editor on the National Endowment for the Humanities–funded *Hemingway Letters Project.*

**Jeromiah Taylor** is a writer from Wichita, Kansas. His work appears in *The Los Angeles Review*, the *Chicago Review of Books*, *U.S. Catholic* magazine, the *Chautauqua Journal, The Millions*, and elsewhere. He works as the editorial assistant at the *National Catholic Reporter.*

**Michaella A. Thornton**'s prose can be read in *Brevity*, *Creative Nonfiction*, *Complete Sentence*, *HAD*, *New South*, *Reckon Review*, the *Southeast Review*, and a few other places. When she's not spending time with her seven-year-old daughter, Kella savors digging in the dirt, kayaking, and second acts. Like her literary idol Kate Chopin once did, Kella lives in St. Louis, Missouri.

**John Edgar Tidwell** is a professor emeritus of English at the University of Kansas. He has published several books, including *Montage of a Dream: The Art and Life of Langston Hughes* (2007, coedited with Cheryl Ragar) and *My Dear Boy: Carrie Hughes's Letters to Langston Hughes, 1926–1938* (2013, coedited with Carmaletta Williams).

**Ava Tomasula y Garcia** was born in 1994 in Chicago. Both sides of her family worked in the steel mills of the Calumet Region, and she grew up in South Bend, Indiana. She was formerly a labor and immigration organizer at Centro de Trabajadores Unidos (United Workers' Center) on the southeast side of Chicago and currently is studying medical anthropology as applied to the so-called undiagnosed illnesses of the Calumet Region. Her writing has appeared in *Best American Experimental Fiction*, *PEN America Best Debut Short Stories*, *Black Warrior Review*, *Belt Magazine*, *CURA.*, and elsewhere.

**Tracy Sanford Tucker** is the director of collections and curation at the National Willa Cather Center in Red Cloud, Nebraska. She is a certified archivist and an affiliate fellow of the Center for Great Plains Studies. Tucker's research, writing, and photography focus on the Plains and have appeared in *Old Northwest Review*, *Midwestern Gothic*, *Whirlwind*, *Open Mic*, *Prairie Fire*, *Willa Cather Review*, *Unknown No More: Essays on Sanora Babb*, and others.

**Nathan Tye** was born and raised in the Platte Valley. A historian by trade, Tye is an associate professor of Nebraska and American West history at the University of Nebraska at Kearney. He writes on Midwestern literary and labor history and serves on the board of the Mari Sandoz Society.

**Greer Veon** is a writer who was raised on the state line between the twin cities of Texarkana, Arkansas, and Texarkana, Texas. She works as the director of residential life at Hendrix

College in Conway, Arkansas. She received her MFA from Sarah Lawrence College in Bronxville, New York, and her work has been featured in *Elle*, *The New Territory*, and *Write or Die Tribe*.

**Leslie VonHolten** is a culture and environmental essayist and the author of *Ambit: Everyday Art History in the Midwest* (blog). She thanks poet Al Ortolani for the map and memory conversations that enlivened this essay.

**Shanley Wells-Rau** earned her MFA in poetry at Oklahoma State University (OSU), where she served as an editorial assistant for *Cimarron Review*. Her poetry has been published or is forthcoming in *The Maine Review*, *Bluestem Magazine*, *Poetry Quarterly*, and *Plants and Poetry*, among others. Following a career in the oil industry, she now teaches literature and writing for Osher Lifelong Learning Institute and OSU and lives with her husband and a clingy dog outside town on a windy hill, where she wanders the prairie to visit with native flora and fauna.

**Matthew A. Werner** is a storyteller and jack of all trades. He grew up on a farm in Union Mills, Indiana—land that once was the outer reaches of the Grand Kankakee Marsh. The area, its people, and its history have inspired much of his writing. He has authored five books: *Season of Upsets*, *How Sweet It Is*, *A White Sox Life*, *The Patch Players*, and *Dispatches from a Northern Hoosier*.

**Elizabeth Wilkinson** is an associate professor at the University of St. Thomas in St. Paul, Minnesota. She researches, writes about, and teaches women's literature—more specifically Native women's literature and the literature of women and sports. She finds that these areas pleasantly collide more often than most people imagine.

**Monique Wingard**, a proud Buckeye and doctoral student at Kent State University's College of Communication and Information, is a digital transformation consultant who amplifies the digital footprint of women-led organizations by shaping effective communication strategies. Her research focuses on news and media literacy among adolescent girls, with the goal of developing curriculum that enhances their critical thinking skills. Visit moniquewingard.com for updates on her research, speaking engagements, conference presentations, and published works.

**Evan Allen Wood**'s writing has appeared in the *Riverfront Times*, *Gunplay*, *Cream Scene Carnival*, and elsewhere. He received an MFA in creative writing from the School of the Art Institute of Chicago.

# PHOTO CREDITS

Photos by the author unless otherwise noted.

**p. 3** House where James Whitcomb Riley—the Hoosier poet—was born on October 7, 1849, on US Route 40. Photo by J. K. Hillers, 1928. Local ID 30-N-34147. Courtesy of the National Archives and Records Administration.

**p. 24** Photo by Barb Kurdna. Courtesy of the National Willa Cather Center in Red Cloud, Nebraska.

**p. 32** Cather's resting place and Mount Monadnock. PHO-4-W689-201. Willa Cather Pioneer Memorial Collection. Courtesy of the National Willa Cather Center in Red Cloud, Nebraska.

**p. 34** Photo by Danielle Head.

**p. 51** Google Maps © 2024, Airbus, Maxar Technologies, Vexcel Imaging.

**p. 68** "Zinc miner's home. Picher, Oklahoma," Arthur Rothstein, May 1936. LC-DIG-fsa-8b38342. Courtesy of the Library of Congress.

**p. 71** Photo by Harvey Payne. Courtesy of the Nature Conservancy.

**p. 74** Photo by Megan Hosmer.

**p. 77** Photo by Abby Boehning.

**p. 89** *Fort Crawford in 1830, Prairie du Chien, Wis.*, Postcard by A. C. Bosselman & Co., 1908. Painting by A. Brower, ca. 1840. From the editor's personal collection.

**p. 99** Photo by T. E. Marr, 1903. Courtesy of the Mark Twain Archive at Elmira College.

**p. 102** Photo by Frank Grace Photography. Courtesy of the Mark Twain House and Museum.

**p. 105** Photo by Becky Dale.

**p. 108** "Gladstone Park, at Dollis Hill, to Be Opened on May 25." *The Illustrated London News*, May 25, 1901.

**p. 113** Photo courtesy of All My Relations Arts and the Native American Community Development Institute.

**p. 115** *World's Largest Buffalo*, by Elmer Petersen, 1959. Photo courtesy of Wikimedia Commons user Ichabod.

**p. 121** Photo by Kit Bütz. Courtesy of Al Johnson's Swedish Restaurant.

**p. 128** Photo by Jim Furley, April 1979. Courtesy of the Hoard Historical Museum and the Friends of Lorine Niedecker, Fort Atkinson, Wisconsin.

**p. 132** Photo by Marianne Connell, May 1976, taken for the *The Independent-Register* (Libertyville, IL). From Lisel Mueller's personal collection. Courtesy of Jenny Mueller.

**p. 136** Photo by Marie Villanueva.

**p. 138** Photo by WestSeven Productions.

**p. 144** Photo by Cameron Smith.

**p. 152** Google Maps © 2022, Airbus, CNES, Landsat, Copernicus, Maxar Technologies.

**p. 159** Photo by Christopher Magson.

**p. 162** Photo by Tom Deater.

**p. 171** *Ambassador Bridge, Windsor, Canada to Detroit, U.S.A.* Curt Teich & Co., 1932. From the editor's personal collection.

**p. 180** *Rose Gardens, Lakeview Park, Lorain, Ohio.* Curt Teich & Co., 1947. Distributed by George R. Klein News Co. ID: Lorain00015. Courtesy of Columbus Metropolitan Library's Ohio Postcard Collection.

**p. 183** *#ClevelandIsTheReason*, by Glen Infante, 2021.

**p. 189** *A New Map of Virginia, Maryland, and the Improved Parts of Pennsylvania and New Jersey.* Christopher Browne, ca. 1685. Courtesy of the Library of Congress, Geography and Map Division.

**p. 192** Anderson Manufacturing Company catalog, ca. 1907–11. Courtesy of the Newberry Library.

**p. 195** Photo by Neil Teixeira. Courtesy of Kurt Vonnegut Museum and Library.

**p. 200** Photo by Eric Kalet.

**p. 202** Racehorse clip art courtesy of Wikimedia Commons users Módis Ágnes Vadszederke and historicair, shared under Creative Commons Attribution-Share Alike 3.0 Unported license. Image has been flipped horizontally.

**p. 210** Courtesy of Wikimedia Commons user Dph414, shared under Creative Commons Share Alike 3.0 Unported license.

**p. 213** Photo by Rebekah Trollinger.

The University of Illinois Press
is a founding member of the
Association of University Presses.

---

Text designed by Kirsten Dennison
Composed in 11/13.5 Adobe Garamond Pro
with Trade Gothic Condensed display
at the University of Illinois Press
Manufactured by Versa Press, Inc.

University of Illinois Press
1325 South Oak Street
Champaign, IL 61820-6903
www.press.uillinois.edu